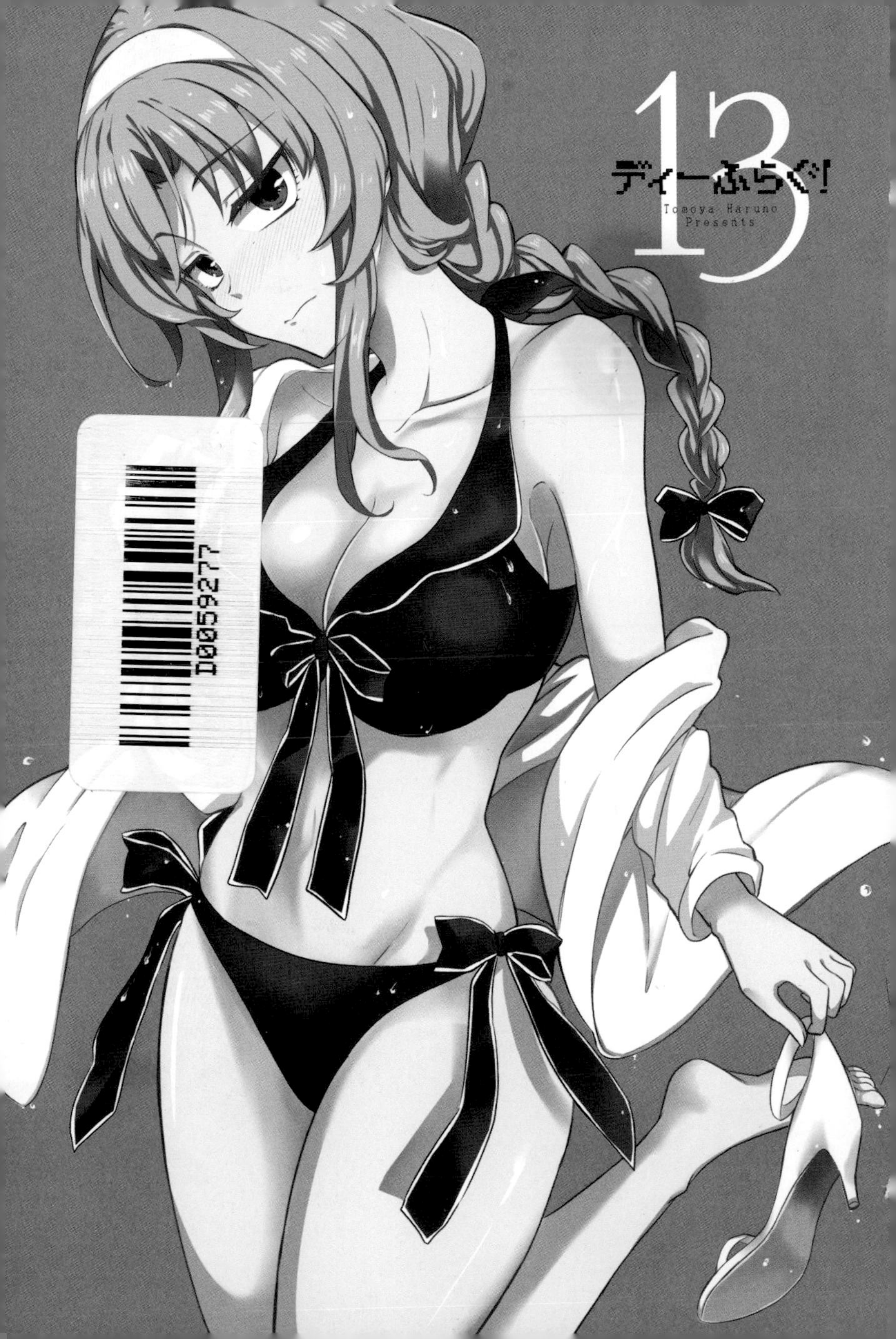
13
ディーふらぐ!
Tomoya Haruno
Presents

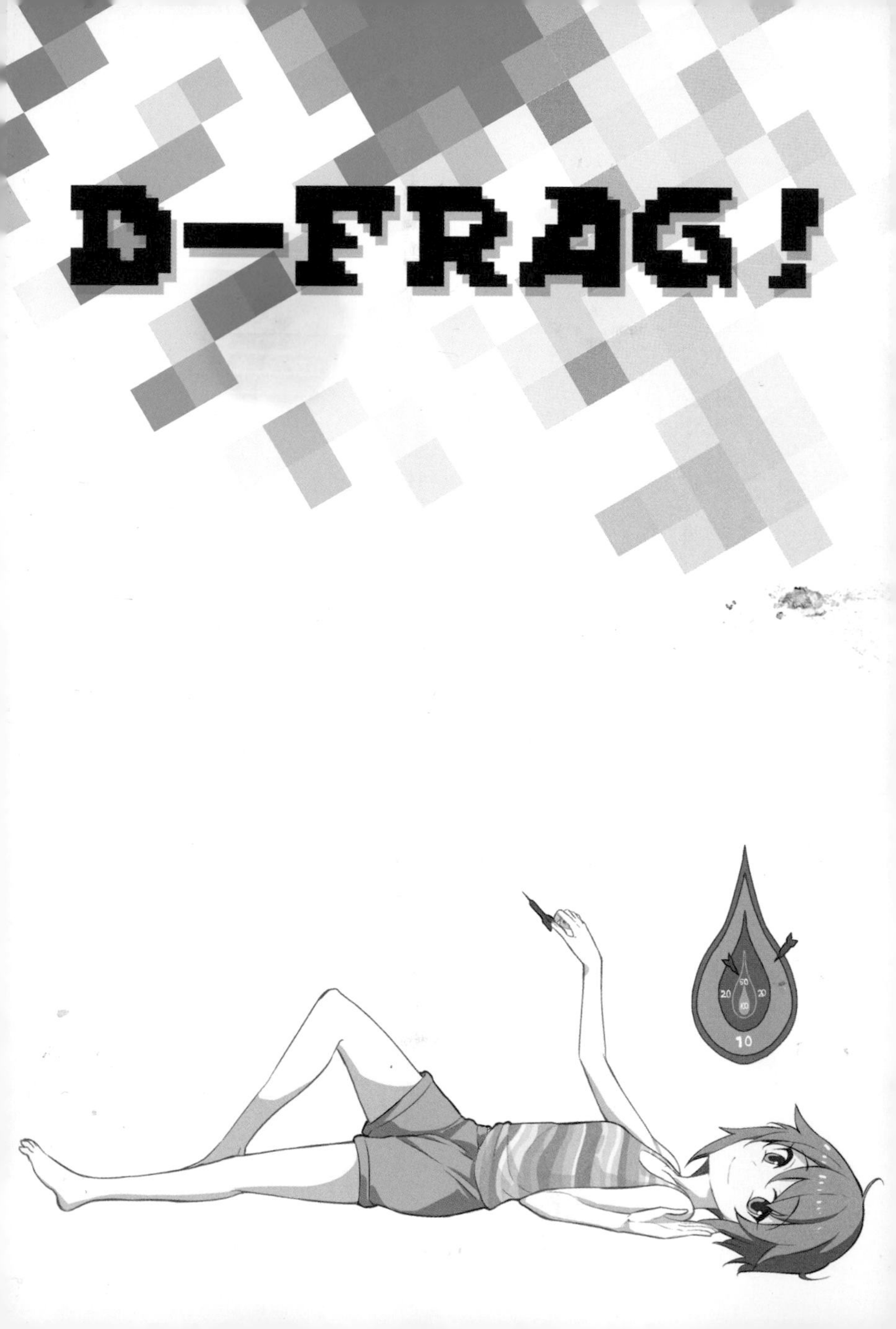
D-FRAG!

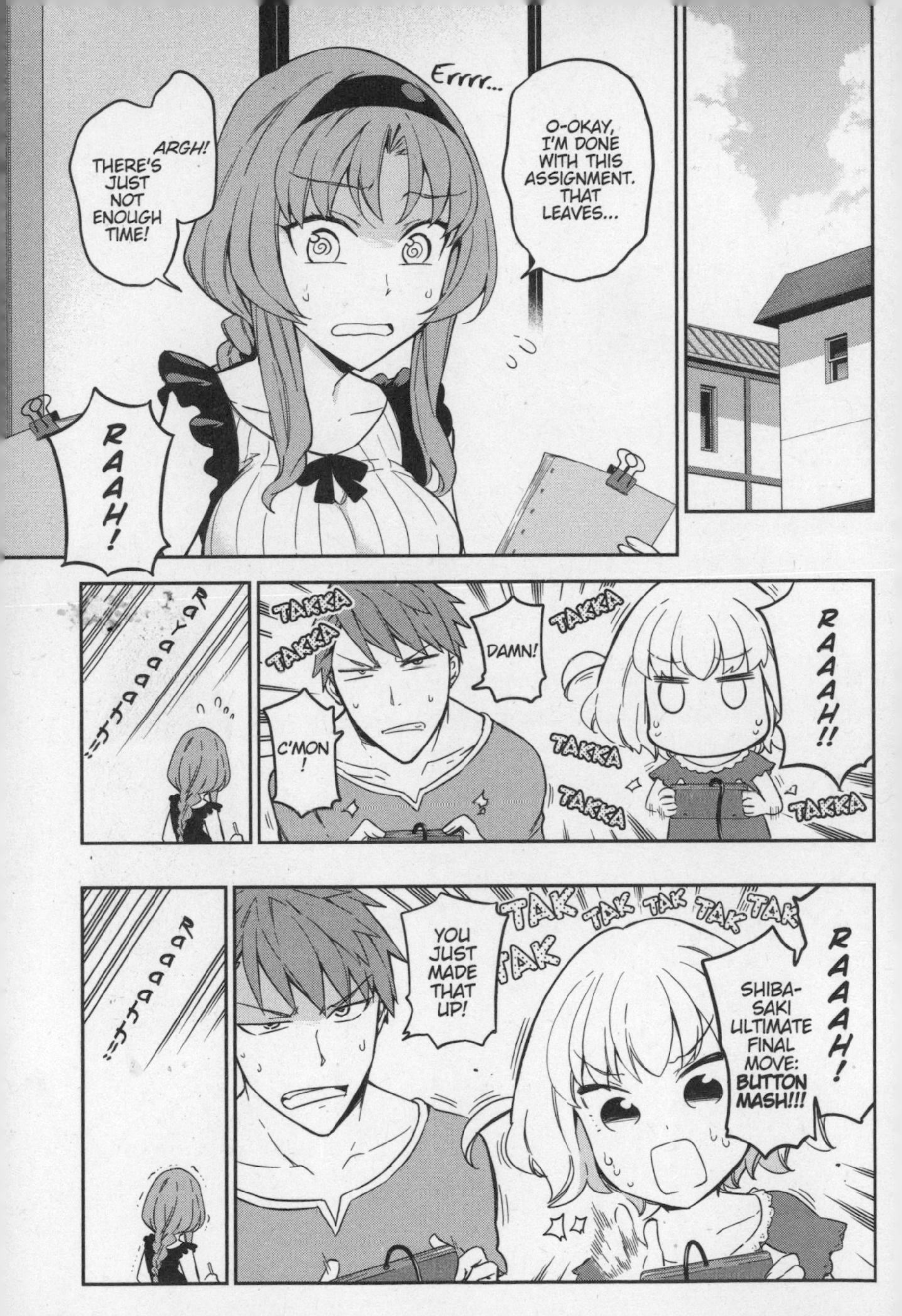
Errrr...
O-OKAY, I'M DONE WITH THIS ASSIGNMENT. THAT LEAVES...
ARGH! THERE'S JUST NOT ENOUGH TIME!
RAAAH!
RAAAAH!!
TAKKA
TAKKA
TAKKA
TAKKA
TAKKA
TAKKA
DAMN!
C'MON!
RAAAAH!
SHIBA-SAKI ULTIMATE FINAL MOVE: BUTTON MASH!!!
TAK TAK TAK TAK TAK TAK
YOU JUST MADE THAT UP!

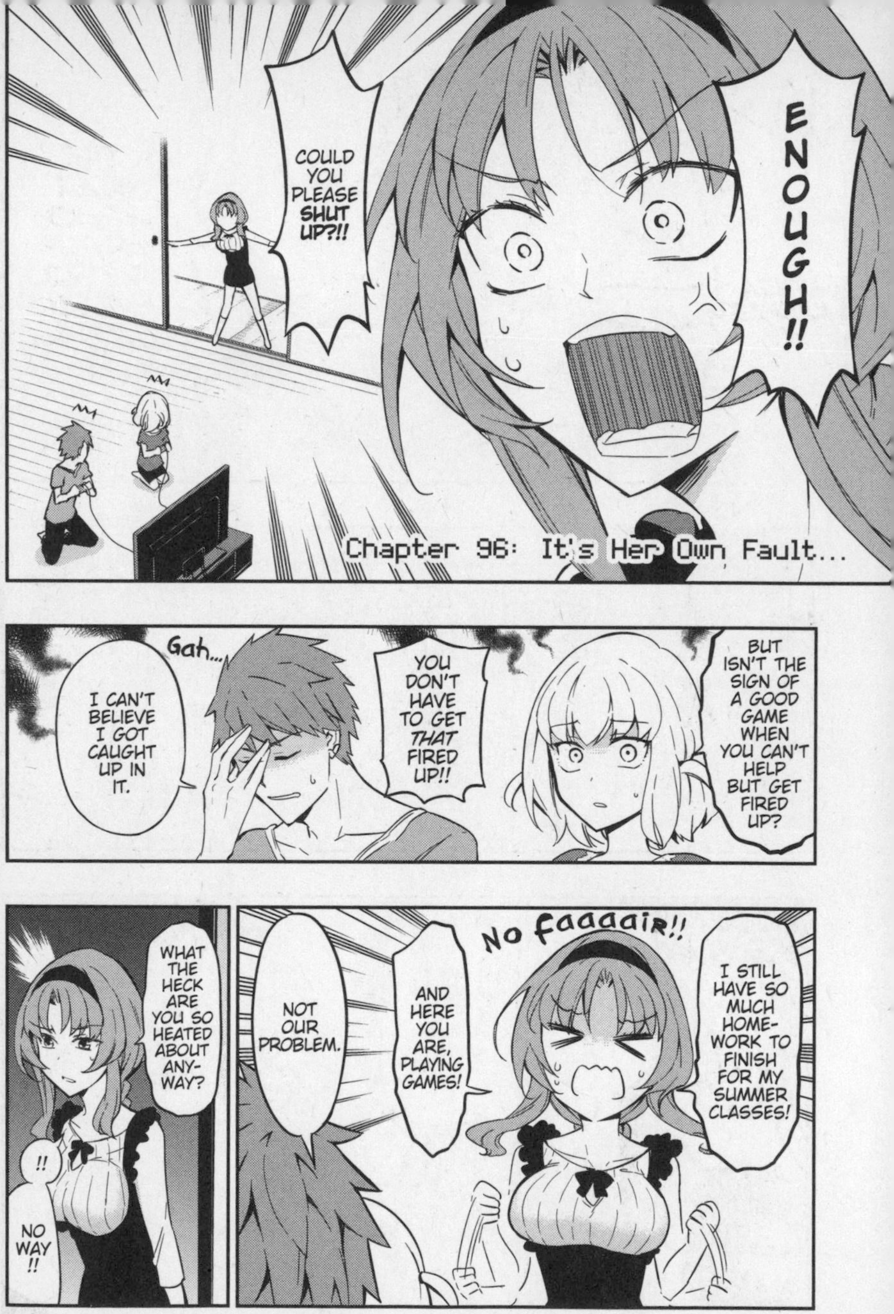
ENOUGH!!
COULD YOU PLEASE SHUT UP?!!
Chapter 96: It's Her Own Fault...
BUT ISN'T THE SIGN OF A GOOD GAME WHEN YOU CAN'T HELP BUT GET FIRED UP?
YOU DON'T HAVE TO GET *THAT* FIRED UP!!
Gah...
I CAN'T BELIEVE I GOT CAUGHT UP IN IT.
I STILL HAVE SO MUCH HOME-WORK TO FINISH FOR MY SUMMER CLASSES!
No faaaair!!
AND HERE YOU ARE, PLAYING GAMES!
NOT OUR PROBLEM.
WHAT THE HECK ARE YOU SO HEATED ABOUT ANY-WAY?
!!
NO WAY !!

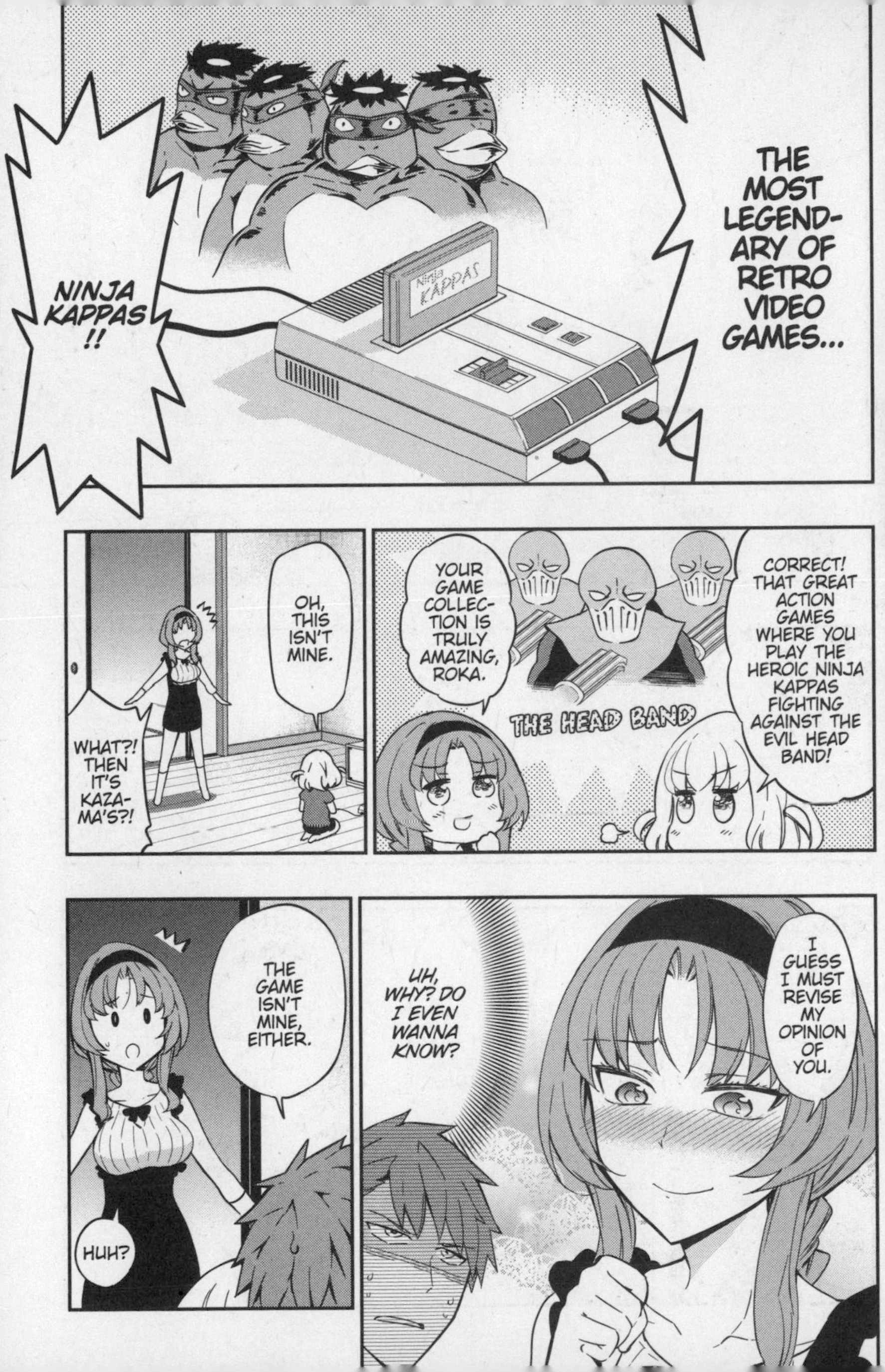
THE MOST LEGENDARY OF RETRO VIDEO GAMES...
Ninja KAPPAS
NINJA KAPPAS!!
CORRECT! THAT GREAT ACTION GAMES WHERE YOU PLAY THE HEROIC NINJA KAPPAS FIGHTING AGAINST THE EVIL HEAD BAND!
YOUR GAME COLLECTION IS TRULY AMAZING, ROKA.
THE HEAD BAND
OH, THIS ISN'T MINE.
WHAT?! THEN IT'S KAZAMA'S?!
I GUESS I MUST REVISE MY OPINION OF YOU.
UH, WHY? DO I EVEN WANNA KNOW?
THE GAME ISN'T MINE, EITHER.
HUH?

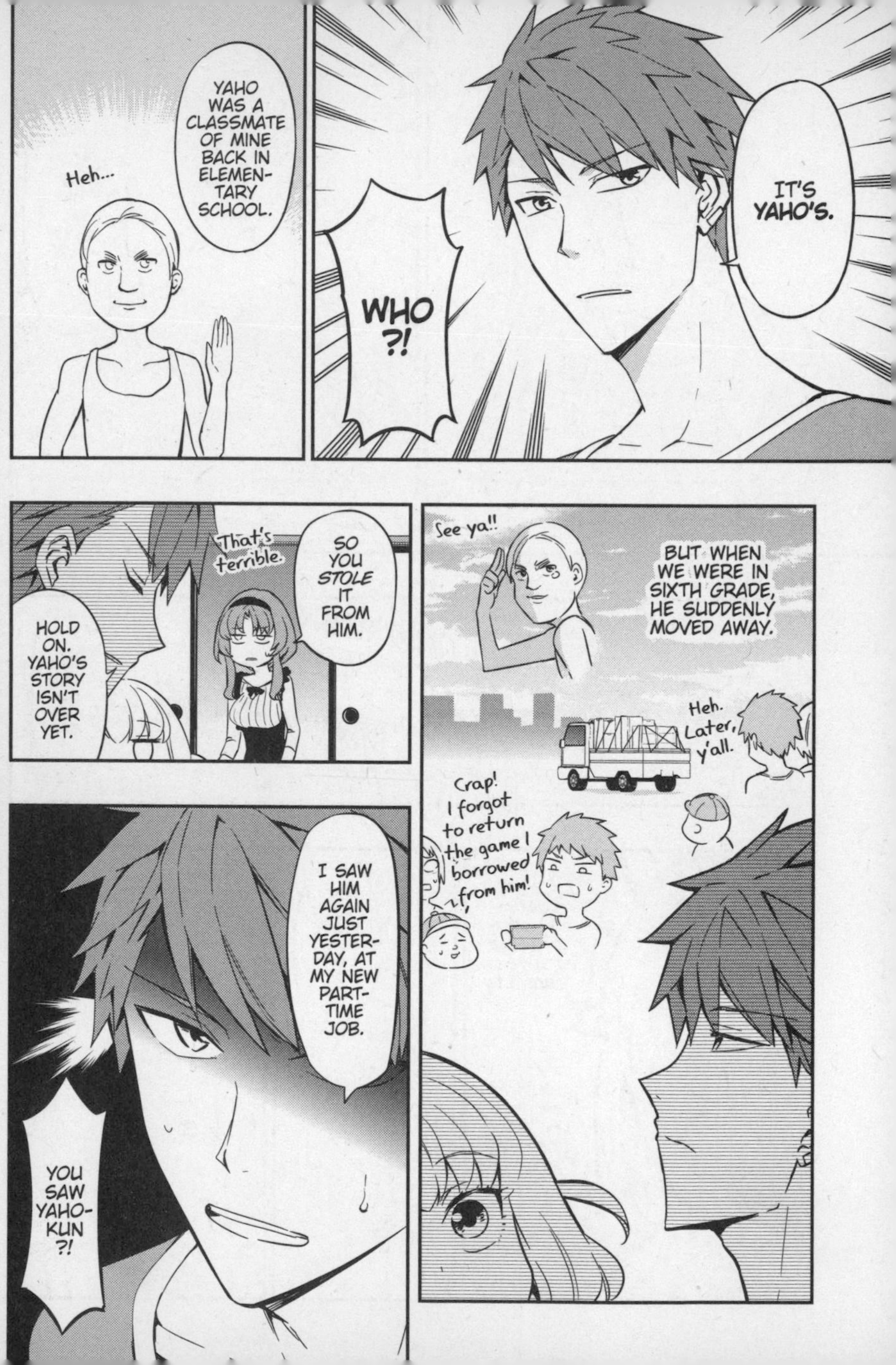
IT'S YAHO'S.
WHO?!
YAHO WAS A CLASSMATE OF MINE BACK IN ELEMENTARY SCHOOL.
Heh...
BUT WHEN WE WERE IN SIXTH GRADE, HE SUDDENLY MOVED AWAY.
See ya!!
Heh. Later, y'all.
Crap! I forgot to return the game I borrowed from him!
SO YOU STOLE IT FROM HIM.
That's terrible.
HOLD ON. YAHO'S STORY ISN'T OVER YET.
I SAW HIM AGAIN JUST YESTERDAY, AT MY NEW PART-TIME JOB.
YOU SAW YAHO-KUN?!

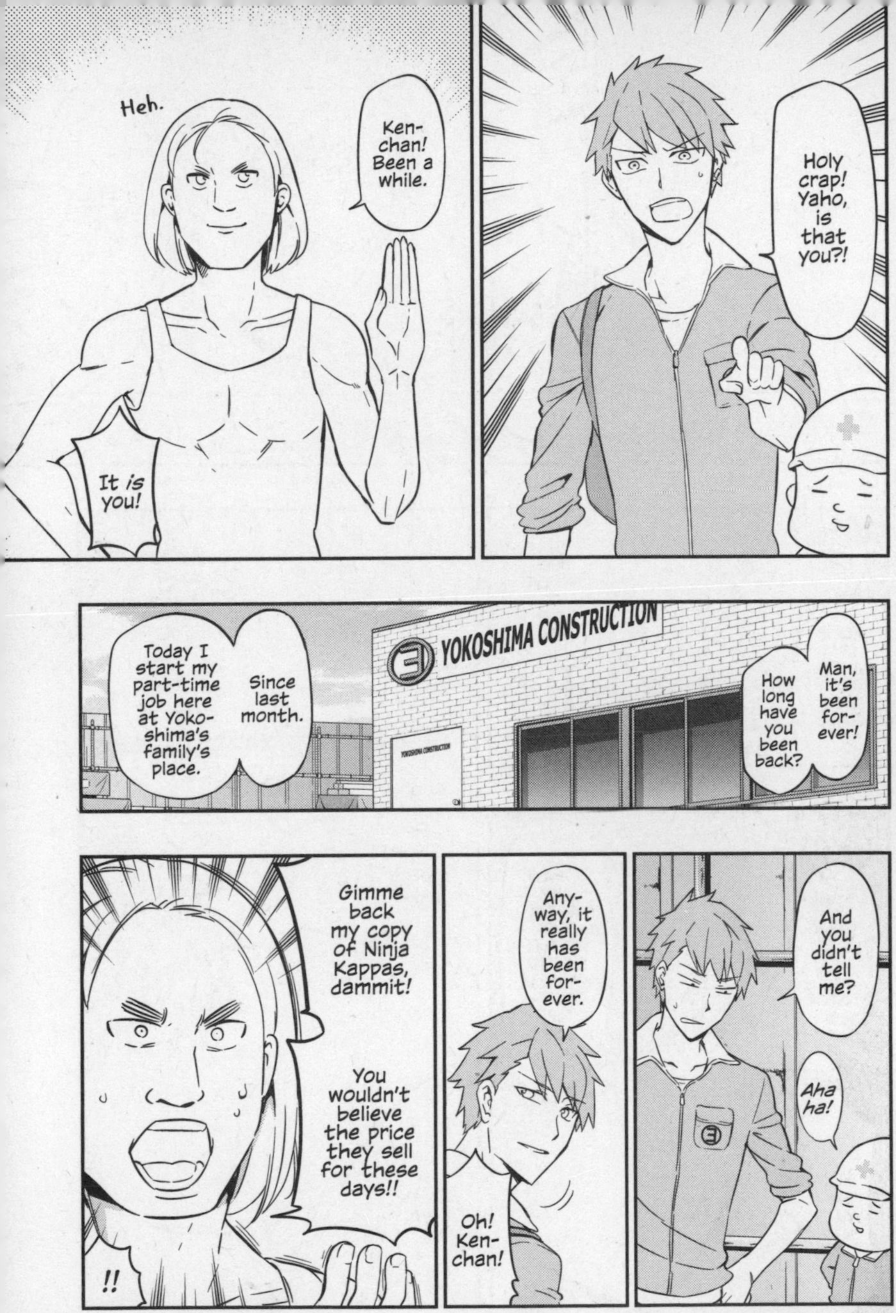
Holy crap! Yaho, is that you?!
Ken-chan! Been a while.
Heh.
It *is* you!
YOKOSHIMA CONSTRUCTION
Man, it's been for-ever!
How long have you been back?
Since last month.
Today I start my part-time job here at Yoko-shima's family's place.
And you didn't tell me?
Aha ha!
Any-way, it really has been for-ever.
Oh! Ken-chan!
Gimme back my copy of Ninja Kappas, dammit!
You wouldn't believe the price they sell for these days!!
!!

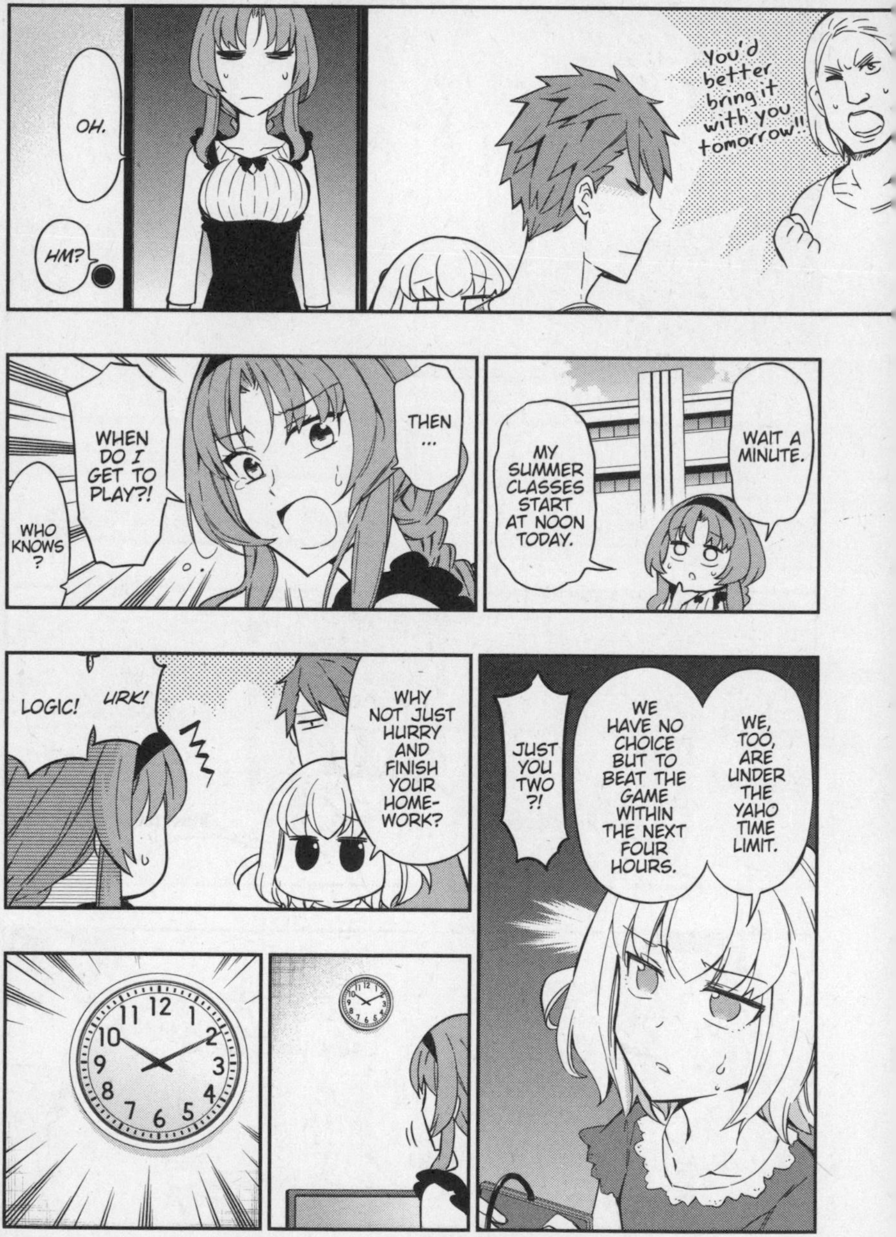
You'd better bring it with you tomorrow!!
OH.
HM?
WAIT A MINUTE.
MY SUMMER CLASSES START AT NOON TODAY.
THEN...
WHEN DO I GET TO PLAY?!
WHO KNOWS?
WE, TOO, ARE UNDER THE YAHO TIME LIMIT.
WE HAVE NO CHOICE BUT TO BEAT THE GAME WITHIN THE NEXT FOUR HOURS.
JUST YOU TWO?!
WHY NOT JUST HURRY AND FINISH YOUR HOME-WORK?
URK!
LOGIC!

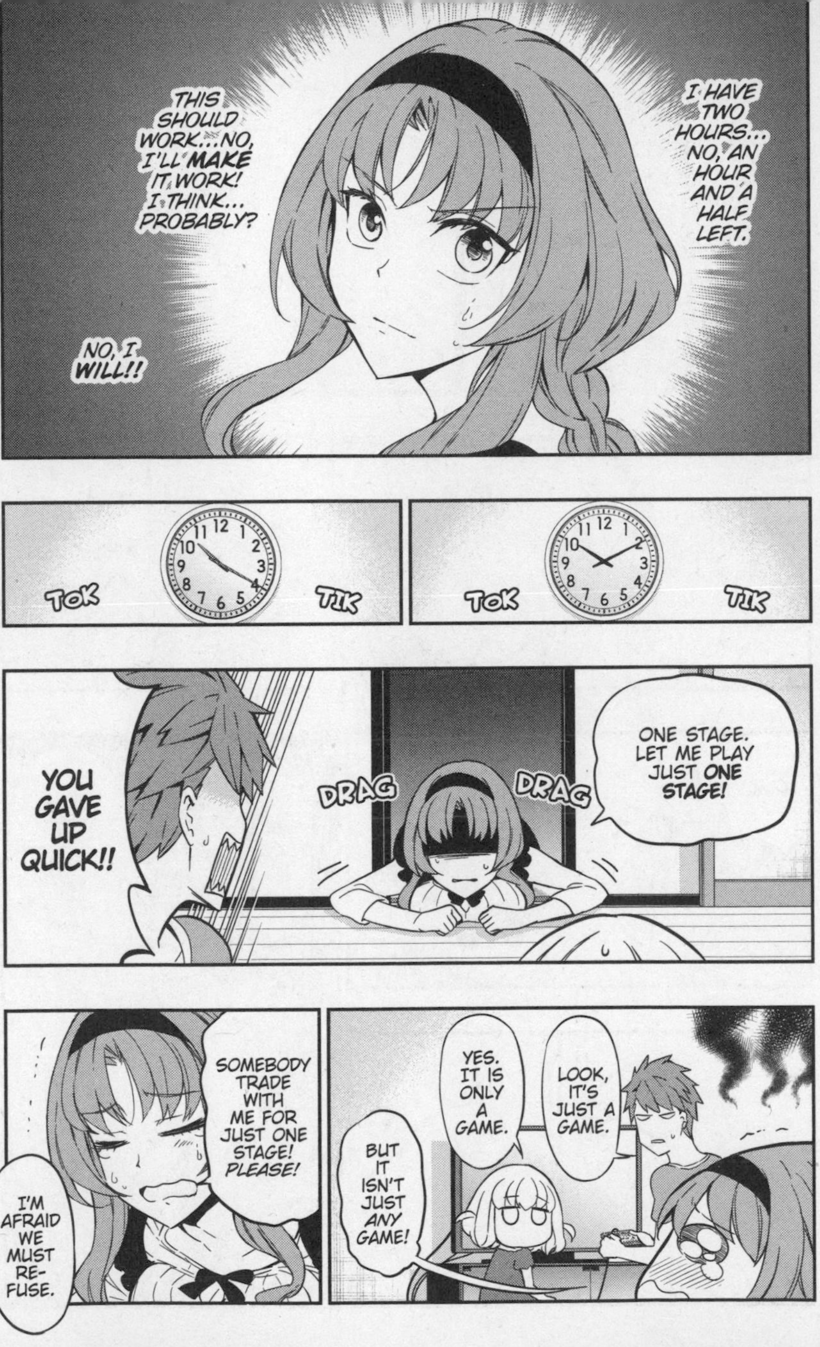
I HAVE TWO HOURS... NO, AN HOUR AND A HALF LEFT.
THIS SHOULD WORK... NO, I'LL **MAKE** IT WORK! I THINK... PROBABLY?
NO, I **WILL**!!
TIK
TOK
TIK
TOK
ONE STAGE. LET ME PLAY JUST **ONE** STAGE!
DRAG
DRAG
YOU GAVE UP QUICK!!
LOOK, IT'S JUST A GAME.
YES. IT IS ONLY A GAME.
BUT IT ISN'T JUST *ANY* GAME!
SOMEBODY TRADE WITH ME FOR JUST ONE STAGE! PLEASE!
I'M AFRAID WE MUST RE-FUSE.

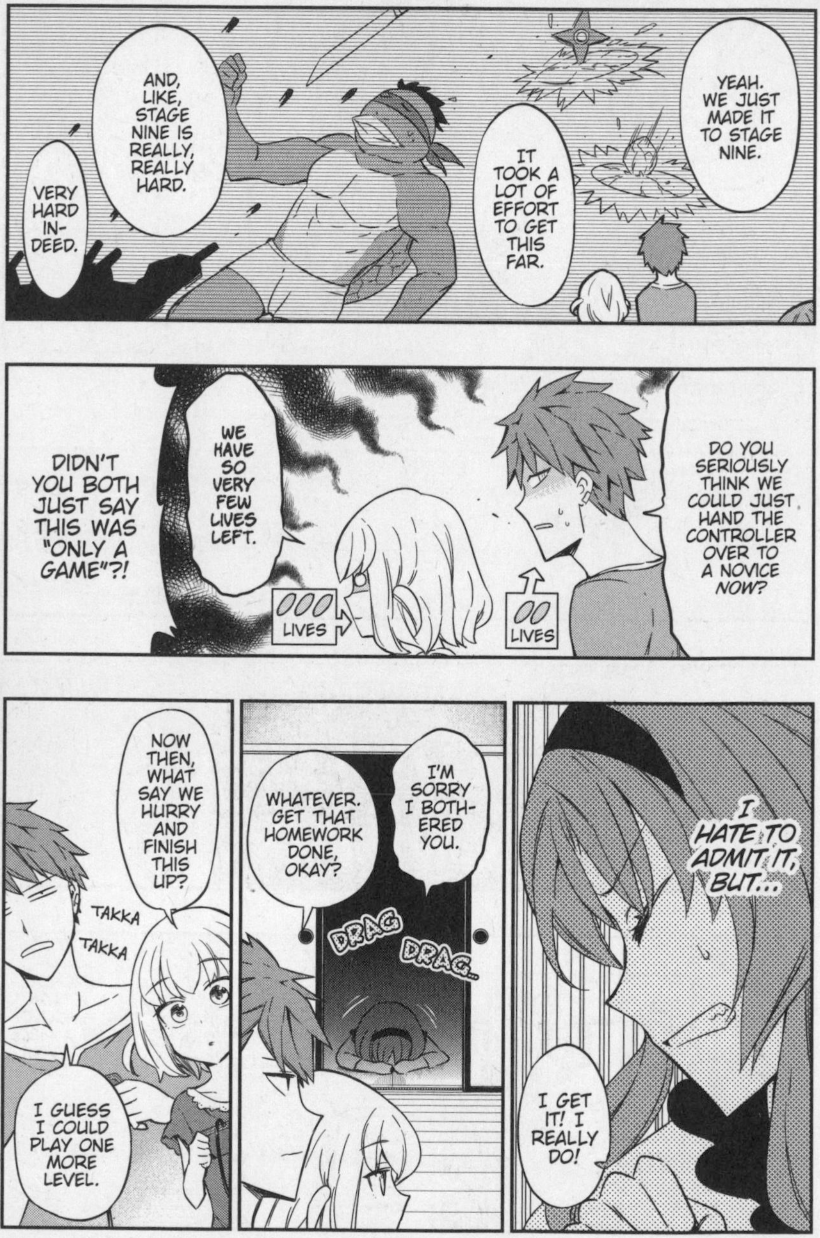
YEAH. WE JUST MADE IT TO STAGE NINE.
IT TOOK A LOT OF EFFORT TO GET THIS FAR.
AND, LIKE, STAGE NINE IS REALLY, REALLY HARD.
VERY HARD IN-DEED.
DO YOU SERIOUSLY THINK WE COULD JUST HAND THE CONTROLLER OVER TO A NOVICE NOW?
LIVES
LIVES
WE HAVE SO VERY FEW LIVES LEFT.
DIDN'T YOU BOTH JUST SAY THIS WAS "ONLY A GAME"?!
I HATE TO ADMIT IT, BUT...
I GET IT! I REALLY DO!
I'M SORRY I BOTHERED YOU.
WHATEVER. GET THAT HOMEWORK DONE, OKAY?
DRAG
DRAG...
NOW THEN, WHAT SAY WE HURRY AND FINISH THIS UP?
TAKKA
TAKKA
I GUESS I COULD PLAY ONE MORE LEVEL.

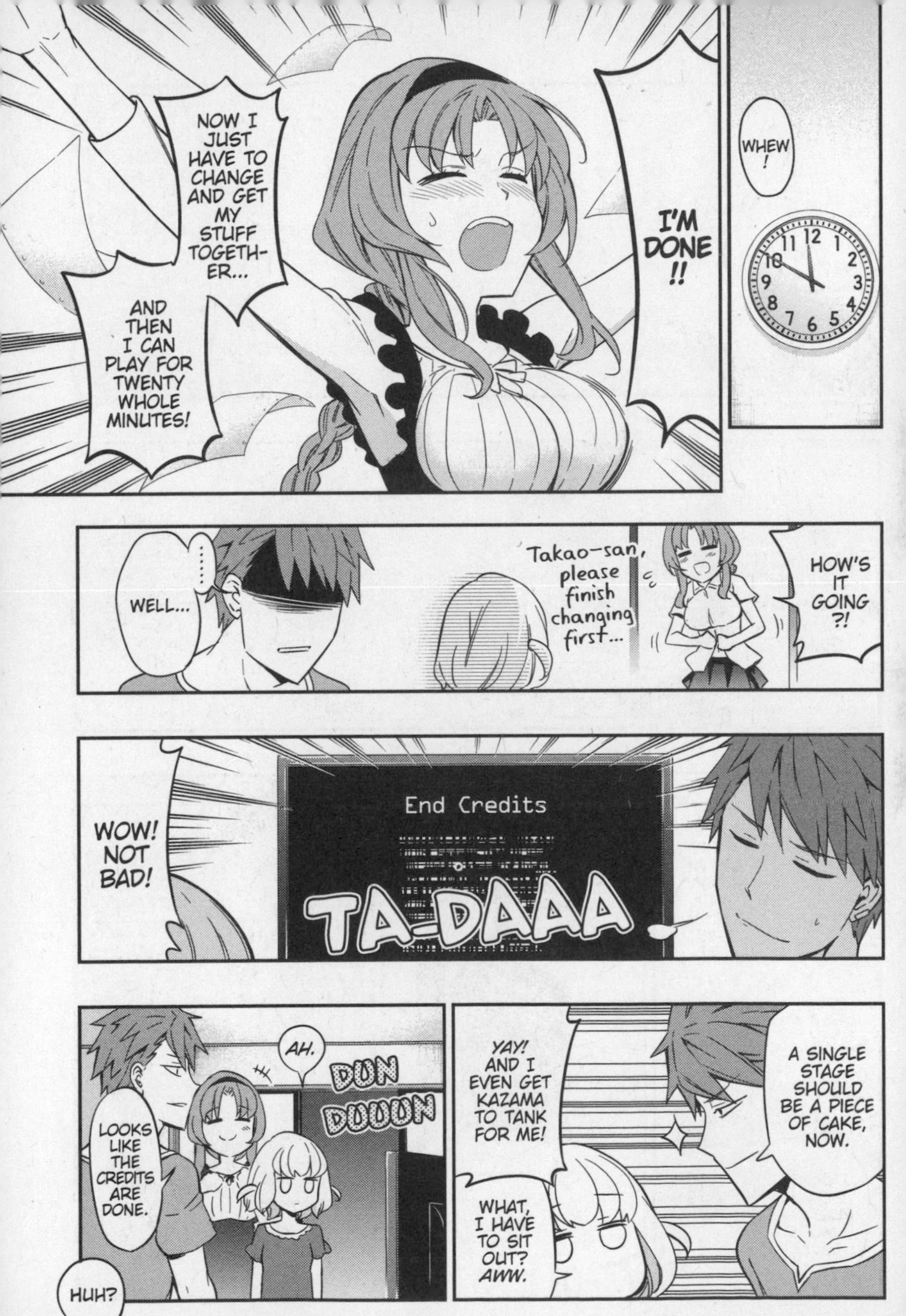
WHEW!
I'M DONE!!
NOW I JUST HAVE TO CHANGE AND GET MY STUFF TOGETHER...
AND THEN I CAN PLAY FOR TWENTY WHOLE MINUTES!
HOW'S IT GOING?!
Takao-san, please finish changing first...
......
WELL...
TA-DAAA
End Credits
WOW! NOT BAD!
A SINGLE STAGE SHOULD BE A PIECE OF CAKE, NOW.
YAY! AND I EVEN GET KAZAMA TO TANK FOR ME!
WHAT, I HAVE TO SIT OUT? AWW.
AH.
DUN DUUUN
LOOKS LIKE THE CREDITS ARE DONE.
HUH?

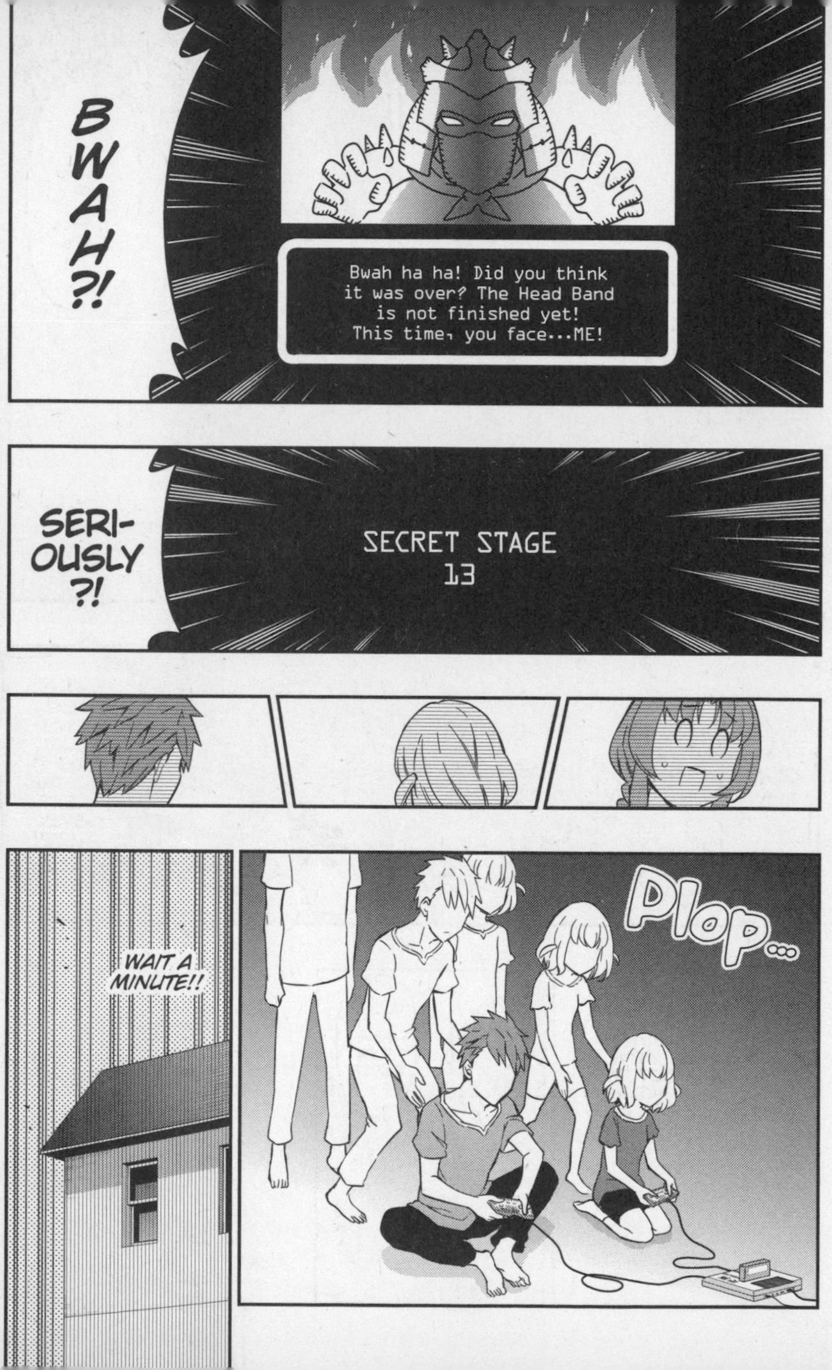
Bwah ha ha! Did you think it was over? The Head Band is not finished yet! This time, you face...ME!
BWAH?!
SECRET STAGE 13
SERI-OUSLY?!
Plop...
WAIT A MINUTE!!

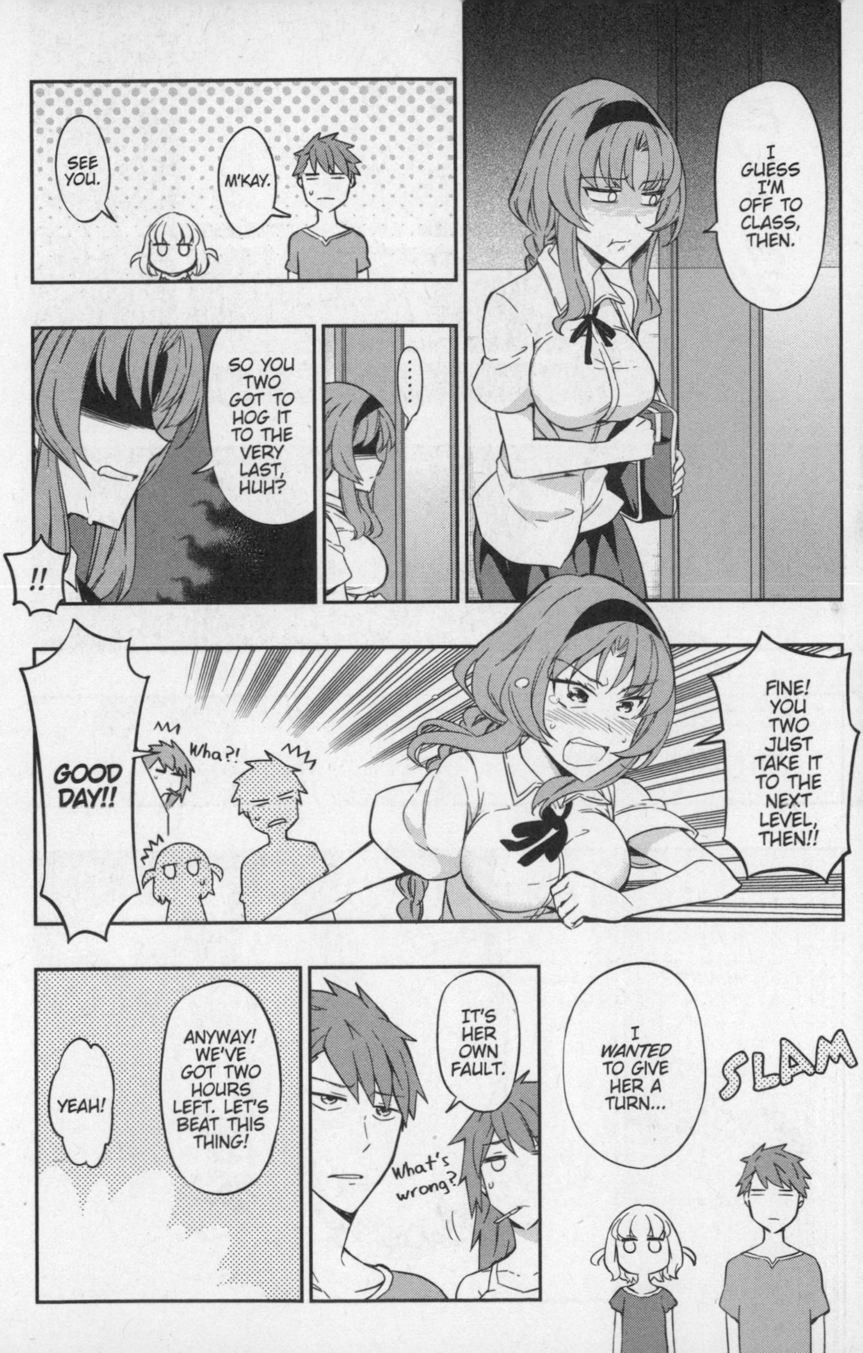
I GUESS I'M OFF TO CLASS, THEN.
M'KAY.
SEE YOU.
......
SO YOU TWO GOT TO HOG IT TO THE VERY LAST, HUH?
!!
FINE! YOU TWO JUST TAKE IT TO THE NEXT LEVEL, THEN!!
Wha?!
GOOD DAY!!
SLAM
I WANTED TO GIVE HER A TURN...
IT'S HER OWN FAULT.
What's wrong?
ANYWAY! WE'VE GOT TWO HOURS LEFT. LET'S BEAT THIS THING!
YEAH!

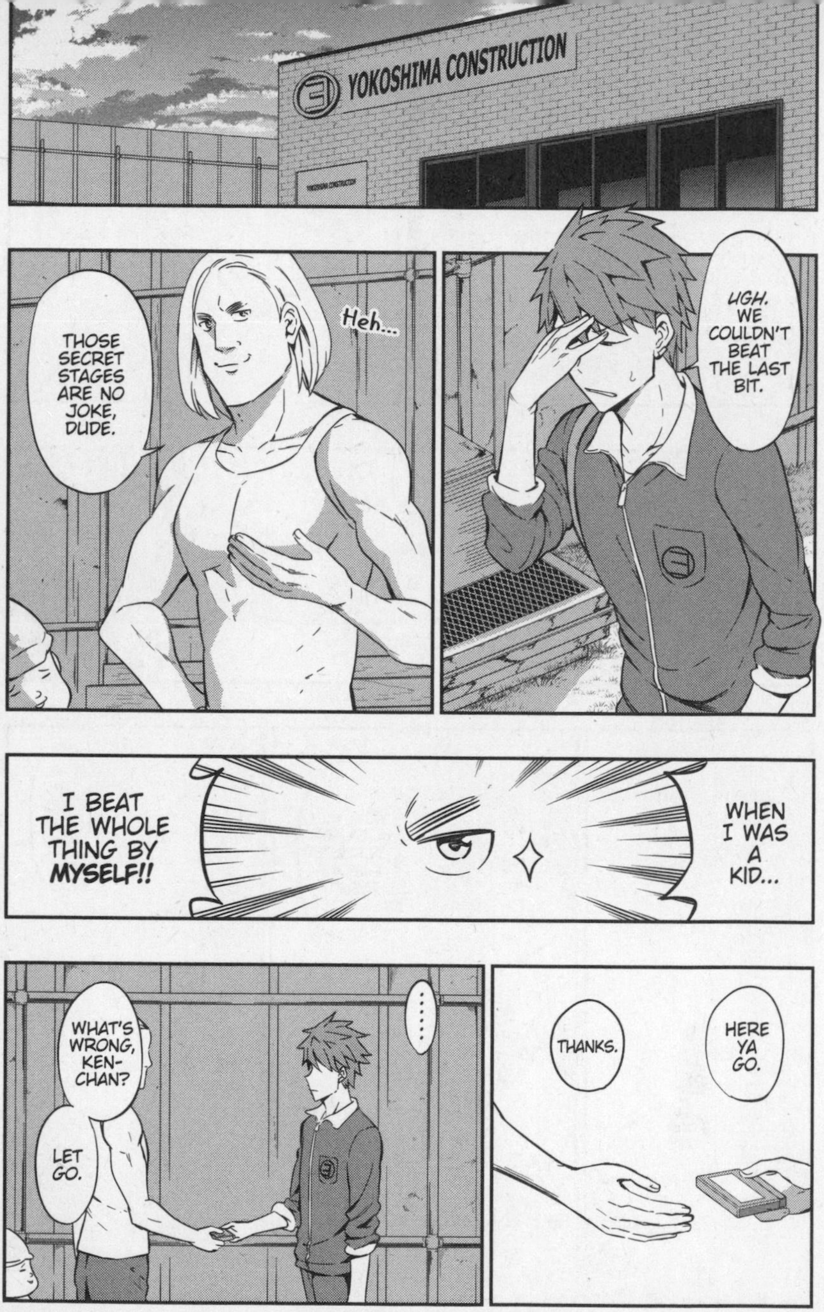
YOKOSHIMA CONSTRUCTION
YOKOSHIMA CONSTRUCTION
UGH. WE COULDN'T BEAT THE LAST BIT.
Heh...
THOSE SECRET STAGES ARE NO JOKE, DUDE.
WHEN I WAS A KID...
I BEAT THE WHOLE THING BY **MYSELF!!**
HERE YA GO.
THANKS.
......
WHAT'S WRONG, KEN-CHAN?
LET GO.

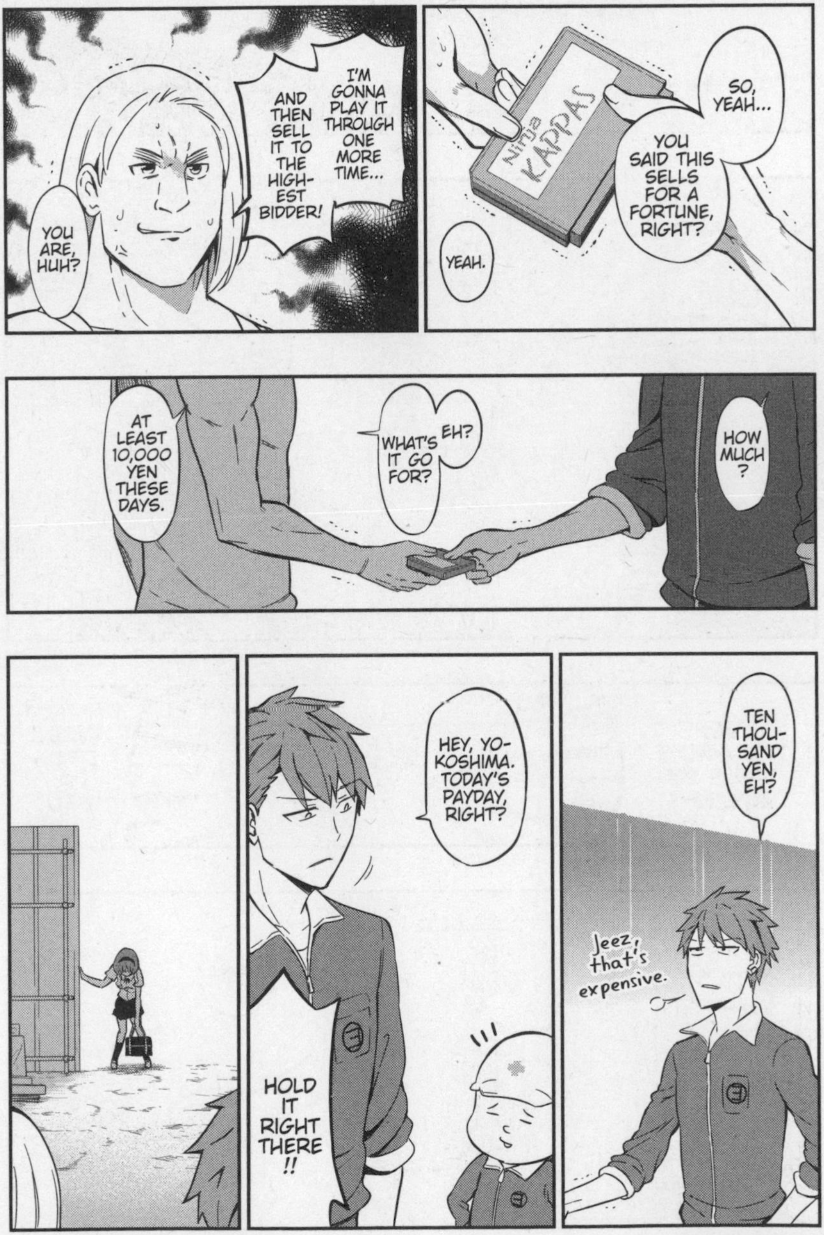
SO, YEAH...
YOU SAID THIS SELLS FOR A FORTUNE, RIGHT?
Ninja KAPPAS
YEAH.
I'M GONNA PLAY IT THROUGH ONE MORE TIME...
AND THEN SELL IT TO THE HIGHEST BIDDER!
YOU ARE, HUH?
HOW MUCH?
EH?
WHAT'S IT GO FOR?
AT LEAST 10,000 YEN THESE DAYS.
TEN THOUSAND YEN, EH?
Jeez, that's expensive.
HEY, YOKOSHIMA. TODAY'S PAYDAY, RIGHT?
HOLD IT RIGHT THERE!!

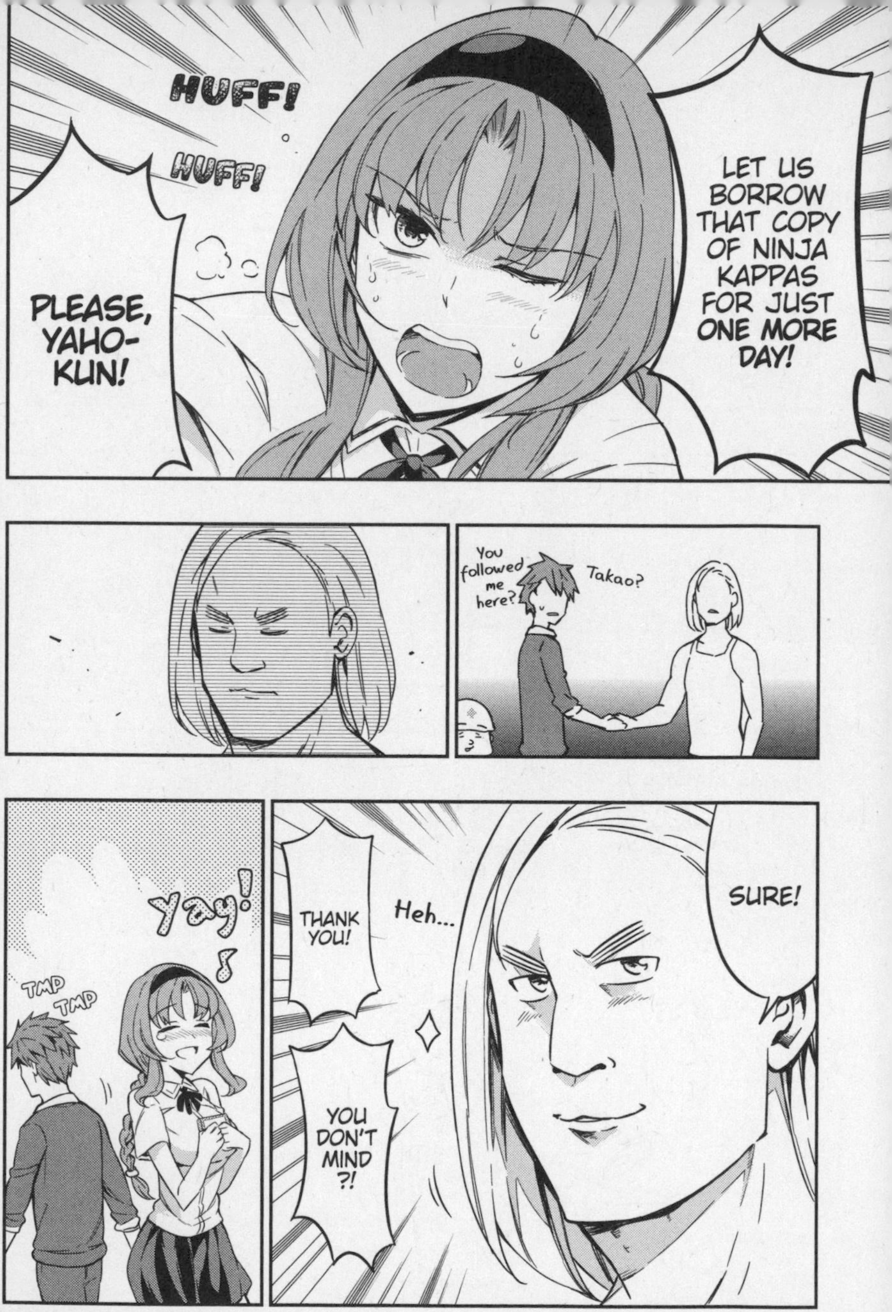
LET US BORROW THAT COPY OF NINJA KAPPAS FOR JUST ONE MORE DAY!
HUFF!
HUFF!
PLEASE, YAHO-KUN!
Takao?
You followed me here?
SURE!
Heh...
THANK YOU!
YOU DON'T MIND?!
Yay! ♪
TMP TMP

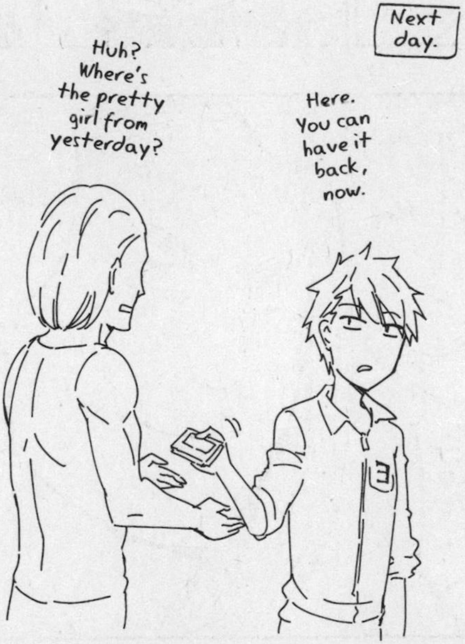
Next day.
Huh? Where's the pretty girl from yesterday?
Here. You can have it back, now.

D-FRAGMENTS

ディーふらぐ!

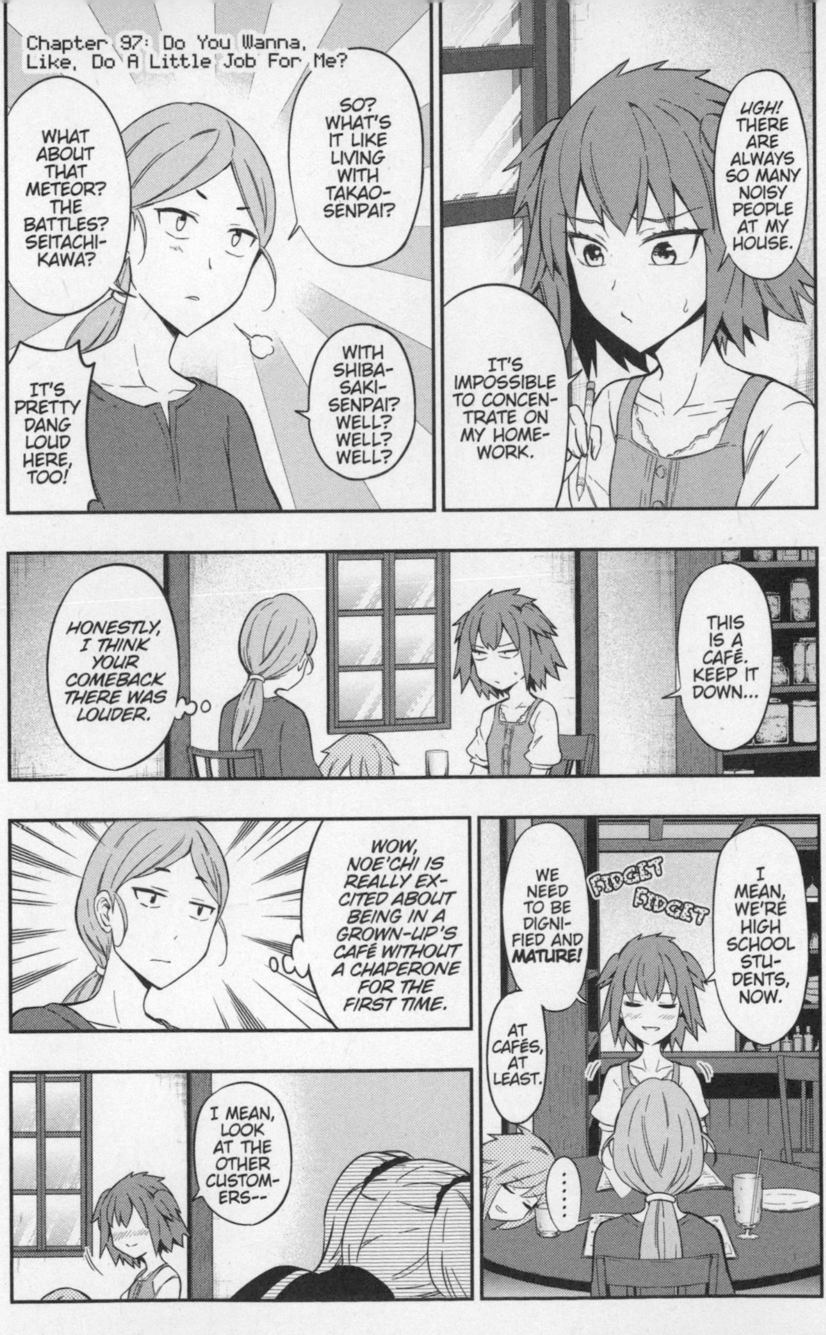
Chapter 97: Do You Wanna, Like, Do A Little Job For Me?
UGH! THERE ARE ALWAYS SO MANY NOISY PEOPLE AT MY HOUSE.
IT'S IMPOSSIBLE TO CONCENTRATE ON MY HOMEWORK.
SO? WHAT'S IT LIKE LIVING WITH TAKAO-SENPAI?
WHAT ABOUT THAT METEOR? THE BATTLES? SEITACHIKAWA?
WITH SHIBASAKI-SENPAI? WELL? WELL? WELL?
IT'S PRETTY DANG LOUD HERE, TOO!
THIS IS A CAFÉ. KEEP IT DOWN...
HONESTLY, I THINK YOUR COMEBACK THERE WAS LOUDER.
I MEAN, WE'RE HIGH SCHOOL STUDENTS, NOW.
FIDGET FIDGET
WE NEED TO BE DIGNIFIED AND MATURE!
AT CAFÉS, AT LEAST.
......
WOW, NOE'CHI IS REALLY EXCITED ABOUT BEING IN A GROWN-UP'S CAFÉ WITHOUT A CHAPERONE FOR THE FIRST TIME.
I MEAN, LOOK AT THE OTHER CUSTOMERS--

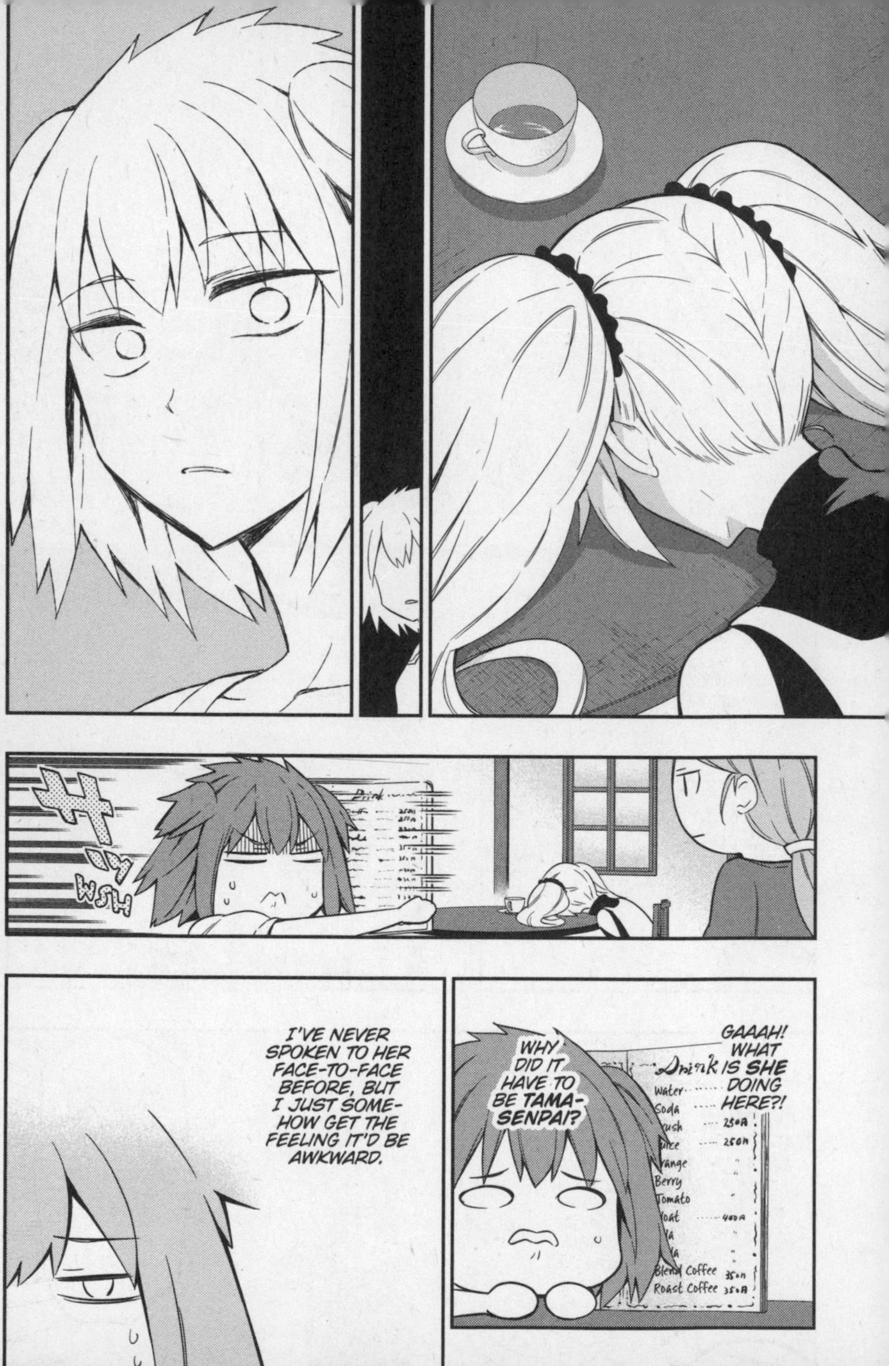
WHSH
GAAAH! WHAT IS SHE DOING HERE?!
WHY DID IT HAVE TO BE TAMA-SENPAI?
Drink
Water
Soda
Berry
Tomato
Blend Coffee 350円
Roast Coffee 350円
I'VE NEVER SPOKEN TO HER FACE-TO-FACE BEFORE, BUT I JUST SOMEHOW GET THE FEELING IT'D BE AWKWARD.

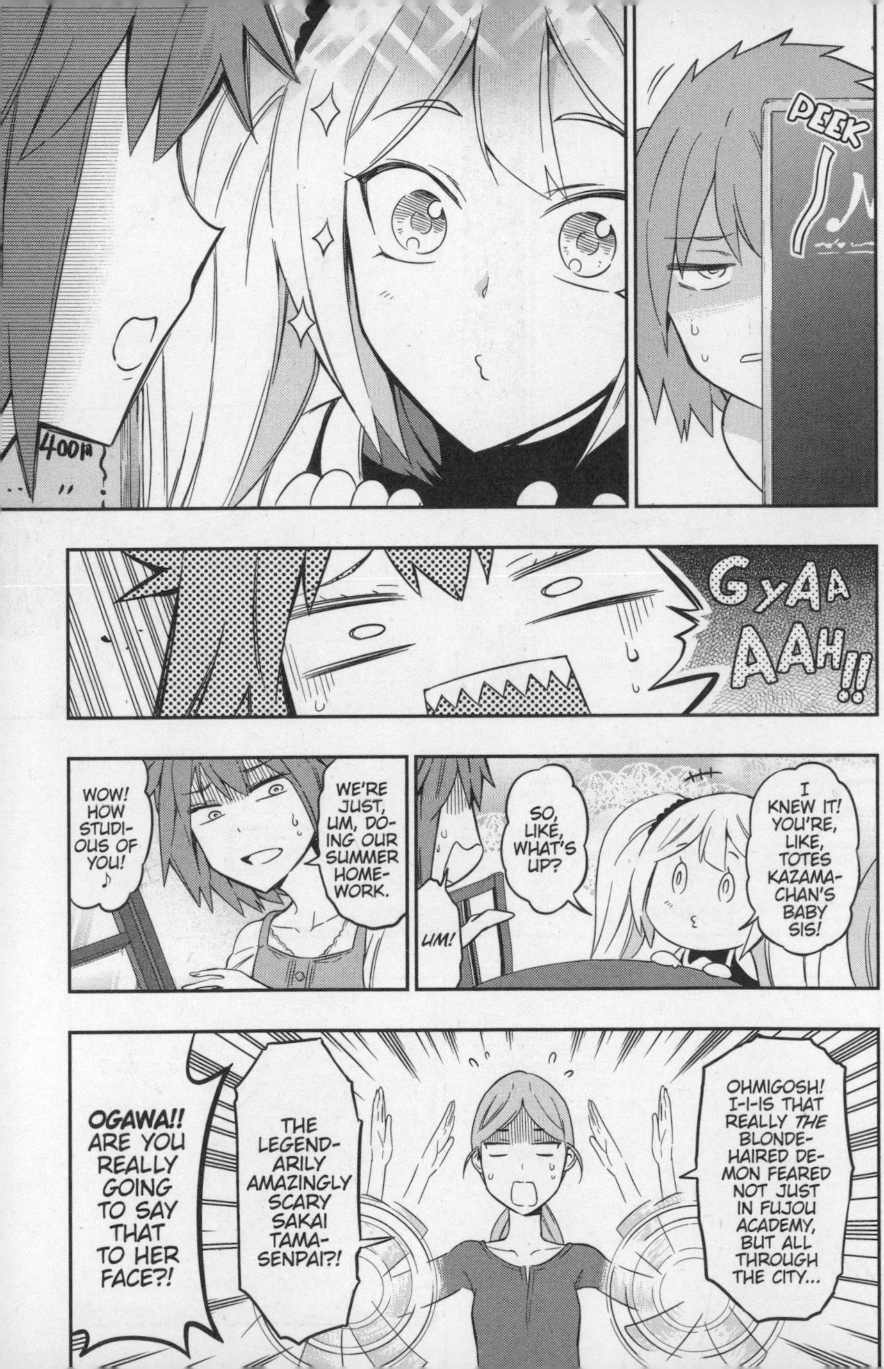
PEEK
400円
GYAAAAH!!
I KNEW IT! YOU'RE, LIKE, TOTES KAZAMA-CHAN'S BABY SIS!
SO, LIKE, WHAT'S UP?
UM!
WE'RE JUST, UM, DOING OUR SUMMER HOMEWORK.
WOW! HOW STUDIOUS OF YOU! ♪
OHMIGOSH! I-I-IS THAT REALLY *THE* BLONDE-HAIRED DEMON FEARED NOT JUST IN FUJOU ACADEMY, BUT ALL THROUGH THE CITY...
THE LEGENDARILY AMAZINGLY SCARY SAKAI TAMA-SENPAI?!
OGAWA!! ARE YOU REALLY GOING TO SAY THAT TO HER FACE?!

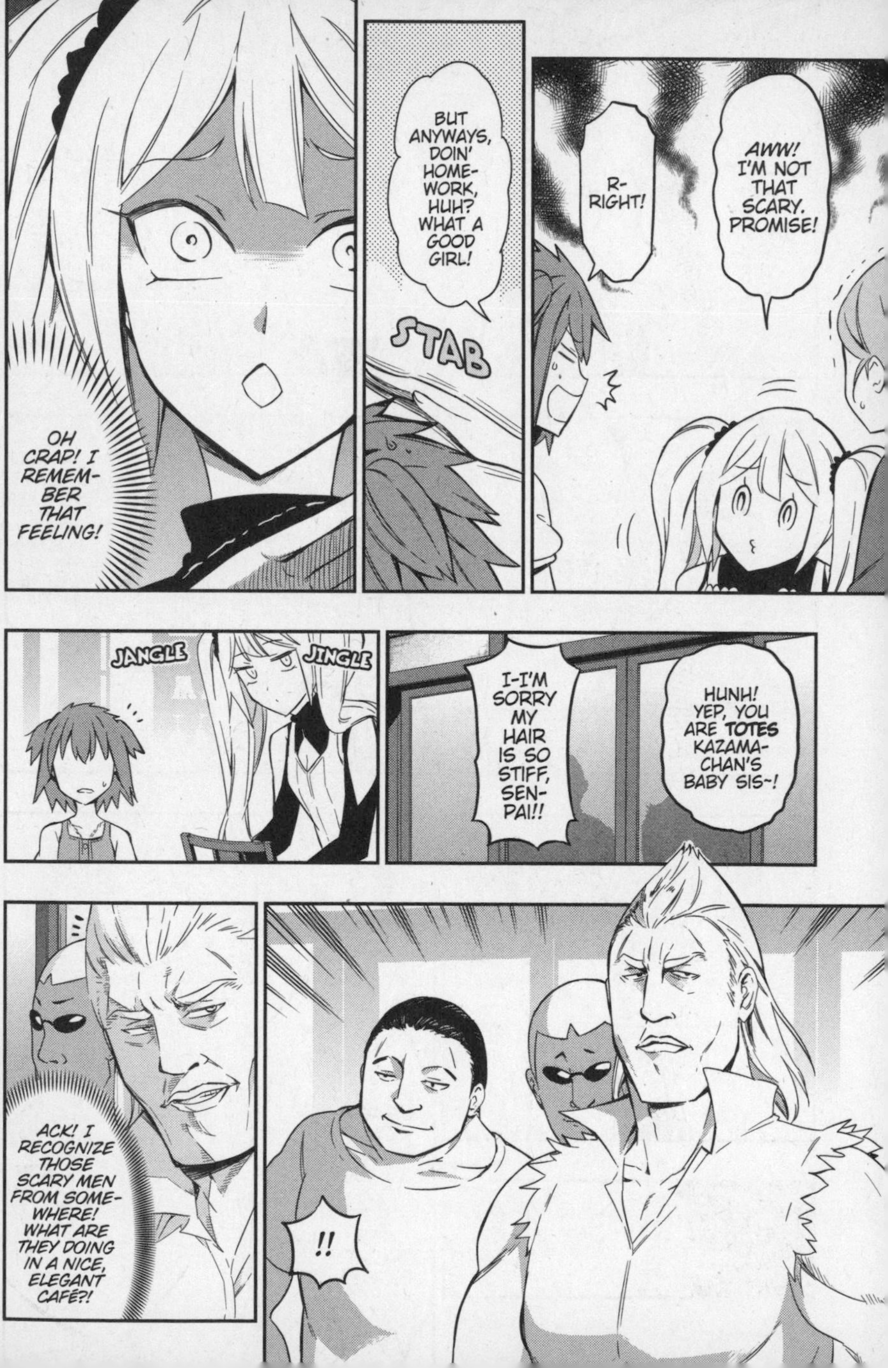
AWW! I'M NOT THAT SCARY. PROMISE!
R-RIGHT!
BUT ANYWAYS, DOIN' HOME-WORK, HUH? WHAT A GOOD GIRL!
STAB
OH CRAP! I REMEMBER THAT FEELING!
HUNH! YEP, YOU ARE **TOTES** KAZAMA-CHAN'S BABY SIS~!
I-I'M SORRY MY HAIR IS SO STIFF, SEN-PAI!!
JINGLE
JANGLE
!!
ACK! I RECOGNIZE THOSE SCARY MEN FROM SOME-WHERE! WHAT ARE THEY DOING IN A NICE, ELEGANT CAFÉ?!

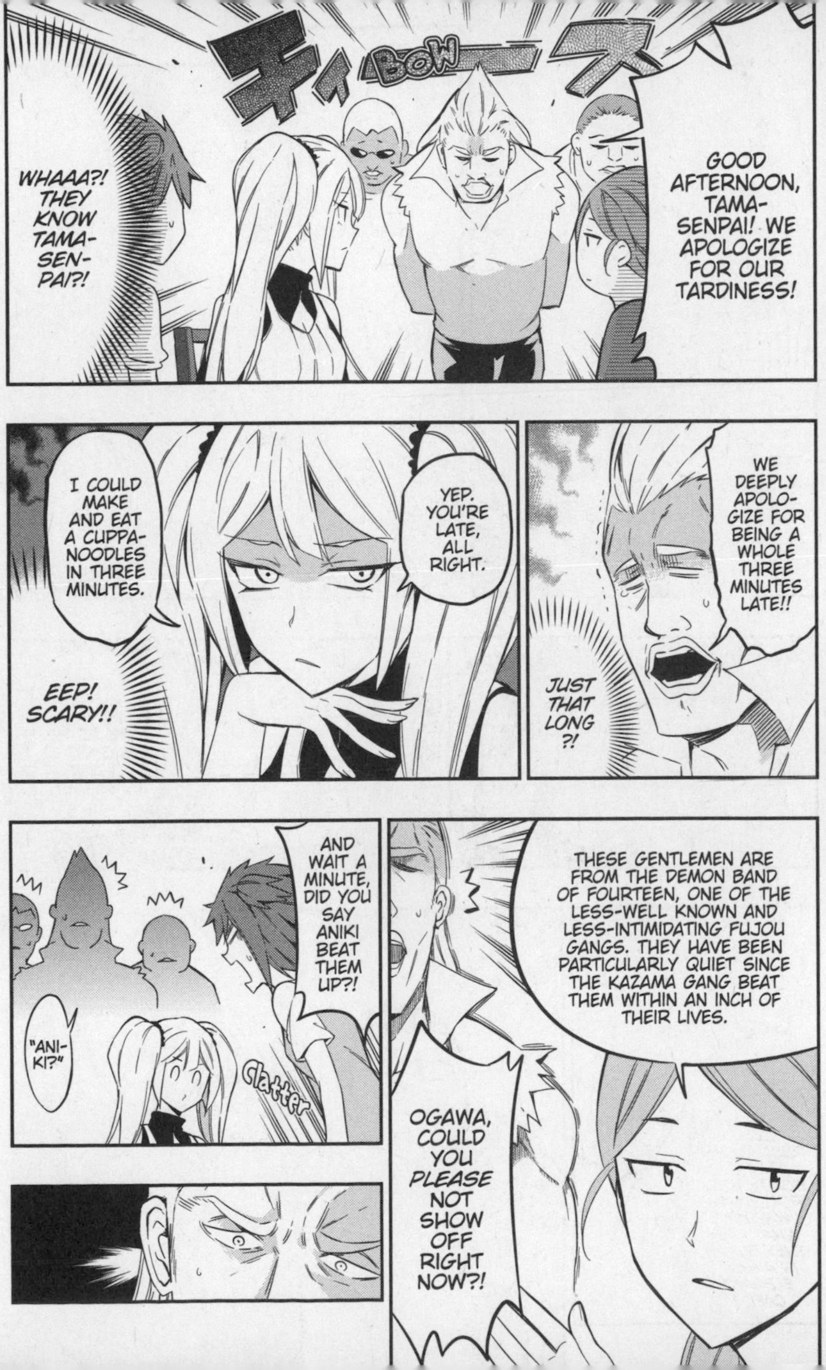

BOW
GOOD AFTERNOON, TAMA-SENPAI! WE APOLOGIZE FOR OUR TARDINESS!
WHAAA?! THEY KNOW TAMA-SENPAI?!
WE DEEPLY APOLOGIZE FOR BEING A WHOLE THREE MINUTES LATE!!
JUST THAT LONG?!
YEP. YOU'RE LATE, ALL RIGHT.
I COULD MAKE AND EAT A CUPPA-NOODLES IN THREE MINUTES.
EEP! SCARY!!
THESE GENTLEMEN ARE FROM THE DEMON BAND OF FOURTEEN, ONE OF THE LESS-WELL KNOWN AND LESS-INTIMIDATING FUJOU GANGS. THEY HAVE BEEN PARTICULARLY QUIET SINCE THE KAZAMA GANG BEAT THEM WITHIN AN INCH OF THEIR LIVES.
OGAWA, COULD YOU PLEASE NOT SHOW OFF RIGHT NOW?!
AND WAIT A MINUTE, DID YOU SAY ANIKI BEAT THEM UP?!
Clatter
"ANIKI?"

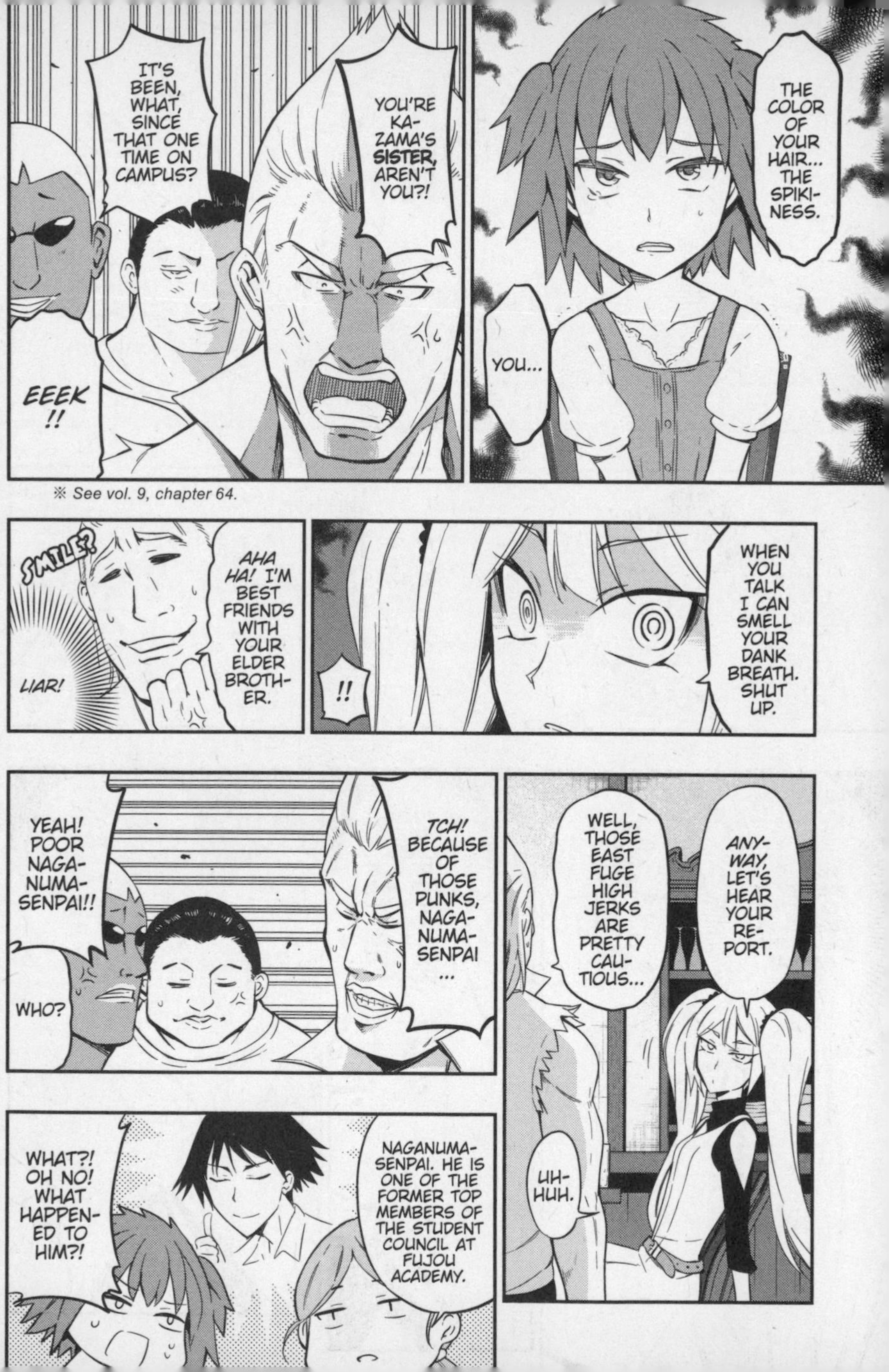
THE COLOR OF YOUR HAIR... THE SPIKINESS.
YOU...
YOU'RE KAZAMA'S **SISTER,** AREN'T YOU?!
IT'S BEEN, WHAT, SINCE THAT ONE TIME ON CAMPUS?
EEEK!!
WHEN YOU TALK I CAN SMELL YOUR DANK BREATH. SHUT UP.
!!
AHA HA! I'M BEST FRIENDS WITH YOUR ELDER BROTHER.
SMILE?
LIAR!
ANYWAY, LET'S HEAR YOUR REPORT.
WELL, THOSE EAST FUGE HIGH JERKS ARE PRETTY CAUTIOUS...
UH-HUH.
TCH! BECAUSE OF THOSE PUNKS, NAGANUMA-SENPAI...
YEAH! POOR NAGANUMA-SENPAI!!
WHO?
NAGANUMA-SENPAI. HE IS ONE OF THE FORMER TOP MEMBERS OF THE STUDENT COUNCIL AT FUJOU ACADEMY.
WHAT?! OH NO! WHAT HAPPENED TO HIM?!

※ *See vol. 9, chapter 64.*

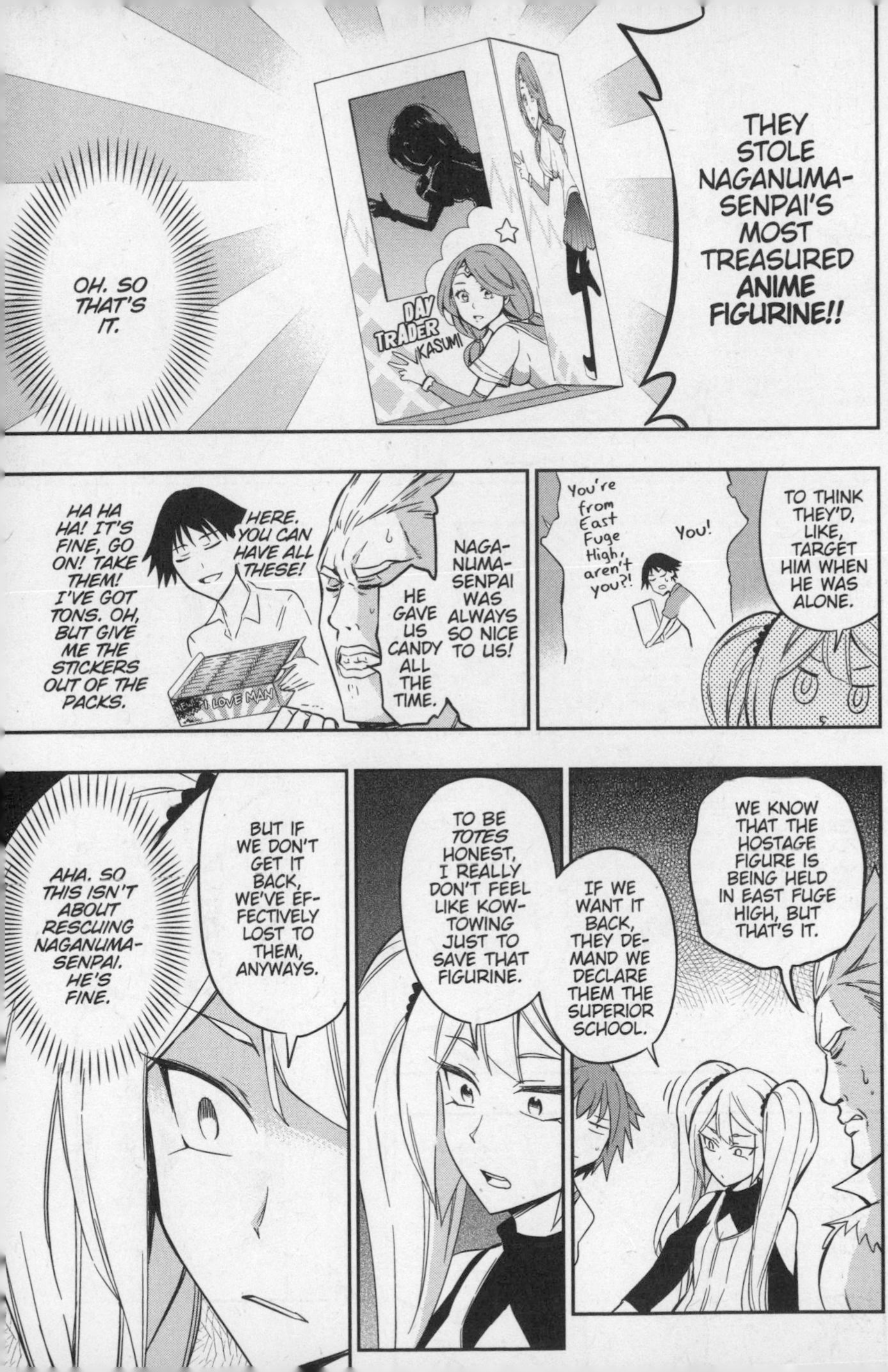
THEY STOLE NAGANUMA-SENPAI'S MOST TREASURED ANIME FIGURINE!!
DAY TRADER KASUMI
OH. SO THAT'S IT.
TO THINK THEY'D, LIKE, TARGET HIM WHEN HE WAS ALONE.
You!
You're from East Fuge High, aren't you?!
NAGANUMA-SENPAI WAS ALWAYS SO NICE TO US!
HE GAVE US CANDY ALL THE TIME.
HERE. YOU CAN HAVE ALL THESE!
I LOVE MAN
HA HA HA! IT'S FINE, GO ON! TAKE THEM! I'VE GOT TONS. OH, BUT GIVE ME THE STICKERS OUT OF THE PACKS.
WE KNOW THAT THE HOSTAGE FIGURE IS BEING HELD IN EAST FUGE HIGH, BUT THAT'S IT.
IF WE WANT IT BACK, THEY DEMAND WE DECLARE THEM THE SUPERIOR SCHOOL.
TO BE *TOTES* HONEST, I REALLY DON'T FEEL LIKE KOWTOWING JUST TO SAVE THAT FIGURINE.
BUT IF WE DON'T GET IT BACK, WE'VE EFFECTIVELY LOST TO THEM, ANYWAYS.
AHA. SO THIS ISN'T ABOUT RESCUING NAGANUMA-SENPAI. HE'S FINE.

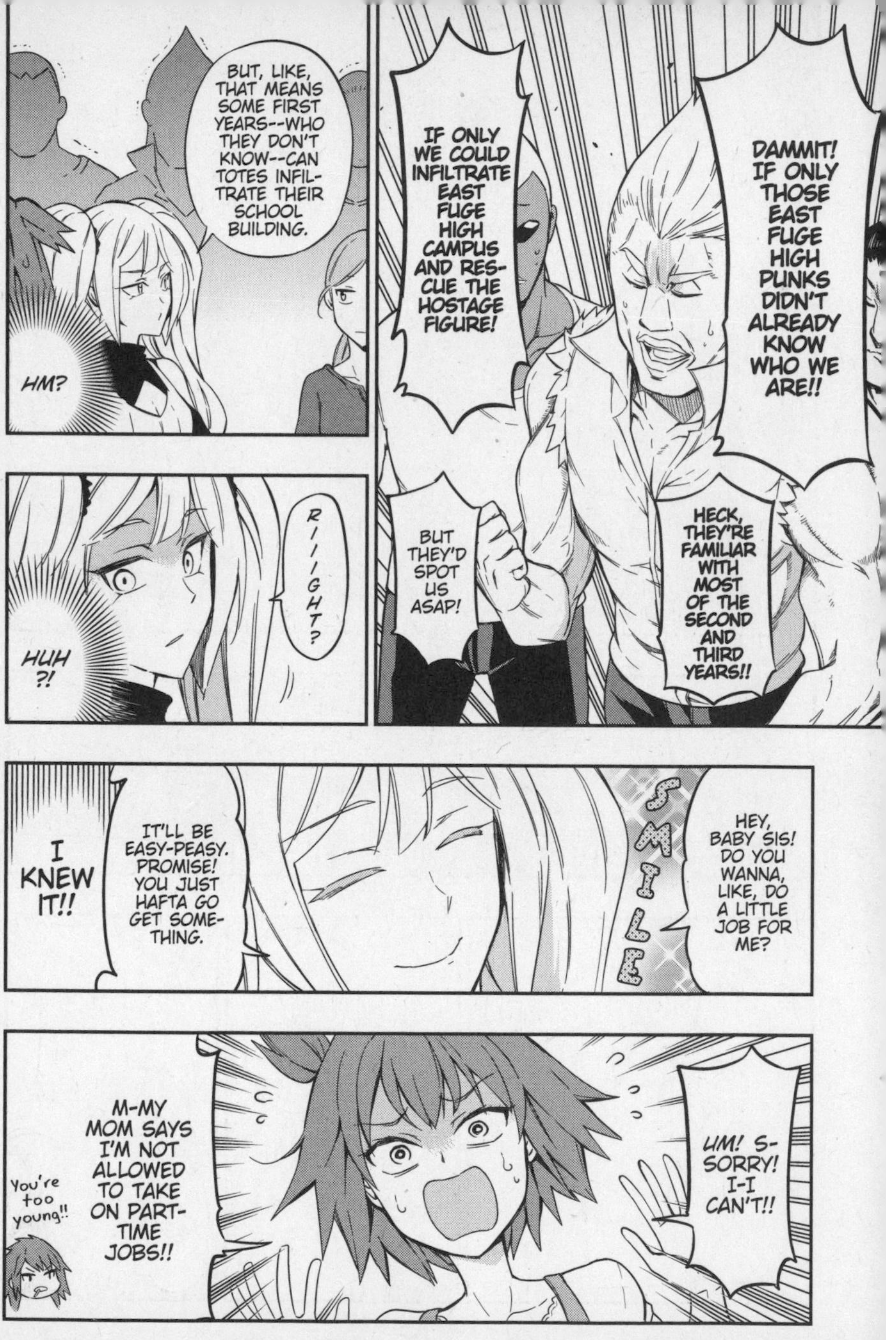
DAMMIT! IF ONLY THOSE EAST FUGE HIGH PUNKS DIDN'T ALREADY KNOW WHO WE ARE!!
IF ONLY WE COULD INFILTRATE EAST FUGE HIGH CAMPUS AND RESCUE THE HOSTAGE FIGURE!
HECK, THEY'RE FAMILIAR WITH MOST OF THE SECOND AND THIRD YEARS!!
BUT THEY'D SPOT US ASAP!
BUT, LIKE, THAT MEANS SOME FIRST YEARS--WHO THEY DON'T KNOW--CAN TOTES INFILTRATE THEIR SCHOOL BUILDING.
HM?
RIIIGHT?
HUH ?!
SMILE
HEY, BABY SIS! DO YOU WANNA, LIKE, DO A LITTLE JOB FOR ME?
IT'LL BE EASY-PEASY. PROMISE! YOU JUST HAFTA GO GET SOMETHING.
I KNEW IT!!
UM! S-SORRY! I-I CAN'T!!
M-MY MOM SAYS I'M NOT ALLOWED TO TAKE ON PART-TIME JOBS!!
You're too young!!

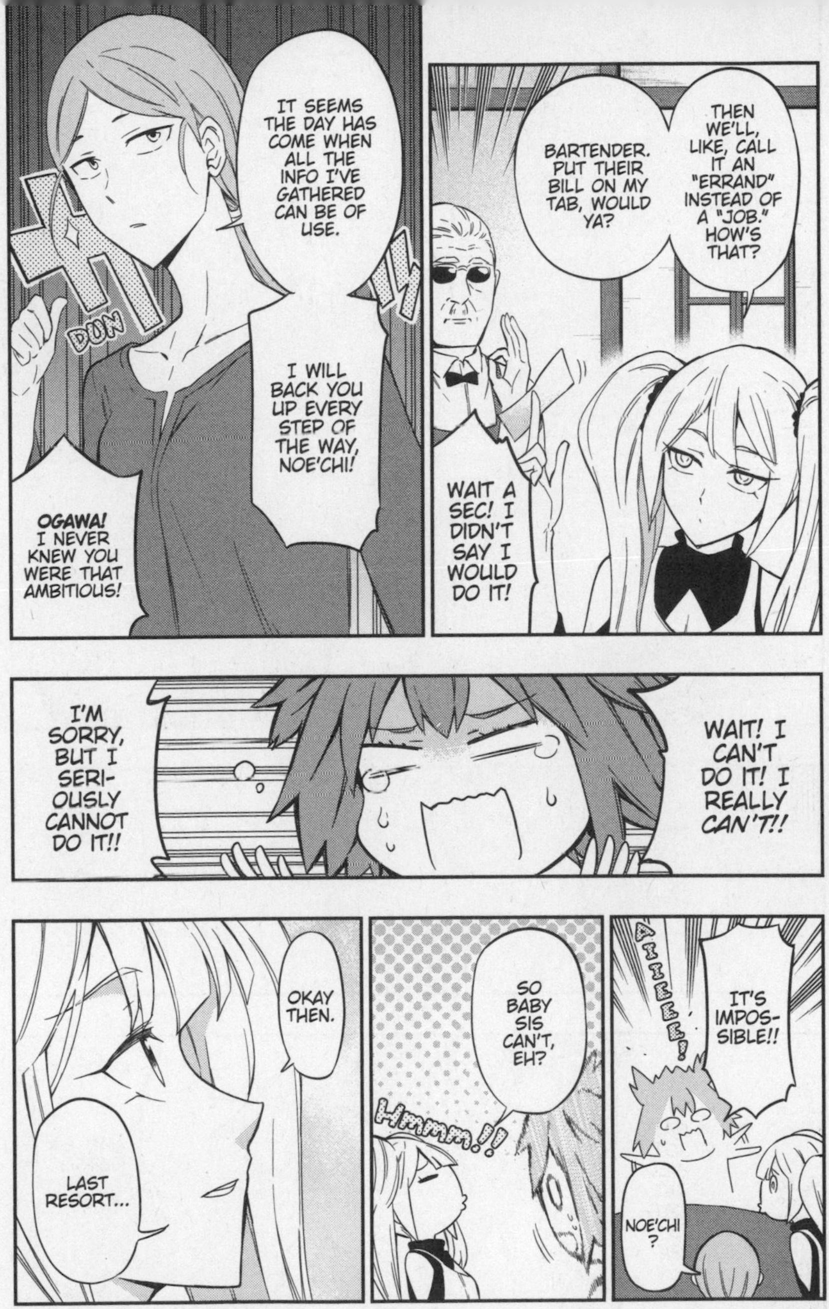
THEN WE'LL, LIKE, CALL IT AN "ERRAND" INSTEAD OF A "JOB." HOW'S THAT?
BARTENDER. PUT THEIR BILL ON MY TAB, WOULD YA?
WAIT A SEC! I DIDN'T SAY I WOULD DO IT!
IT SEEMS THE DAY HAS COME WHEN ALL THE INFO I'VE GATHERED CAN BE OF USE.
I WILL BACK YOU UP EVERY STEP OF THE WAY, NOE'CHI!
DUN
OGAWA! I NEVER KNEW YOU WERE THAT AMBITIOUS!
WAIT! I CAN'T DO IT! I REALLY CAN'T!!
I'M SORRY, BUT I SERI-OUSLY CANNOT DO IT!!
IT'S IMPOS-SIBLE!!
AIIEEE!
NOE'CHI?
SO BABY SIS CAN'T, EH?
Hmmm!!
OKAY THEN.
LAST RESORT...

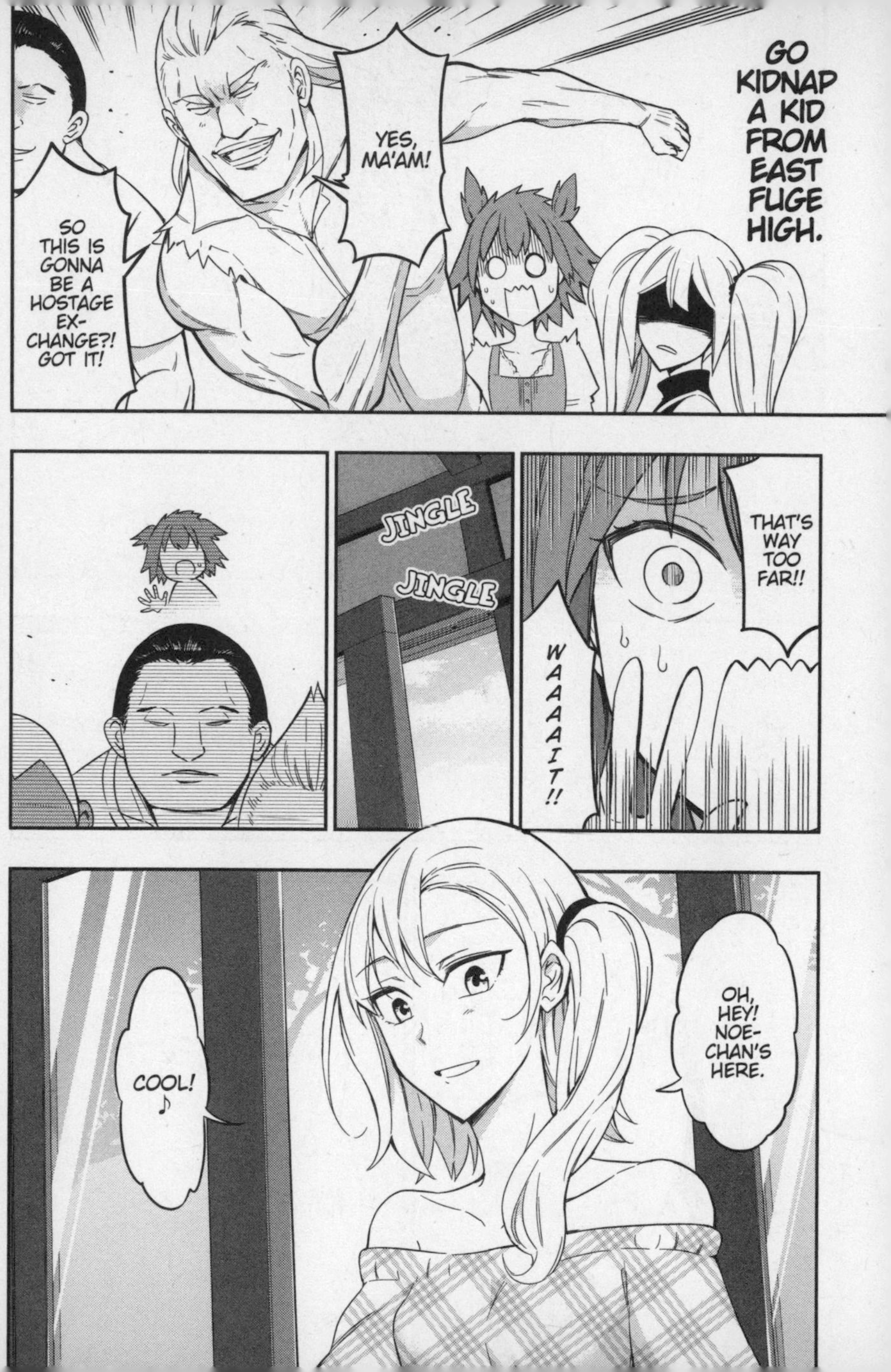
GO KIDNAP A KID FROM EAST FUGE HIGH.
YES, MA'AM!
SO THIS IS GONNA BE A HOSTAGE EX-CHANGE?! GOT IT!
THAT'S WAY TOO FAR!!
WAAAAAIT!!
JINGLE
JINGLE
OH, HEY! NOE-CHAN'S HERE.
COOL! ♪

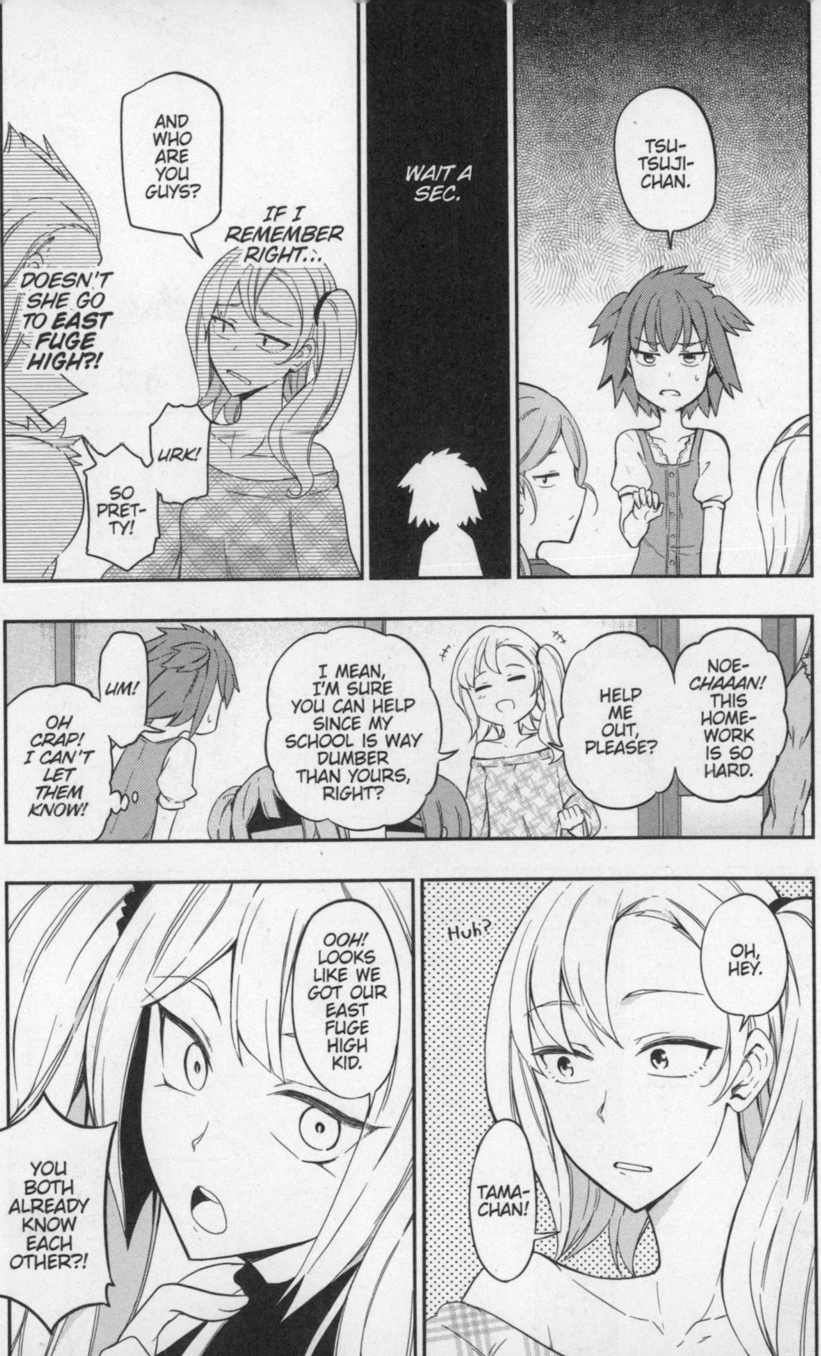
TSU-TSUJI-CHAN.
WAIT A SEC.
IF I REMEMBER RIGHT...
AND WHO ARE YOU GUYS?
DOESN'T SHE GO TO EAST FUGE HIGH?!
URK!
SO PRETTY!
NOE-CHAAAN! THIS HOMEWORK IS SO HARD.
HELP ME OUT, PLEASE?
I MEAN, I'M SURE YOU CAN HELP SINCE MY SCHOOL IS WAY DUMBER THAN YOURS, RIGHT?
UM!
OH CRAP! I CAN'T LET THEM KNOW!
OH, HEY.
Huh?
TAMA-CHAN!
OOH! LOOKS LIKE WE GOT OUR EAST FUGE HIGH KID.
YOU BOTH ALREADY KNOW EACH OTHER?!

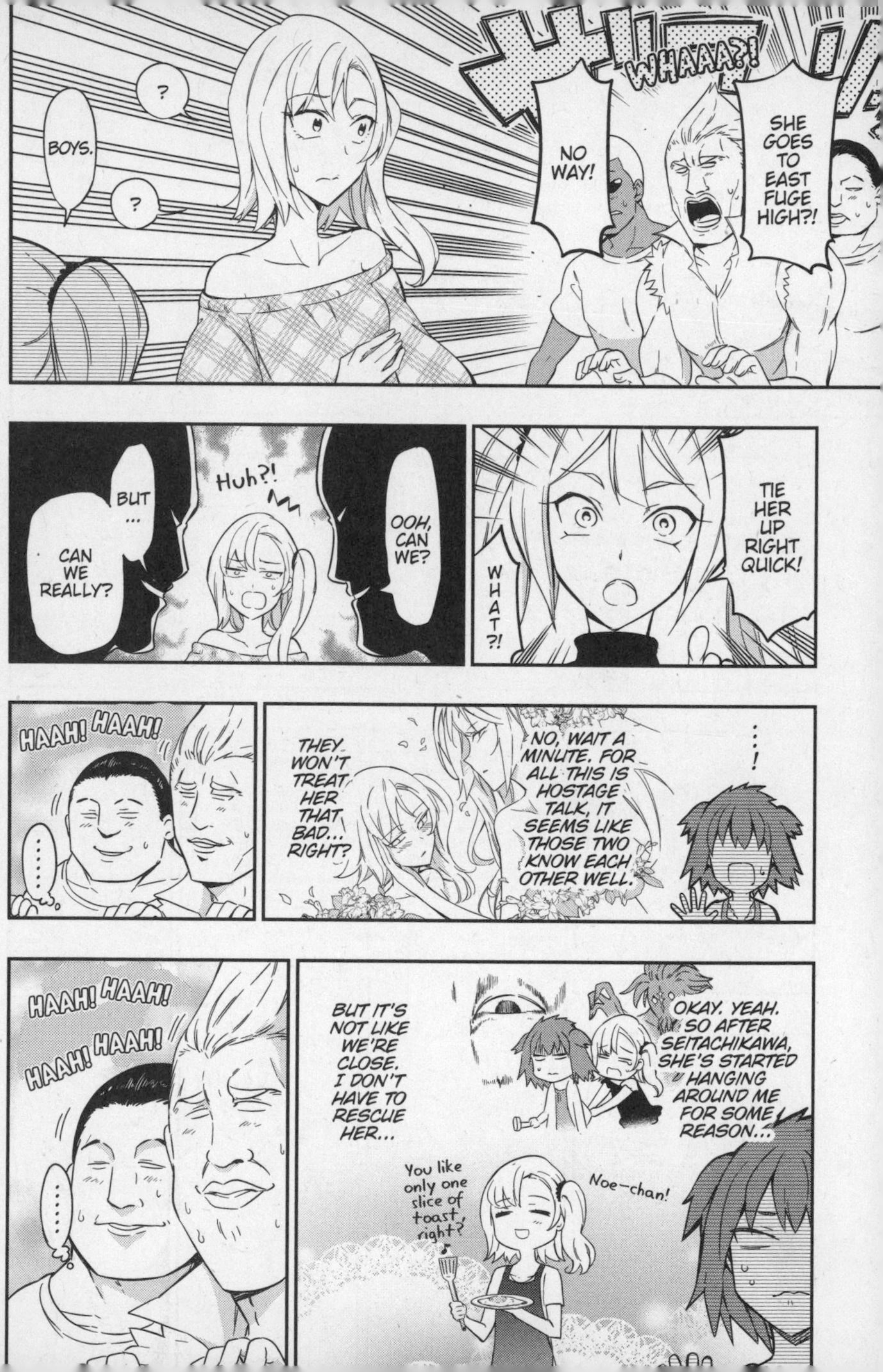

SHE GOES TO EAST FUGE HIGH?!
WHAAAA?!
NO WAY!
?
BOYS.
?
TIE HER UP RIGHT QUICK!
WHAT?!
OOH, CAN WE?
Huh?!
BUT ...
CAN WE REALLY?
...!
NO, WAIT A MINUTE. FOR ALL THIS IS HOSTAGE TALK, IT SEEMS LIKE THOSE TWO KNOW EACH OTHER WELL.
THEY WON'T TREAT HER THAT BAD... RIGHT?
HAAH! HAAH!
......
OKAY. YEAH. SO AFTER SEITACHIKAWA, SHE'S STARTED HANGING AROUND ME FOR SOME REASON...
BUT IT'S NOT LIKE WE'RE CLOSE. I DON'T HAVE TO RESCUE HER...
Noe-chan!
You like only one slice of toast, right?
HAAH! HAAH!
HAAH! HAAH!
......

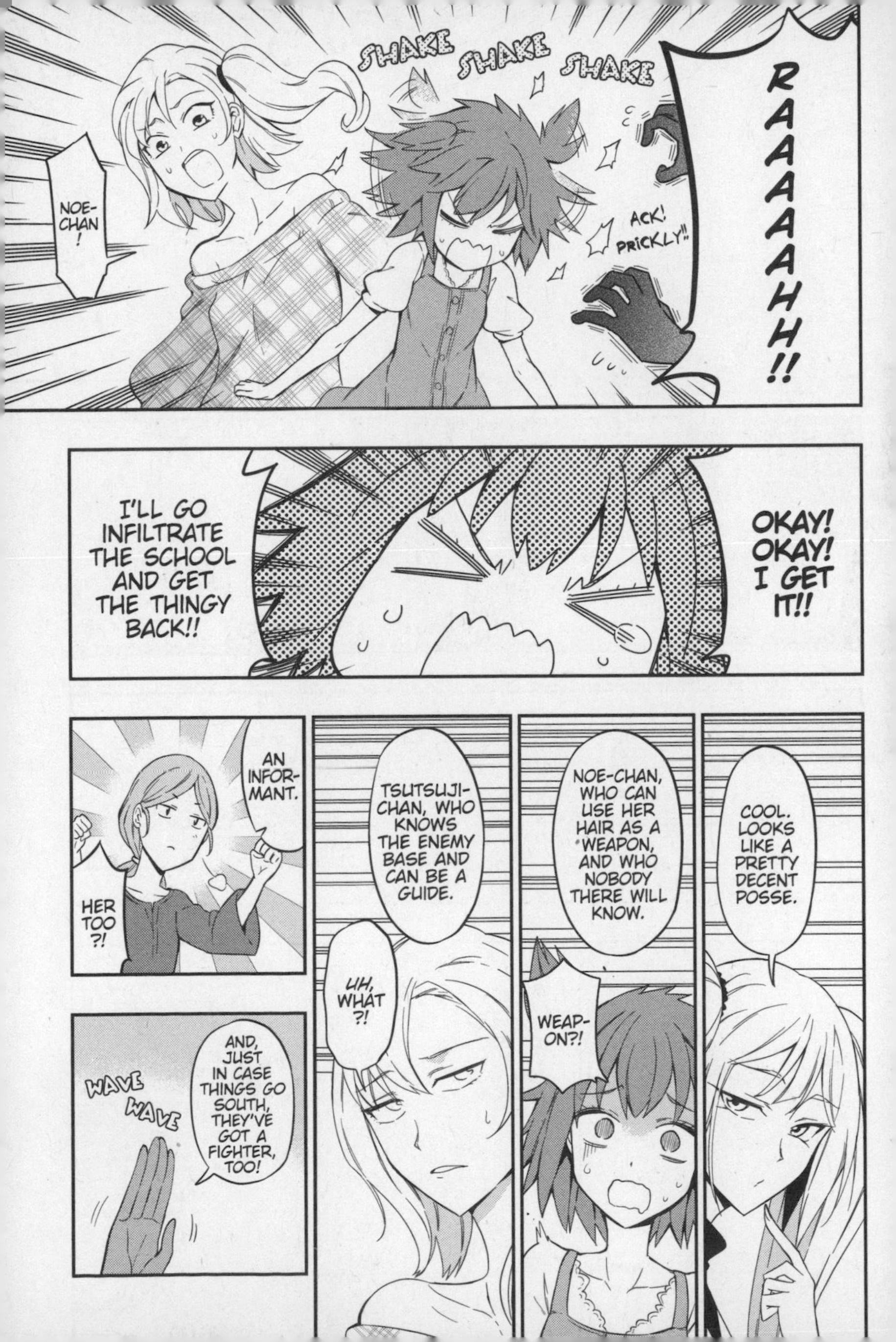
RAAAAAAHH!!
SHAKE SHAKE SHAKE
ACK! PRICKLY!!
NOE-CHAN!
OKAY! OKAY! I GET IT!!
I'LL GO INFILTRATE THE SCHOOL AND GET THE THINGY BACK!!
COOL. LOOKS LIKE A PRETTY DECENT POSSE.
NOE-CHAN, WHO CAN USE HER HAIR AS A WEAPON, AND WHO NOBODY THERE WILL KNOW.
WEAP-ON?!
TSUTSUJI-CHAN, WHO KNOWS THE ENEMY BASE AND CAN BE A GUIDE.
UH, WHAT?!
AN INFOR-MANT.
HER TOO?!
AND, JUST IN CASE THINGS GO SOUTH, THEY'VE GOT A FIGHTER, TOO!
WAVE WAVE

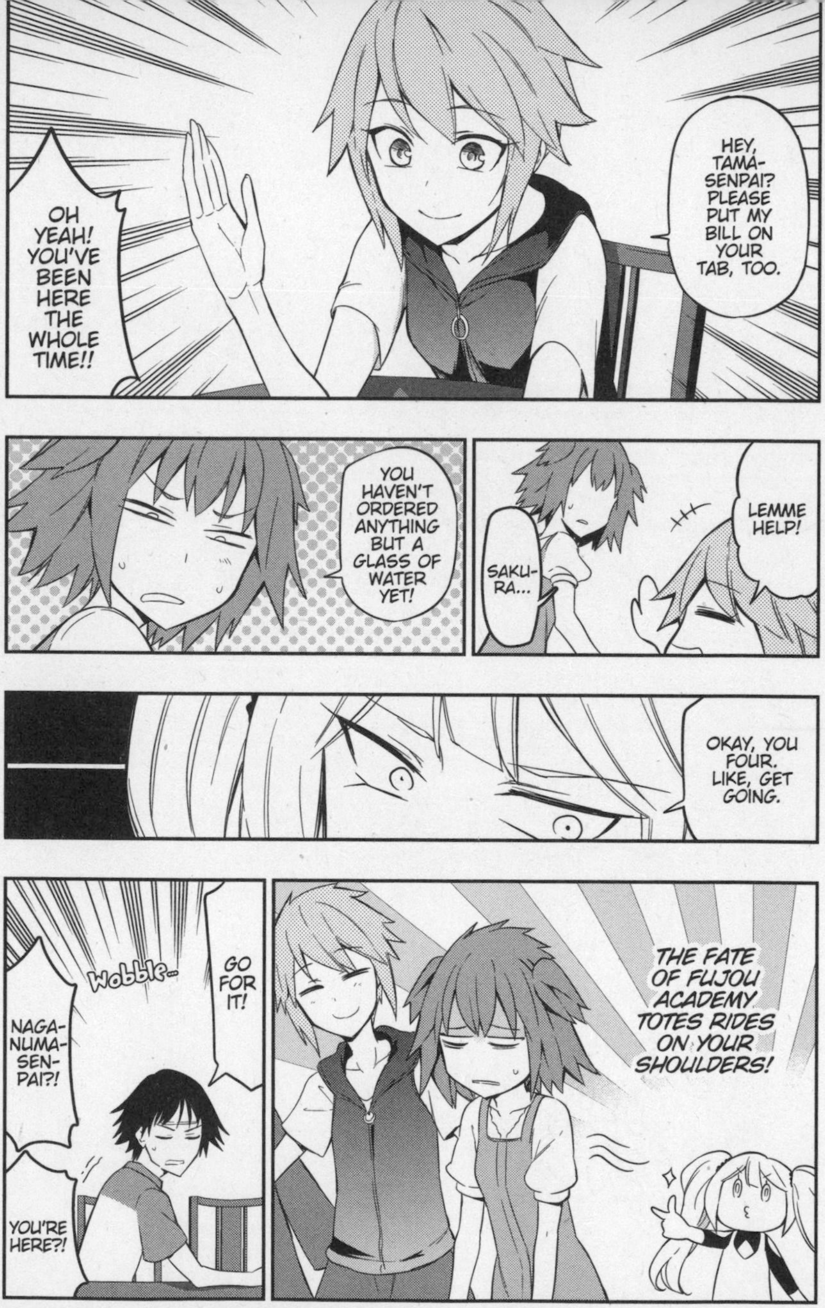
HEY, TAMA-SENPAI? PLEASE PUT MY BILL ON YOUR TAB, TOO.
OH YEAH! YOU'VE BEEN HERE THE WHOLE TIME!!
LEMME HELP!
SAKURA...
YOU HAVEN'T ORDERED ANYTHING BUT A GLASS OF WATER YET!
OKAY, YOU FOUR. LIKE, GET GOING.
THE FATE OF FUJOU ACADEMY TOTES RIDES ON YOUR SHOULDERS!
GO FOR IT!
Wobble...
NAGANUMA-SENPAI?!
YOU'RE HERE?!

TROMP
TROMP
TROMP
TROMP

D-FRAGMENTS

ディーふらぐ!

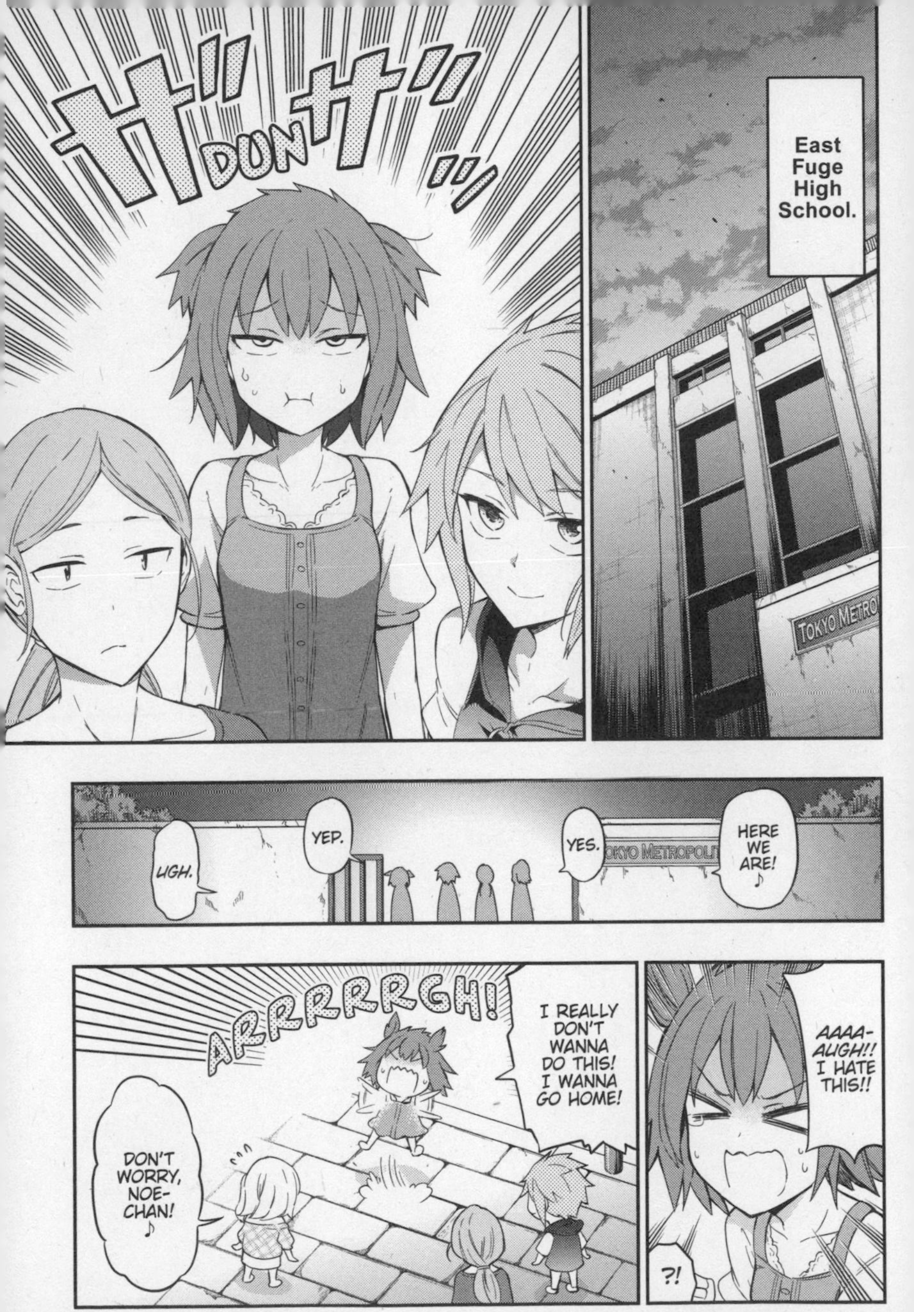
East Fuge High School.
TOKYO METRO
DON
HERE WE ARE! ♪
YES.
TOKYO METROPOLIT
YEP.
UGH.
AAAA-AUGH!! I HATE THIS!!
?!
I REALLY DON'T WANNA DO THIS! I WANNA GO HOME!
ARRRRRGH!
DON'T WORRY, NOE-CHAN! ♪

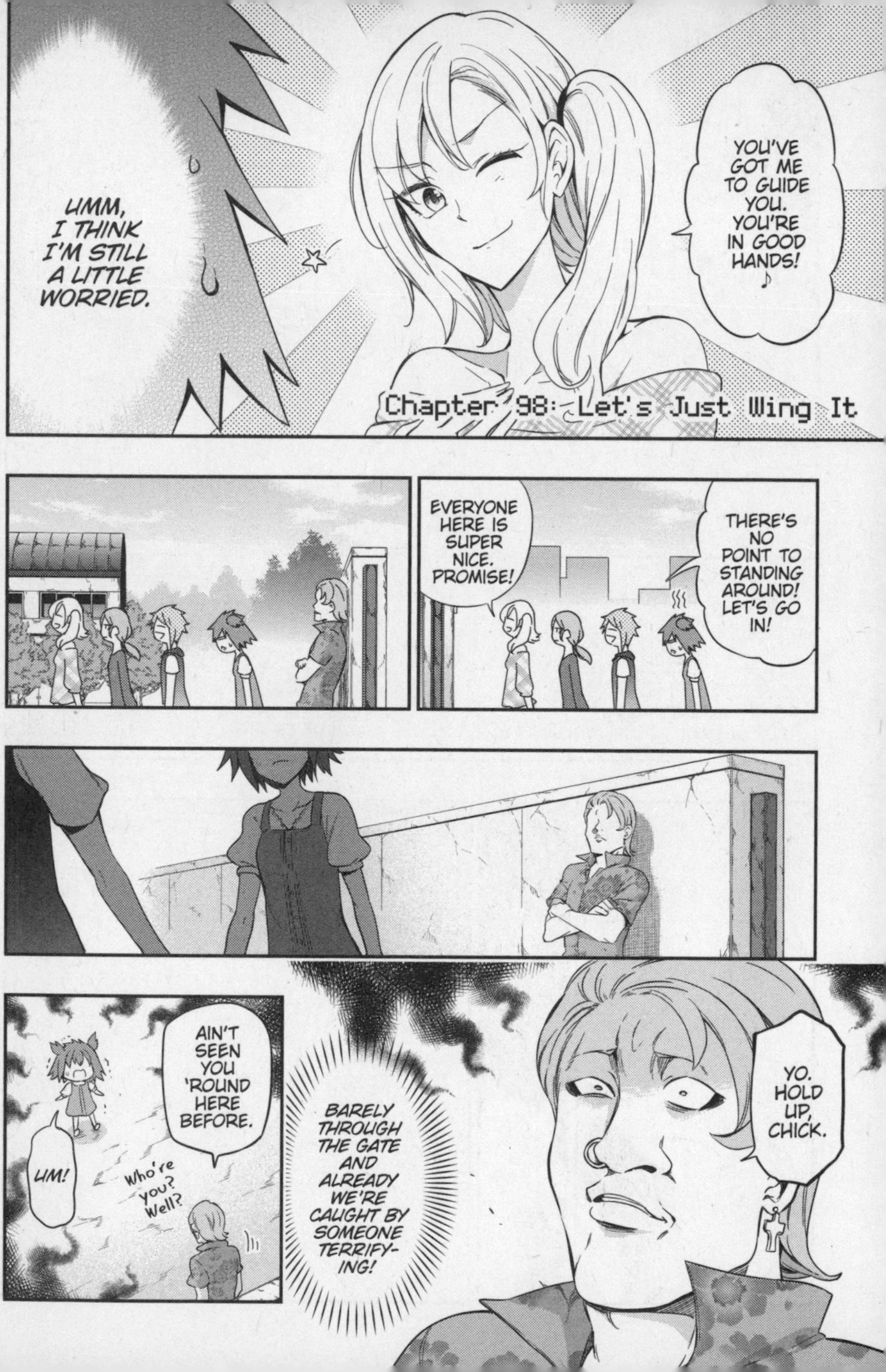
YOU'VE GOT ME TO GUIDE YOU. YOU'RE IN GOOD HANDS! ♪
UMM, I THINK I'M STILL A LITTLE WORRIED.
Chapter 98: Let's Just Wing It
THERE'S NO POINT TO STANDING AROUND! LET'S GO IN!
EVERYONE HERE IS SUPER NICE. PROMISE!
YO. HOLD UP, CHICK.
BARELY THROUGH THE GATE AND ALREADY WE'RE CAUGHT BY SOMEONE TERRIFYING!
AIN'T SEEN YOU 'ROUND HERE BEFORE.
Who're you? Well?
UM!

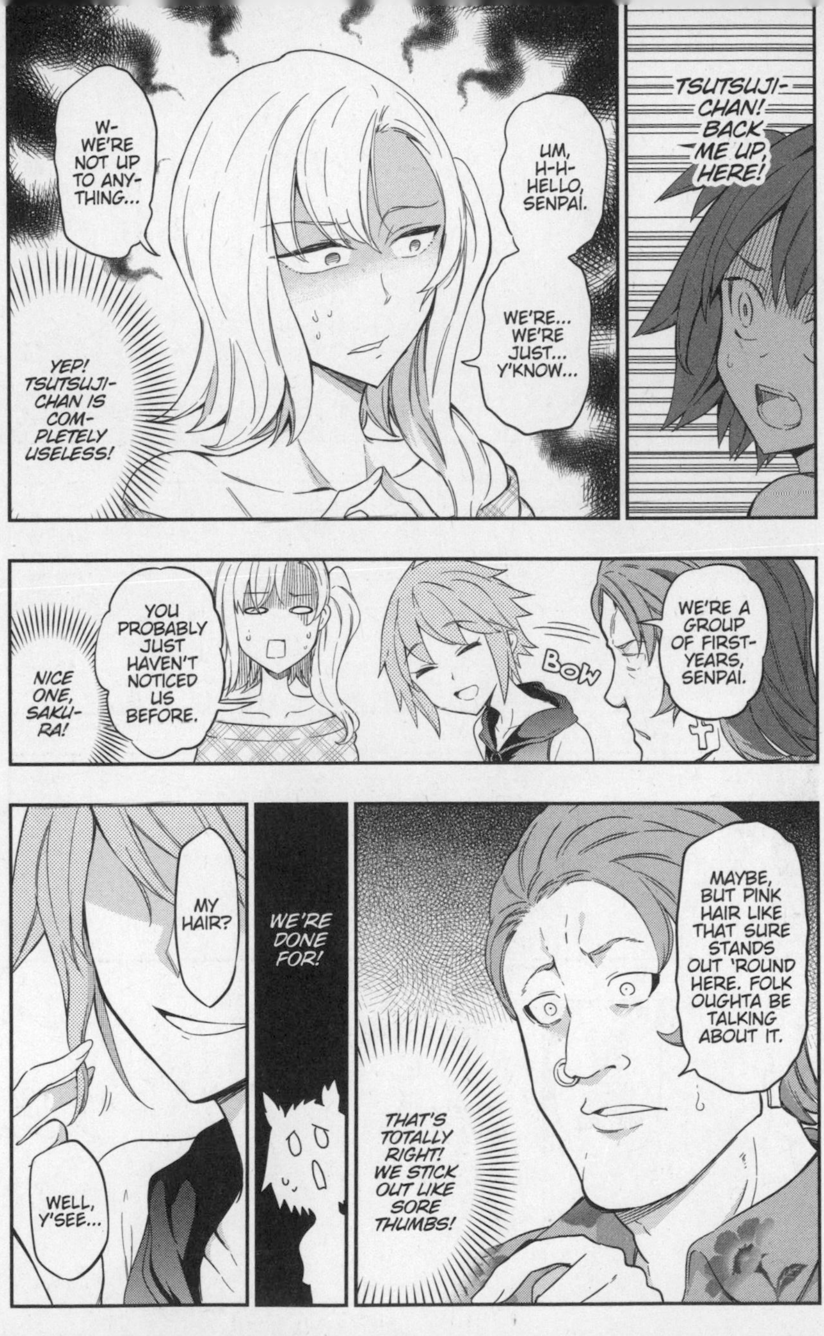
TSUTSUJI-CHAN! BACK ME UP, HERE!
UM, H-H-HELLO, SENPAI.
W-WE'RE NOT UP TO ANYTHING...
WE'RE... WE'RE JUST... Y'KNOW...
YEP! TSUTSUJI-CHAN IS COMPLETELY USELESS!
WE'RE A GROUP OF FIRST-YEARS, SENPAI.
BOW
YOU PROBABLY JUST HAVEN'T NOTICED US BEFORE.
NICE ONE, SAKURA!
MAYBE, BUT PINK HAIR LIKE THAT SURE STANDS OUT 'ROUND HERE. FOLK OUGHTA BE TALKING ABOUT IT.
THAT'S TOTALLY RIGHT! WE STICK OUT LIKE SORE THUMBS!
WE'RE DONE FOR!
MY HAIR?
WELL, Y'SEE...

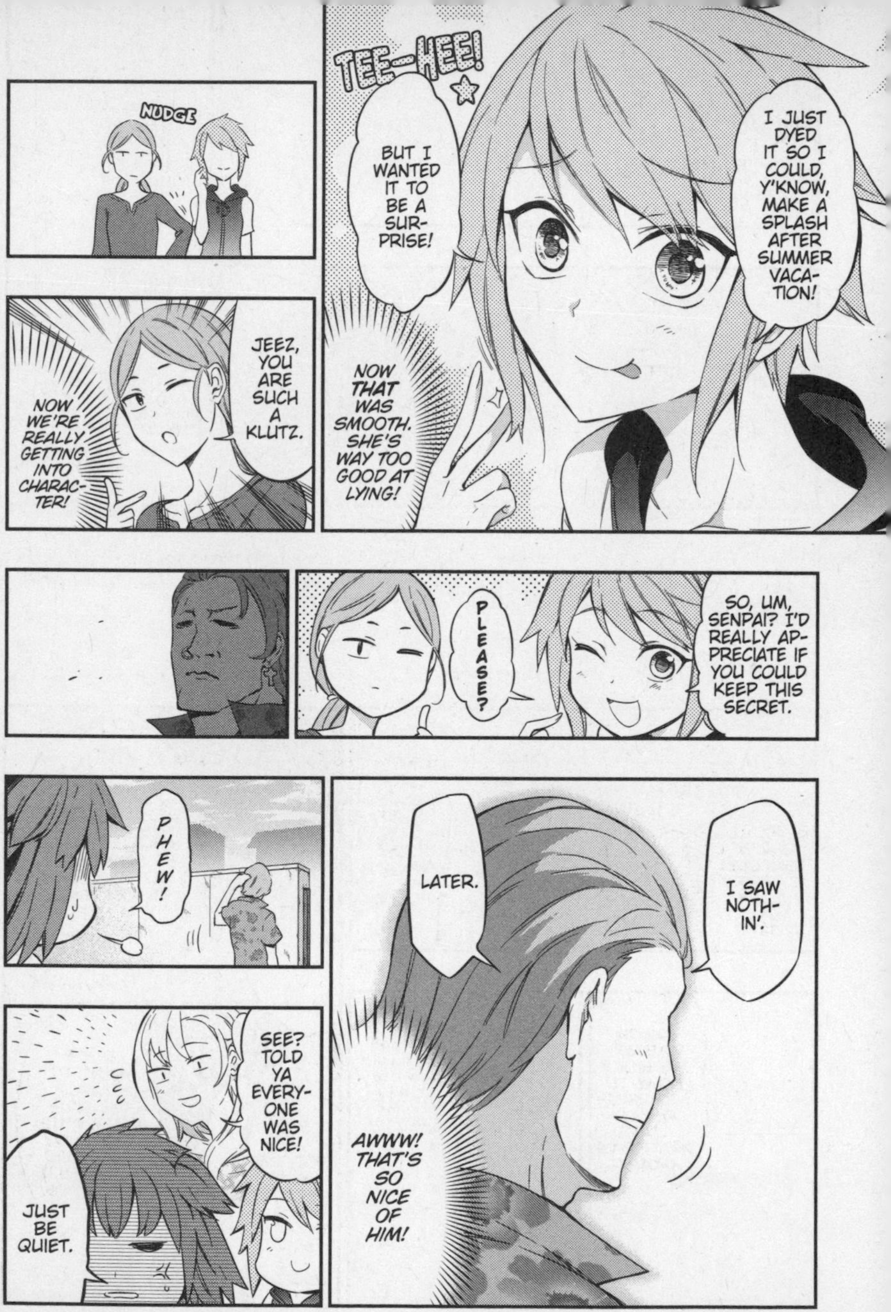
TEE-HEE!
I JUST DYED IT SO I COULD, Y'KNOW, MAKE A SPLASH AFTER SUMMER VACATION!
BUT I WANTED IT TO BE A SURPRISE!
NOW THAT WAS SMOOTH. SHE'S WAY TOO GOOD AT LYING!
NUDGE
JEEZ, YOU ARE SUCH A KLUTZ.
NOW WE'RE REALLY GETTING INTO CHARACTER!
SO, UM, SENPAI? I'D REALLY APPRECIATE IF YOU COULD KEEP THIS SECRET.
PLEASE?
I SAW NOTHIN'.
LATER.
AWWW! THAT'S SO NICE OF HIM!
PHEW!
SEE? TOLD YA EVERYONE WAS NICE!
JUST BE QUIET.

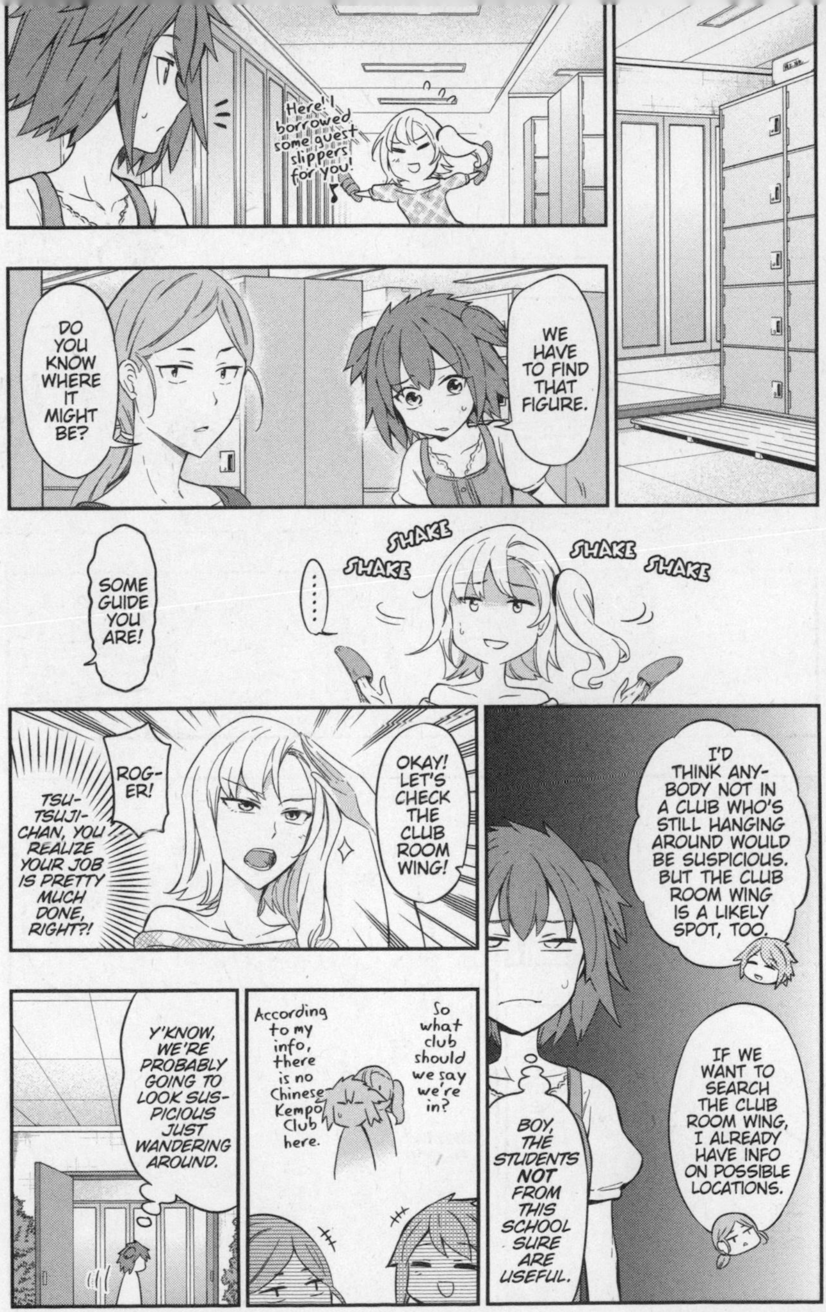
Here! I borrowed some guest slippers for you!
WE HAVE TO FIND THAT FIGURE.
DO YOU KNOW WHERE IT MIGHT BE?
SHAKE
SHAKE
SHAKE
SHAKE
......
SOME GUIDE YOU ARE!
I'D THINK ANYBODY NOT IN A CLUB WHO'S STILL HANGING AROUND WOULD BE SUSPICIOUS. BUT THE CLUB ROOM WING IS A LIKELY SPOT, TOO.
IF WE WANT TO SEARCH THE CLUB ROOM WING, I ALREADY HAVE INFO ON POSSIBLE LOCATIONS.
BOY, THE STUDENTS NOT FROM THIS SCHOOL SURE ARE USEFUL.
OKAY! LET'S CHECK THE CLUB ROOM WING!
ROGER!
TSUTSUJI-CHAN, YOU REALIZE YOUR JOB IS PRETTY MUCH DONE, RIGHT?!
So what club should we say we're in?
According to my info, there is no Chinese Kempo Club here.
Y'KNOW, WE'RE PROBABLY GOING TO LOOK SUSPICIOUS JUST WANDERING AROUND.

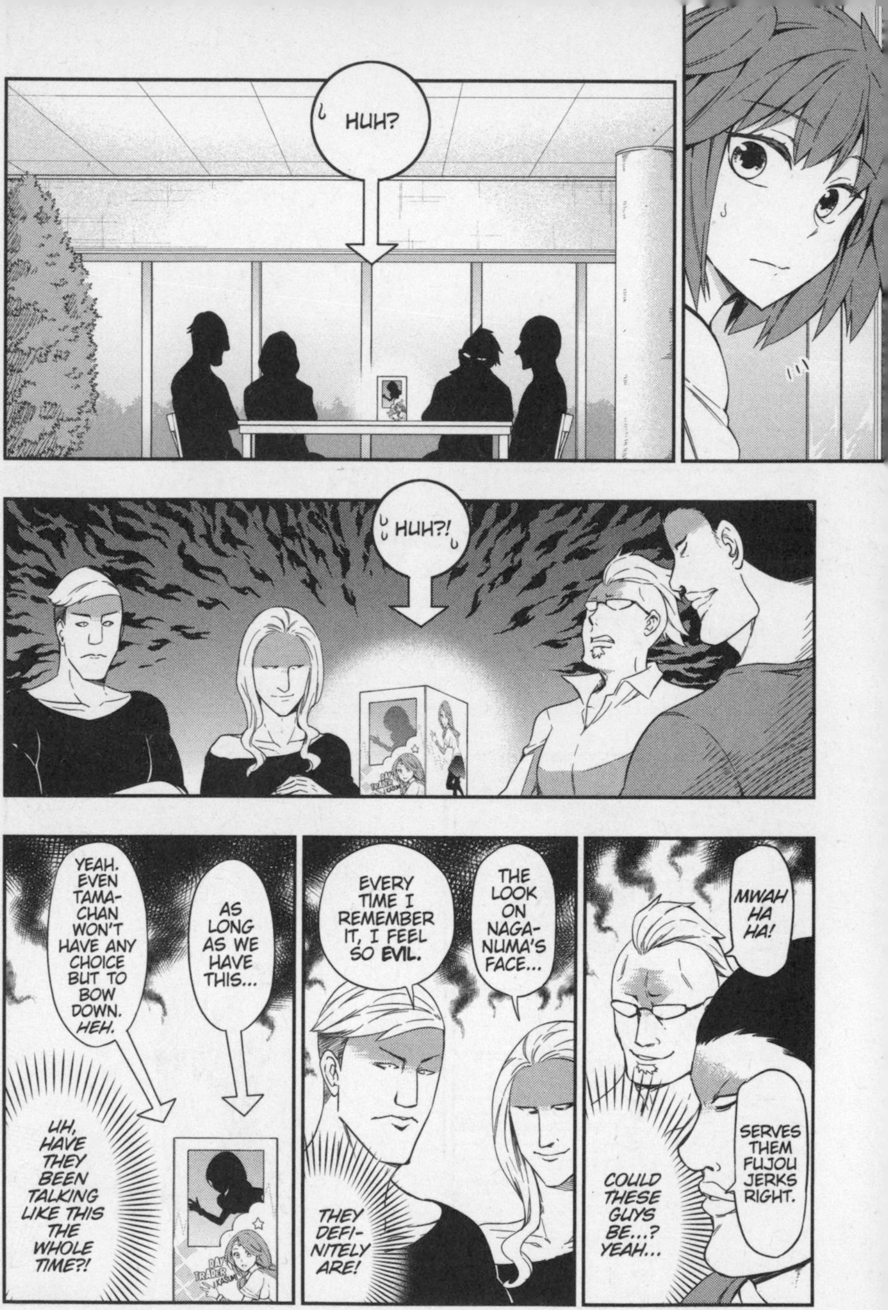
HUH?
HUH?!
MWAH HA HA!
SERVES THEM FUJOU JERKS RIGHT.
COULD THESE GUYS BE...? YEAH...
THE LOOK ON NAGANUMA'S FACE...
EVERY TIME I REMEMBER IT, I FEEL SO **EVIL.**
THEY DEFINITELY ARE!
AS LONG AS WE HAVE THIS...
YEAH. EVEN TAMA-CHAN WON'T HAVE ANY CHOICE BUT TO BOW DOWN. HEH.
UH, HAVE THEY BEEN TALKING LIKE THIS THE WHOLE TIME?!

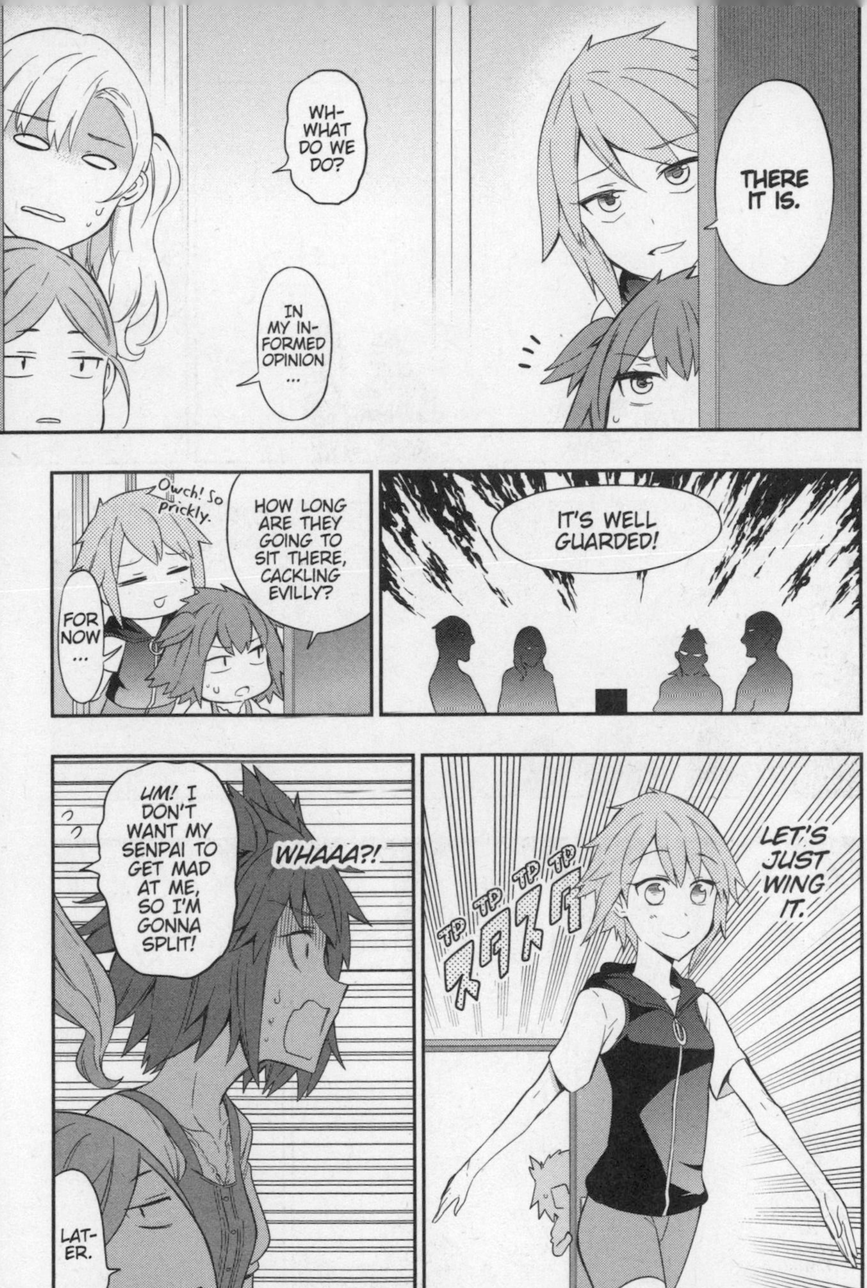
THERE IT IS.
WH-WHAT DO WE DO?
IN MY IN-FORMED OPINION ...
IT'S WELL GUARDED!
HOW LONG ARE THEY GOING TO SIT THERE, CACKLING EVILLY?
Owch! So prickly.
FOR NOW ...
LET'S JUST WING IT.
TP TP TP TP
UM! I DON'T WANT MY SENPAI TO GET MAD AT ME, SO I'M GONNA SPLIT!
WHAAA?!
LAT-ER.

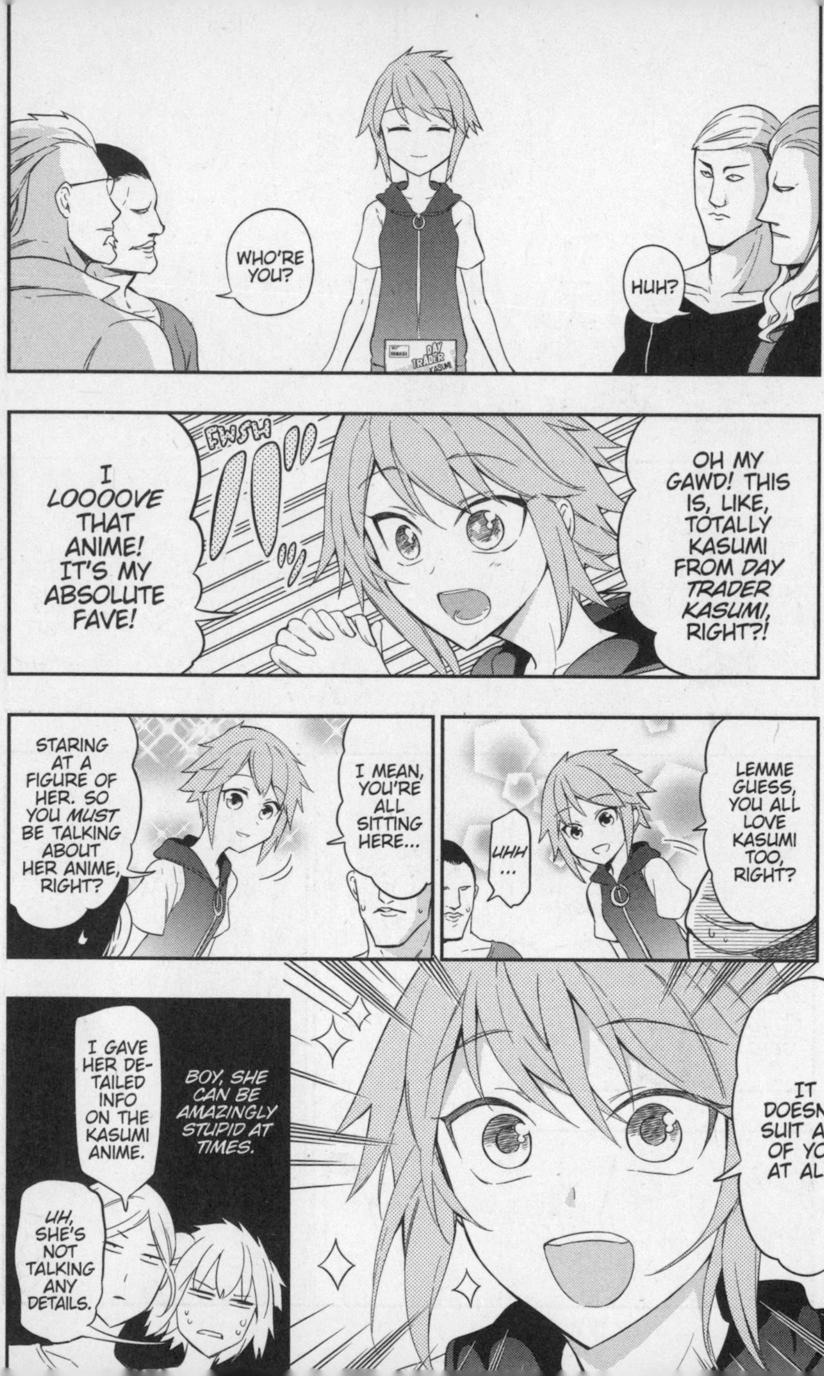
HUH?
WHO'RE YOU?
DAY TRADER KASUMI
OH MY GAWD! THIS IS, LIKE, TOTALLY KASUMI FROM *DAY TRADER KASUMI*, RIGHT?!
FWSH
I *LOOOOVE* THAT ANIME! IT'S MY ABSOLUTE FAVE!
LEMME GUESS, YOU ALL LOVE KASUMI TOO, RIGHT?
UHH ...
I MEAN, YOU'RE ALL SITTING HERE...
STARING AT A FIGURE OF HER. SO YOU *MUST* BE TALKING ABOUT HER ANIME, RIGHT?
IT DOESN'T SUIT ANY OF YOU AT ALL!
BOY, SHE CAN BE AMAZINGLY STUPID AT TIMES.
I GAVE HER DE-TAILED INFO ON THE KASUMI ANIME.
UH, SHE'S NOT TALKING ANY DETAILS.

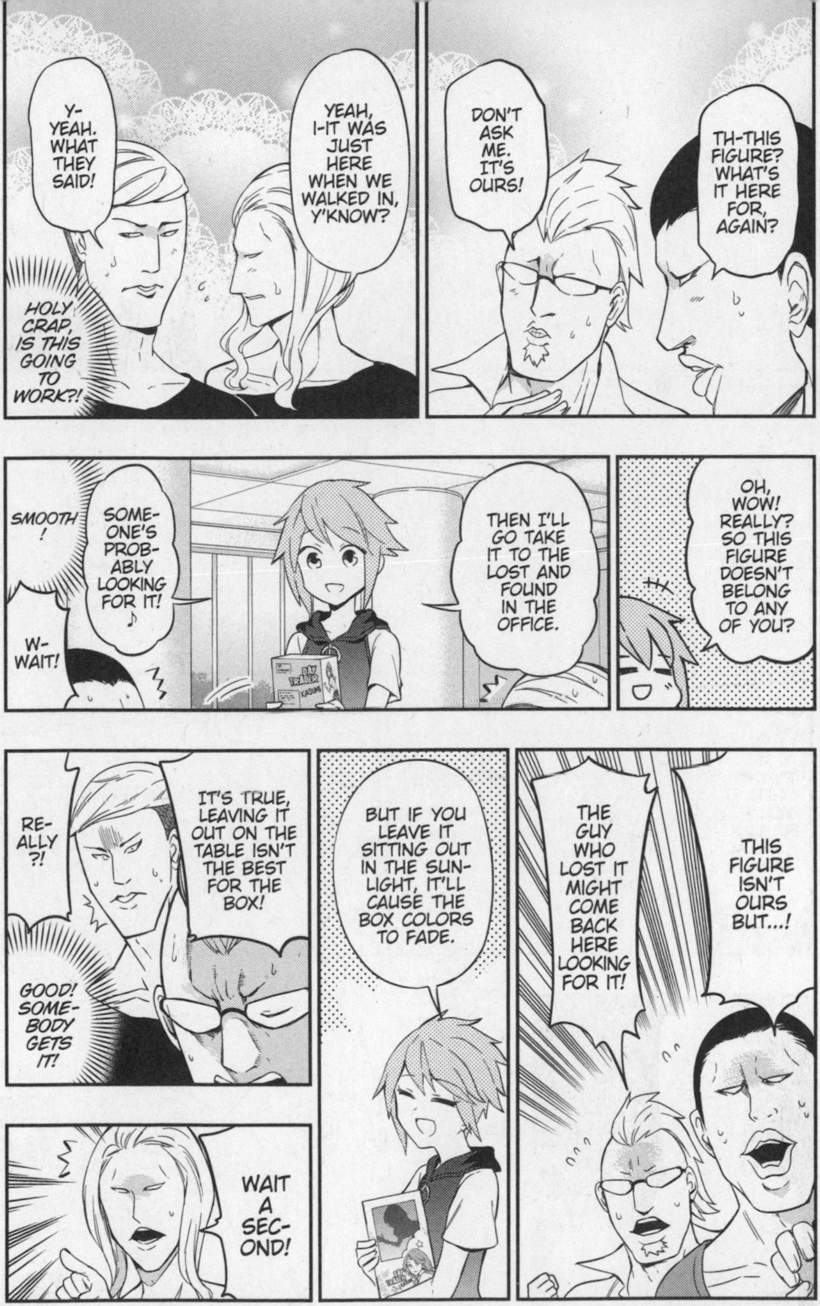
TH-THIS FIGURE? WHAT'S IT HERE FOR, AGAIN?
DON'T ASK ME. IT'S OURS!
YEAH, I-IT WAS JUST HERE WHEN WE WALKED IN, Y'KNOW?
Y-YEAH. WHAT THEY SAID!
HOLY CRAP, IS THIS GOING TO WORK?!
OH, WOW! REALLY? SO THIS FIGURE DOESN'T BELONG TO ANY OF YOU?
THEN I'LL GO TAKE IT TO THE LOST AND FOUND IN THE OFFICE.
SOMEONE'S PROBABLY LOOKING FOR IT! ♪
SMOOTH!
W-WAIT!
THIS FIGURE ISN'T OURS BUT...!
THE GUY WHO LOST IT MIGHT COME BACK HERE LOOKING FOR IT!
BUT IF YOU LEAVE IT SITTING OUT IN THE SUNLIGHT, IT'LL CAUSE THE BOX COLORS TO FADE.
IT'S TRUE, LEAVING IT OUT ON THE TABLE ISN'T THE BEST FOR THE BOX!
REALLY?!
GOOD! SOMEBODY GETS IT!
WAIT A SECOND!

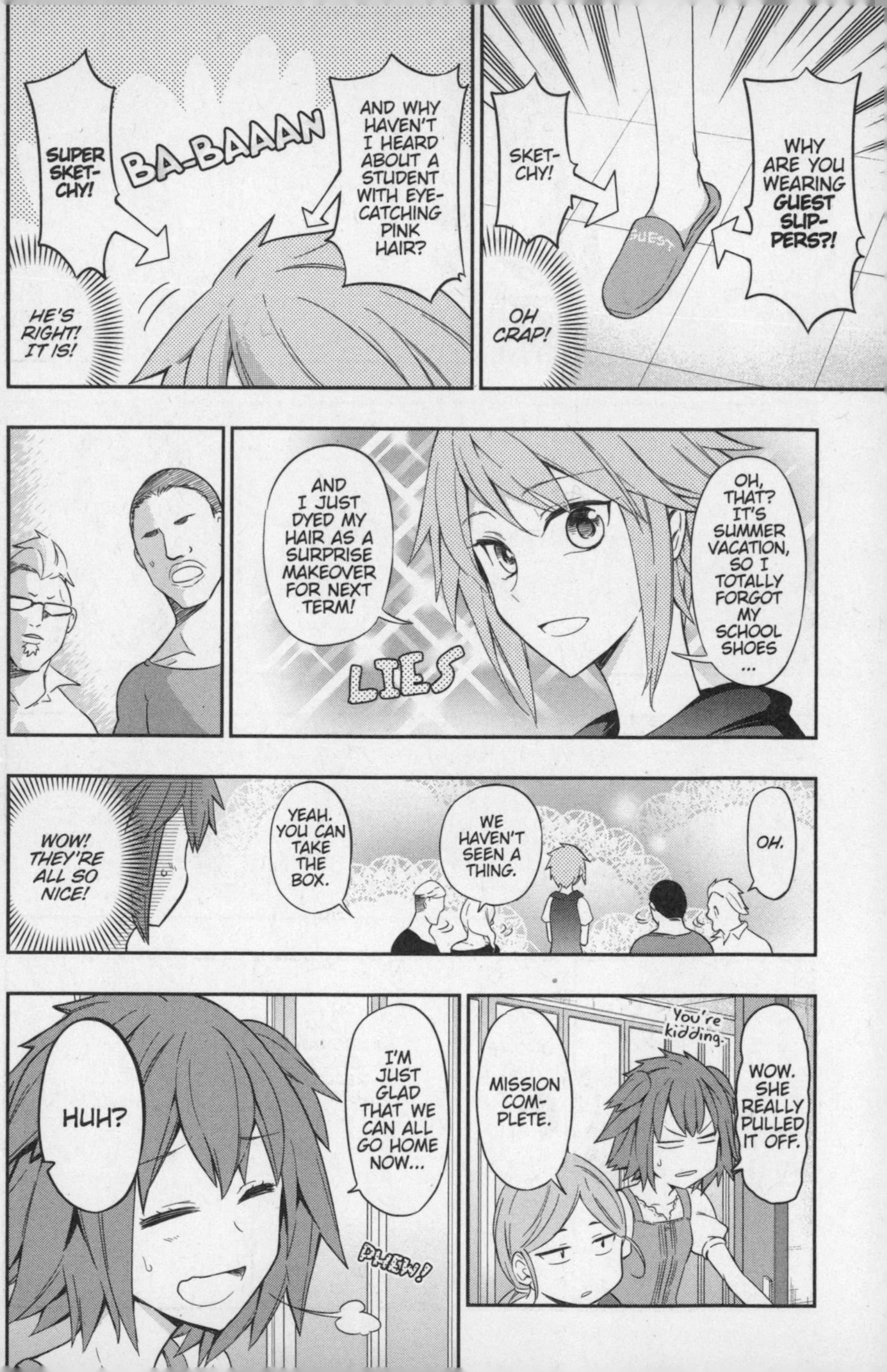
WHY ARE YOU WEARING GUEST SLIPPERS?!
SKET-CHY!
GUEST
OH CRAP!
AND WHY HAVEN'T I HEARD ABOUT A STUDENT WITH EYE-CATCHING PINK HAIR?
BA-BAAAN
SUPER SKET-CHY!
HE'S RIGHT! IT IS!
OH, THAT? IT'S SUMMER VACATION, SO I TOTALLY FORGOT MY SCHOOL SHOES ...
AND I JUST DYED MY HAIR AS A SURPRISE MAKEOVER FOR NEXT TERM!
LIES
OH.
WE HAVEN'T SEEN A THING.
YEAH. YOU CAN TAKE THE BOX.
WOW! THEY'RE ALL SO NICE!
WOW. SHE REALLY PULLED IT OFF.
You're kidding.
MISSION COMPLETE.
I'M JUST GLAD THAT WE CAN ALL GO HOME NOW...
HUH?
PHEW!

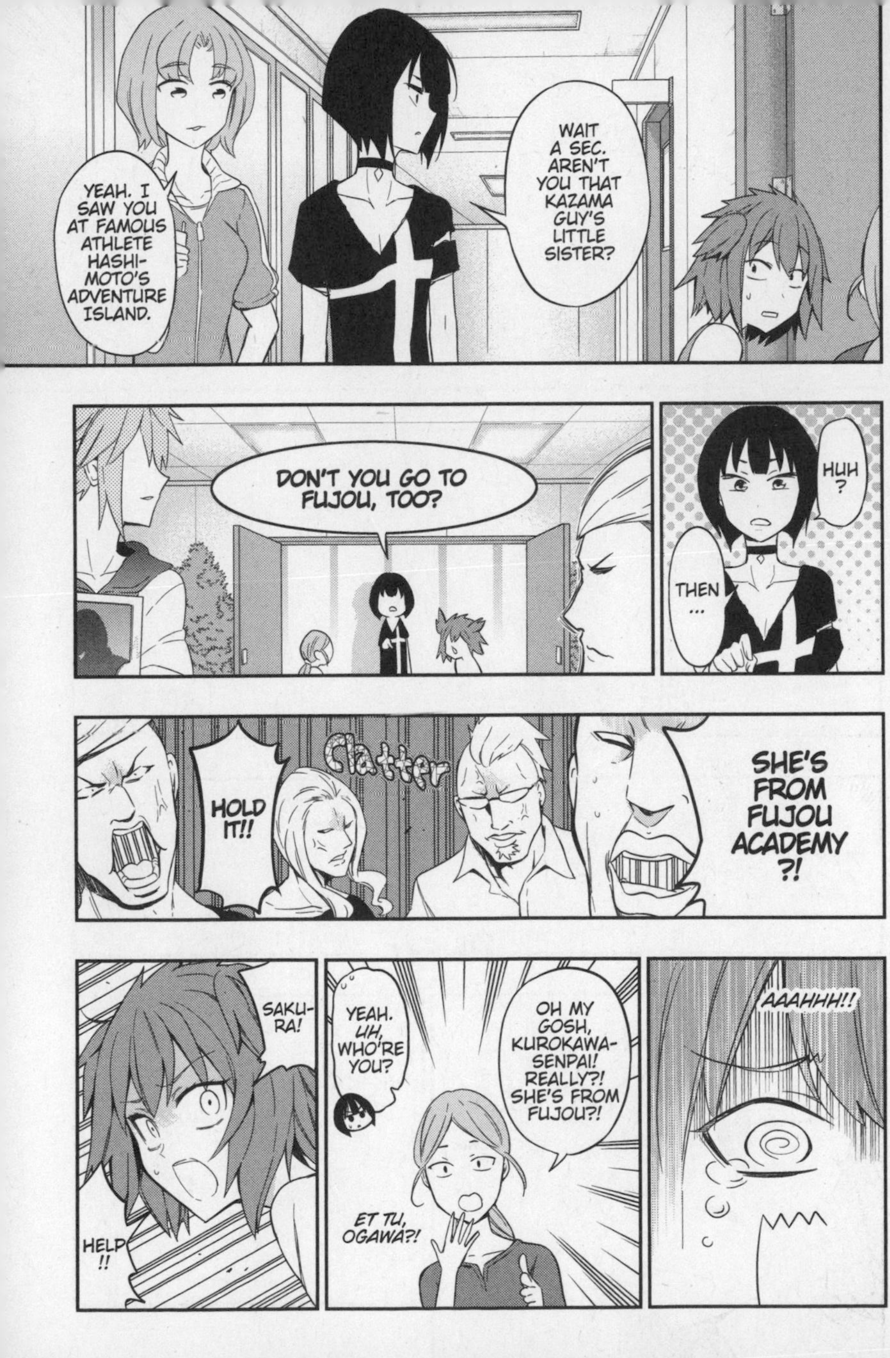
WAIT A SEC. AREN'T YOU THAT KAZAMA GUY'S LITTLE SISTER?
YEAH. I SAW YOU AT FAMOUS ATHLETE HASHI-MOTO'S ADVENTURE ISLAND.
HUH?
THEN...
DON'T YOU GO TO FUJOU, TOO?
SHE'S FROM FUJOU ACADEMY?!
Clatter
HOLD IT!!
AAAHHH!!
OH MY GOSH, KUROKAWA-SENPAI! REALLY?! SHE'S FROM FUJOU?!
YEAH. UH, WHO'RE YOU?
ET TU, OGAWA?!
SAKU-RA!
HELP!!

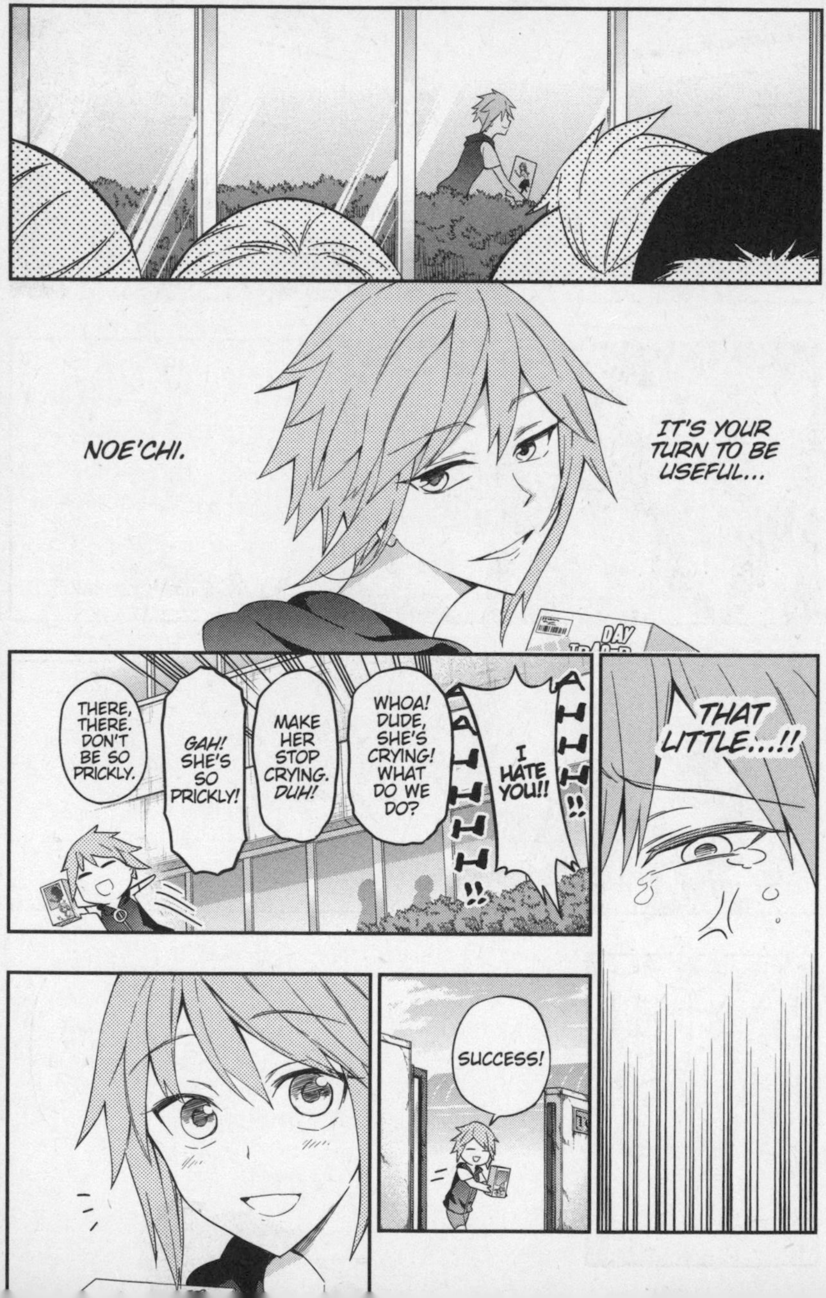
IT'S YOUR TURN TO BE USEFUL...
NOE'CHI.
DAY
THAT LITTLE...!!
AHHHH!!
I HATE YOU!!
AHHHHHH!!
WHOA! DUDE, SHE'S CRYING! WHAT DO WE DO?
MAKE HER STOP CRYING. DUH!
GAH! SHE'S SO PRICKLY!
THERE, THERE. DON'T BE SO PRICKLY.
SUCCESS!

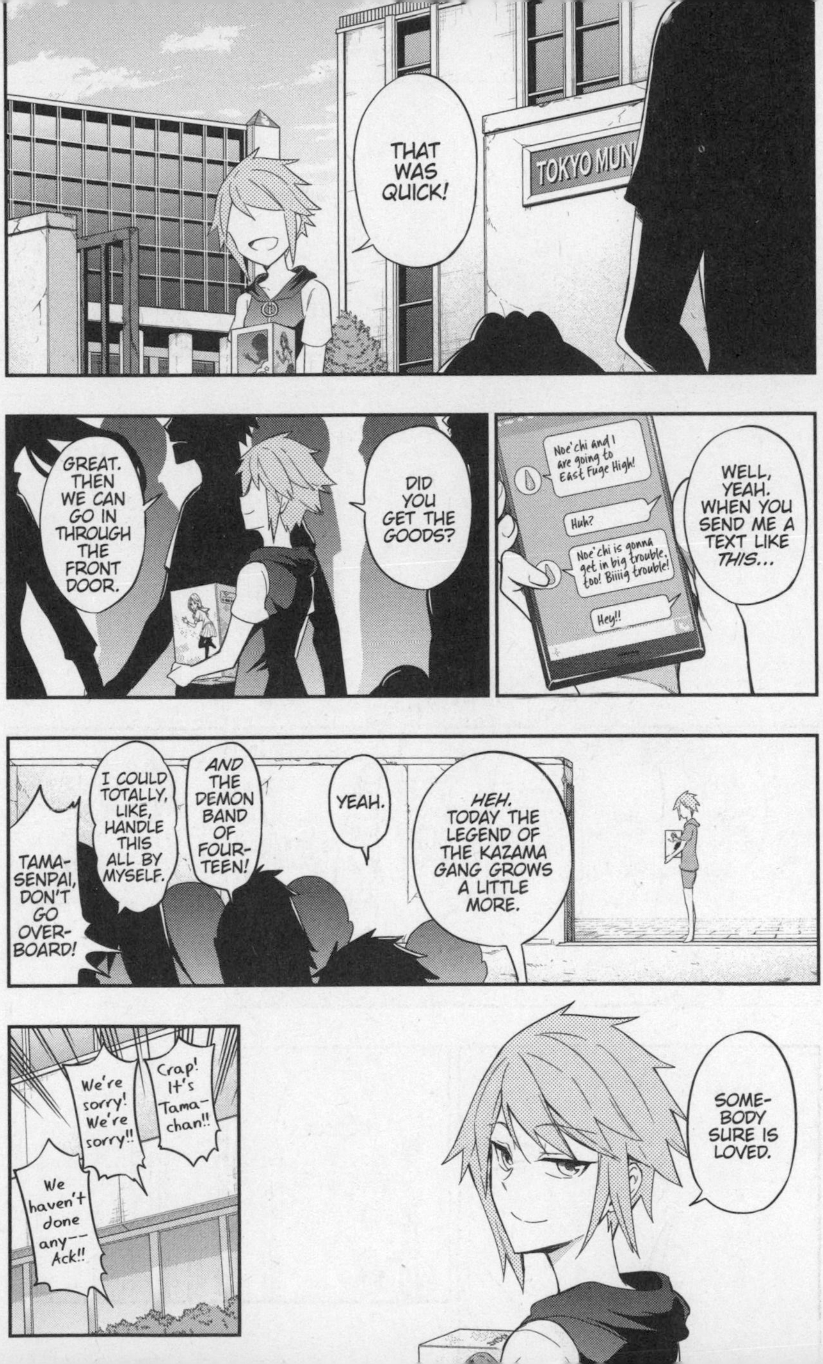
THAT WAS QUICK!
TOKYO MUN
WELL, YEAH. WHEN YOU SEND ME A TEXT LIKE *THIS*...
Noe'chi and I are going to East Fuge High!
Huh?
Noe'chi is gonna get in big trouble, too! Biiiig trouble!
Hey!!
DID YOU GET THE GOODS?
GREAT. THEN WE CAN GO IN THROUGH THE FRONT DOOR.
HEH. TODAY THE LEGEND OF THE KAZAMA GANG GROWS A LITTLE MORE.
YEAH.
AND THE DEMON BAND OF FOURTEEN!
I COULD TOTALLY, LIKE, HANDLE THIS ALL BY MYSELF.
TAMA-SENPAI, DON'T GO OVERBOARD!
SOMEBODY SURE IS LOVED.
Crap! It's Tama-chan!!
We're sorry! We're sorry!!
We haven't done any-- Ack!!

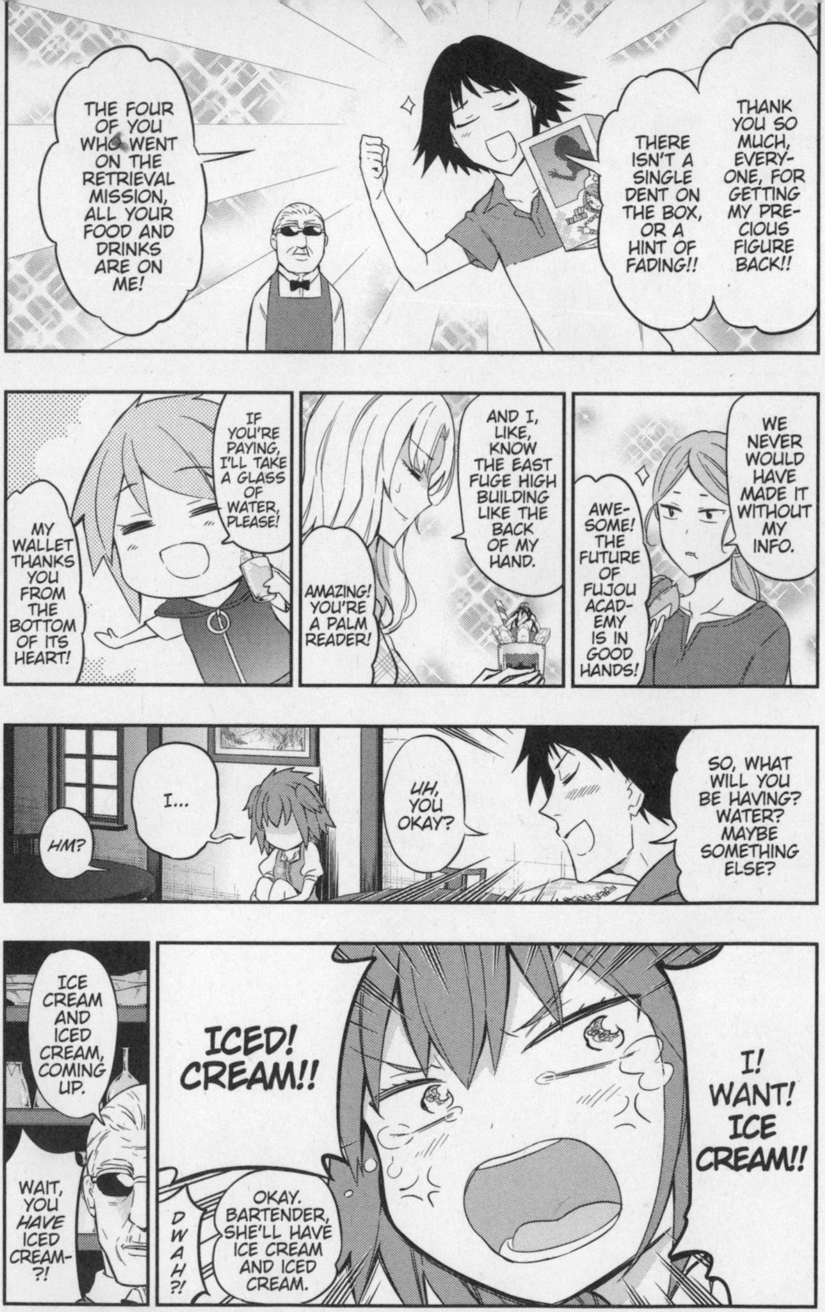
THANK YOU SO MUCH, EVERYONE, FOR GETTING MY PRECIOUS FIGURE BACK!!
THERE ISN'T A SINGLE DENT ON THE BOX, OR A HINT OF FADING!!
THE FOUR OF YOU WHO WENT ON THE RETRIEVAL MISSION, ALL YOUR FOOD AND DRINKS ARE ON ME!
WE NEVER WOULD HAVE MADE IT WITHOUT MY INFO.
AWESOME! THE FUTURE OF FUJOU ACADEMY IS IN GOOD HANDS!
AND I, LIKE, KNOW THE EAST FUGE HIGH BUILDING LIKE THE BACK OF MY HAND.
AMAZING! YOU'RE A PALM READER!
IF YOU'RE PAYING, I'LL TAKE A GLASS OF WATER, PLEASE!
MY WALLET THANKS YOU FROM THE BOTTOM OF ITS HEART!
SO, WHAT WILL YOU BE HAVING? WATER? MAYBE SOMETHING ELSE?
UH, YOU OKAY?
I...
HM?
I! WANT! ICE CREAM!!
ICED! CREAM!!
OKAY. BARTENDER, SHE'LL HAVE ICE CREAM AND ICED CREAM.
DWAH?!
ICE CREAM AND ICED CREAM, COMING UP.
WAIT, YOU *HAVE* ICED CREAM-?!

Oh dear. I'm sorry, but I'm fresh out of the ingredients for iced cream.

Now I want to know what they were!!

D-FRAGMENTS

ディーふらぐ!

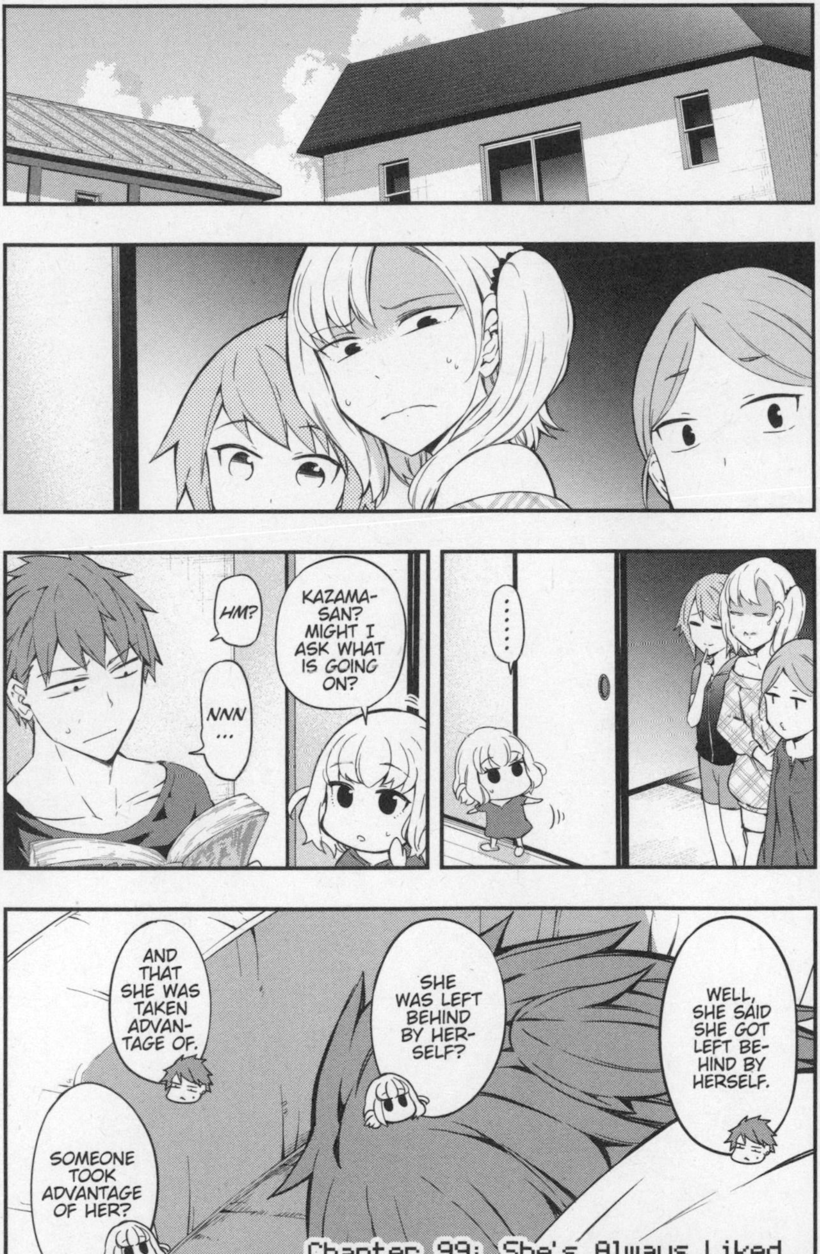
......
KAZAMA-SAN? MIGHT I ASK WHAT IS GOING ON?
HM?
NNN ...
WELL, SHE SAID SHE GOT LEFT BE-HIND BY HERSELF.
SHE WAS LEFT BEHIND BY HER-SELF?
AND THAT SHE WAS TAKEN ADVAN-TAGE OF.
SOMEONE TOOK ADVANTAGE OF HER?

Chapter 99: She's Always Liked Her Ice Cream Frozen Solid

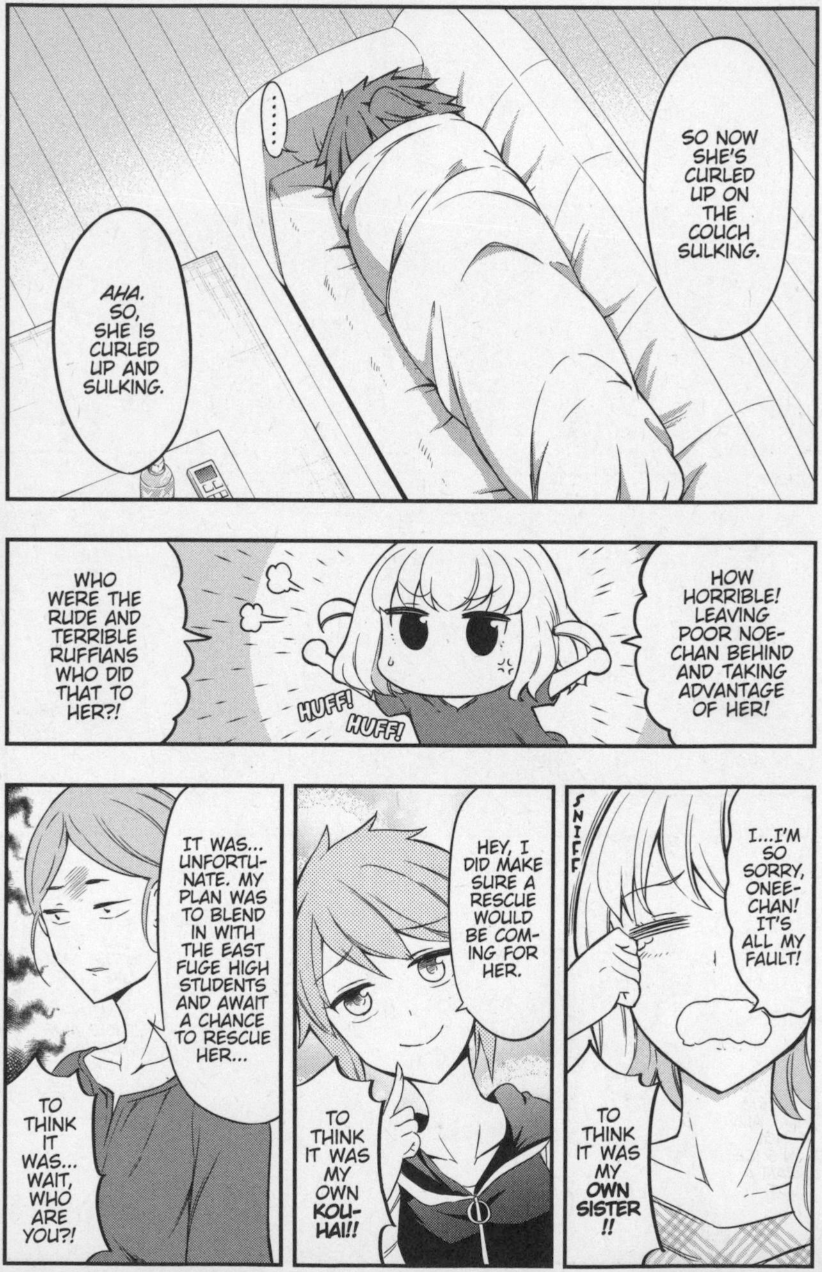
SO NOW SHE'S CURLED UP ON THE COUCH SULKING.
......
AHA. SO, SHE IS CURLED UP AND SULKING.
HOW HORRIBLE! LEAVING POOR NOE-CHAN BEHIND AND TAKING ADVANTAGE OF HER!
HUFF! HUFF!
WHO WERE THE RUDE AND TERRIBLE RUFFIANS WHO DID THAT TO HER?!
SNIFF
I...I'M SO SORRY, ONEE-CHAN! IT'S ALL MY FAULT!
TO THINK IT WAS MY OWN SISTER!!
HEY, I DID MAKE SURE A RESCUE WOULD BE COMING FOR HER.
TO THINK IT WAS MY OWN KOUHAI!!
IT WAS... UNFORTUNATE. MY PLAN WAS TO BLEND IN WITH THE EAST FUGE HIGH STUDENTS AND AWAIT A CHANCE TO RESCUE HER...
TO THINK IT WAS... WAIT, WHO ARE YOU?!

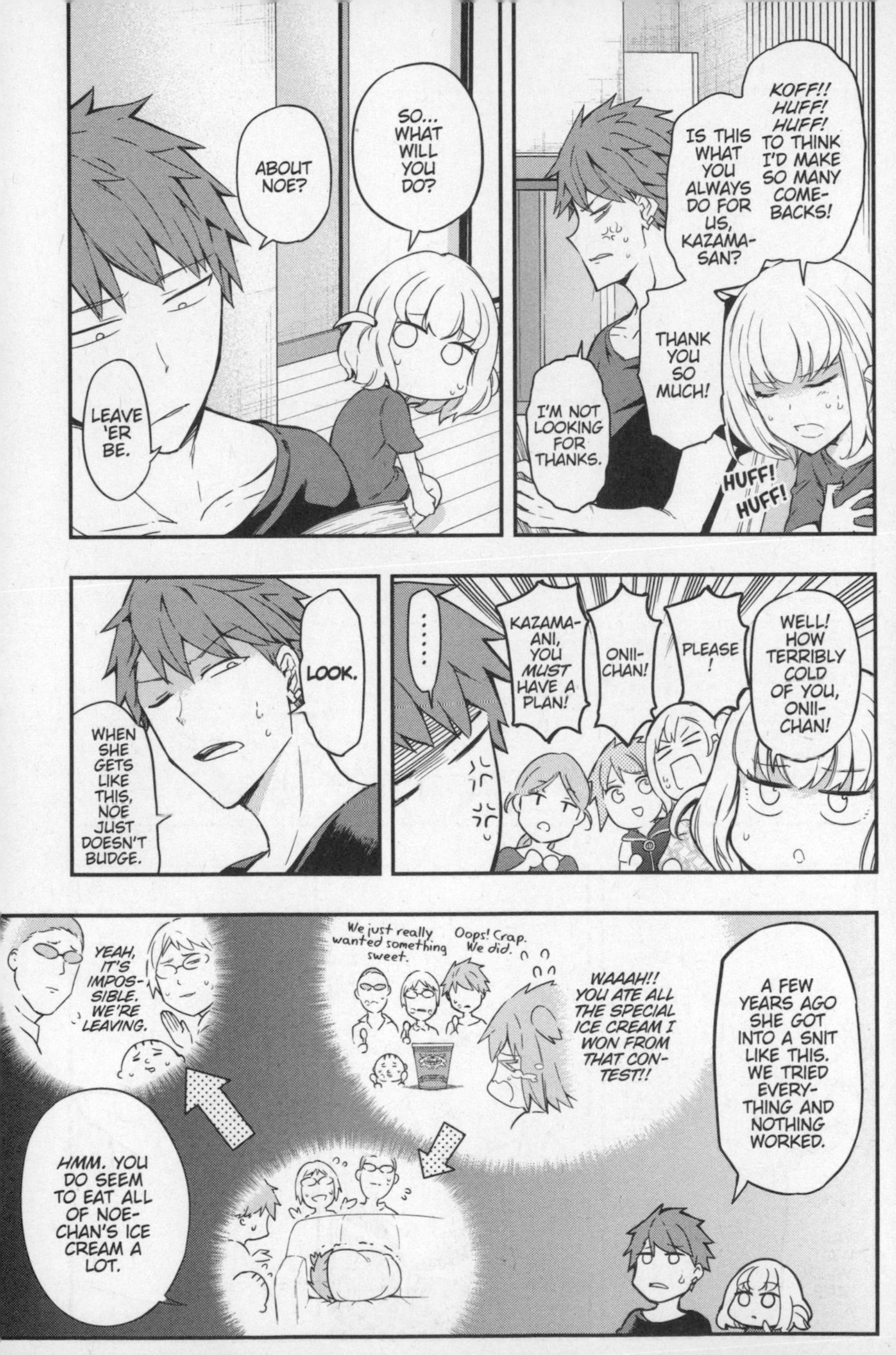
KOFF!! HUFF! HUFF! TO THINK I'D MAKE SO MANY COME-BACKS!
IS THIS WHAT YOU ALWAYS DO FOR US, KAZAMA-SAN?
THANK YOU SO MUCH!
I'M NOT LOOKING FOR THANKS.
HUFF! HUFF!
SO... WHAT WILL YOU DO?
ABOUT NOE?
LEAVE 'ER BE.
WELL! HOW TERRIBLY COLD OF YOU, ONII-CHAN!
PLEASE!
ONII-CHAN!
KAZAMA-ANI, YOU MUST HAVE A PLAN!
......
LOOK.
WHEN SHE GETS LIKE THIS, NOE JUST DOESN'T BUDGE.
A FEW YEARS AGO SHE GOT INTO A SNIT LIKE THIS. WE TRIED EVERY-THING AND NOTHING WORKED.
WAAAH!! YOU ATE ALL THE SPECIAL ICE CREAM I WON FROM THAT CON-TEST!!
Oops! Crap. We did.
We just really wanted something sweet.
YEAH, IT'S IMPOS-SIBLE. WE'RE LEAVING.
HMM. YOU DO SEEM TO EAT ALL OF NOE-CHAN'S ICE CREAM A LOT.

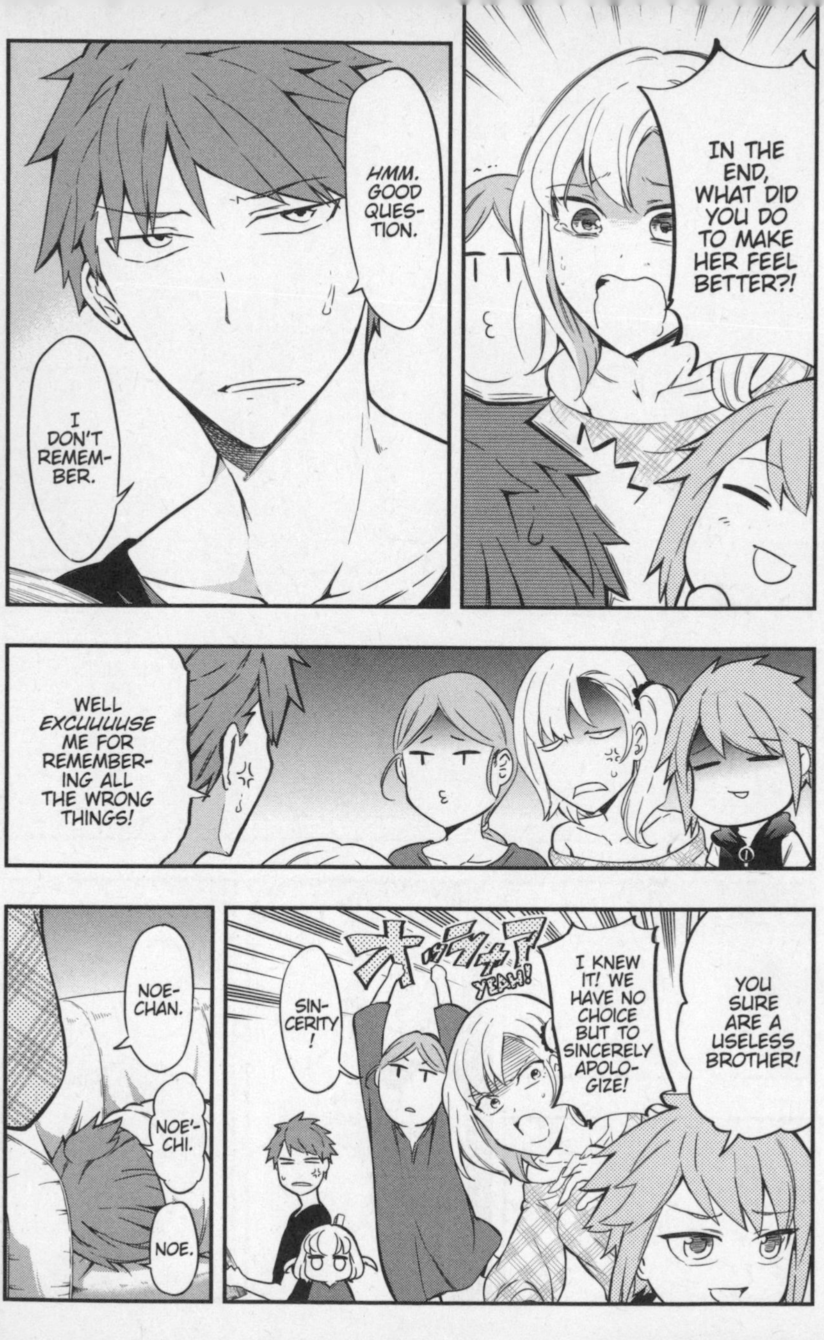
IN THE END, WHAT DID YOU DO TO MAKE HER FEEL BETTER?!
HMM. GOOD QUES-TION.
I DON'T REMEM-BER.
WELL EXCUUUUSE ME FOR REMEMBER-ING ALL THE WRONG THINGS!
YOU SURE ARE A USELESS BROTHER!
I KNEW IT! WE HAVE NO CHOICE BUT TO SINCERELY APOLO-GIZE!
YEAH!
SIN-CERITY!
NOE-CHAN.
NOE'-CHI.
NOE.

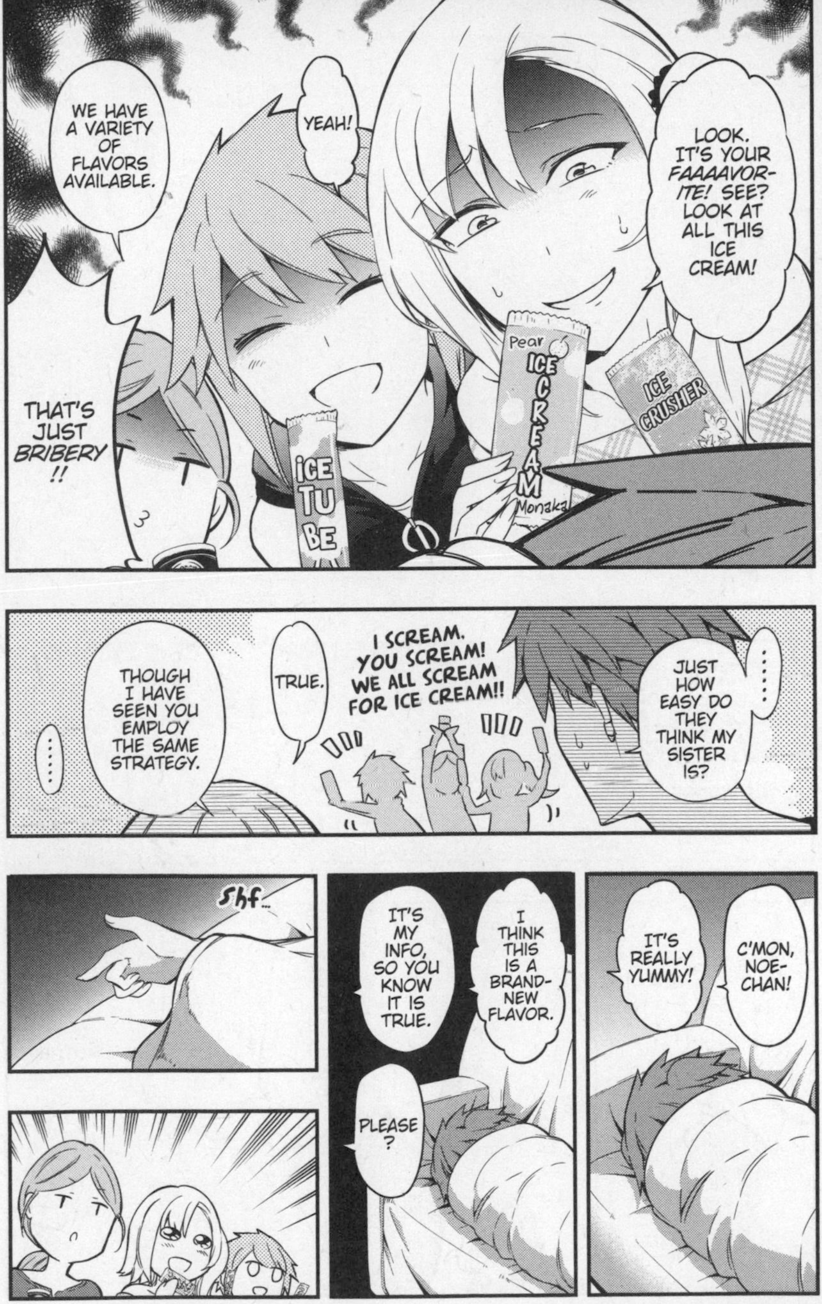

LOOK. IT'S YOUR FAAAAVOR-ITE! SEE? LOOK AT ALL THIS ICE CREAM!
YEAH!
WE HAVE A VARIETY OF FLAVORS AVAILABLE.
ICE CRUSHER
Pear ICE CREAM Monaka
THAT'S JUST BRIBERY!!
iCE TUBE
......
JUST HOW EASY DO THEY THINK MY SISTER IS?
I SCREAM. YOU SCREAM! WE ALL SCREAM FOR ICE CREAM!!
TRUE.
THOUGH I HAVE SEEN YOU EMPLOY THE SAME STRATEGY.
......
C'MON, NOE-CHAN!
IT'S REALLY YUMMY!
I THINK THIS IS A BRAND-NEW FLAVOR.
IT'S MY INFO, SO YOU KNOW IT IS TRUE.
PLEASE?
Shf..

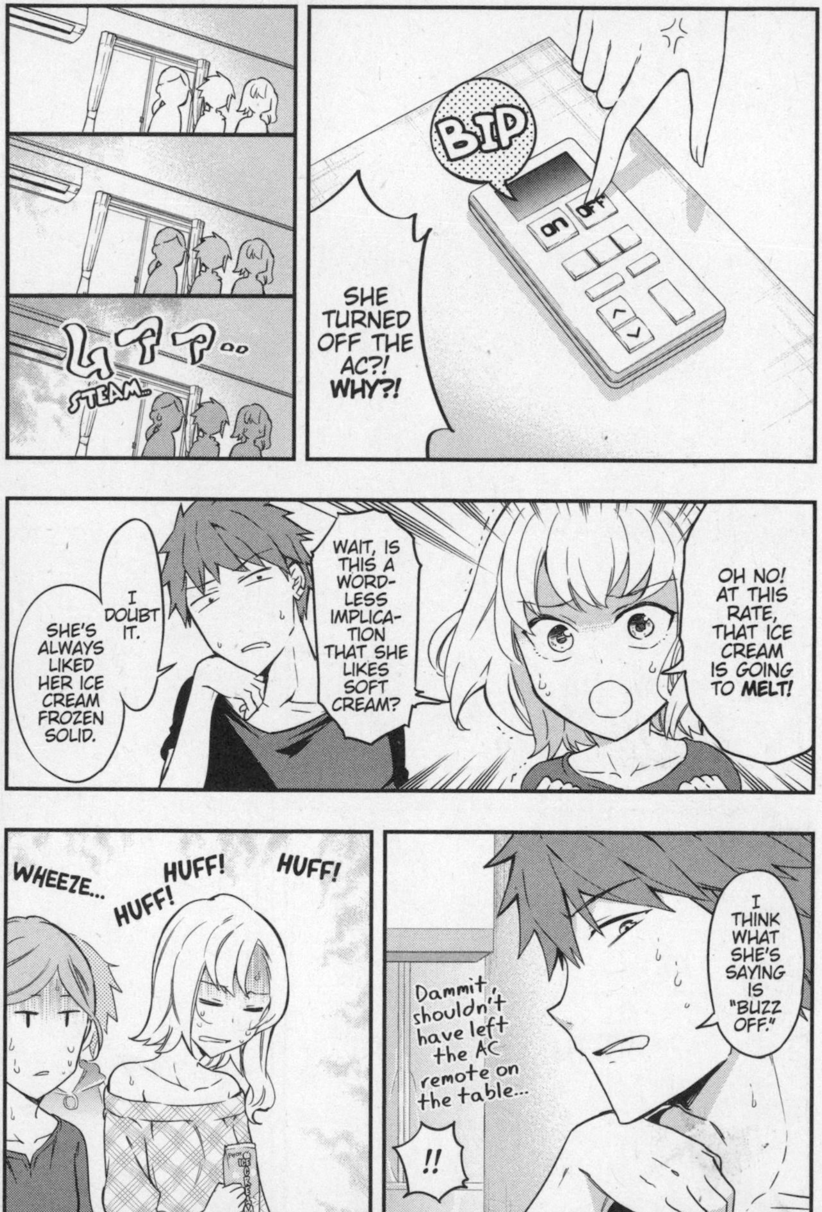
BIP
SHE TURNED OFF THE AC?! **WHY?!**
STEAM...
OH NO! AT THIS RATE, THAT ICE CREAM IS GOING TO **MELT!**
WAIT, IS THIS A WORDLESS IMPLICATION THAT SHE LIKES SOFT CREAM?
I DOUBT IT.
SHE'S ALWAYS LIKED HER ICE CREAM FROZEN SOLID.
I THINK WHAT SHE'S SAYING IS "BUZZ OFF."
Dammit, shouldn't have left the AC remote on the table...
!!
HUFF!
HUFF!
HUFF!
WHEEZE...

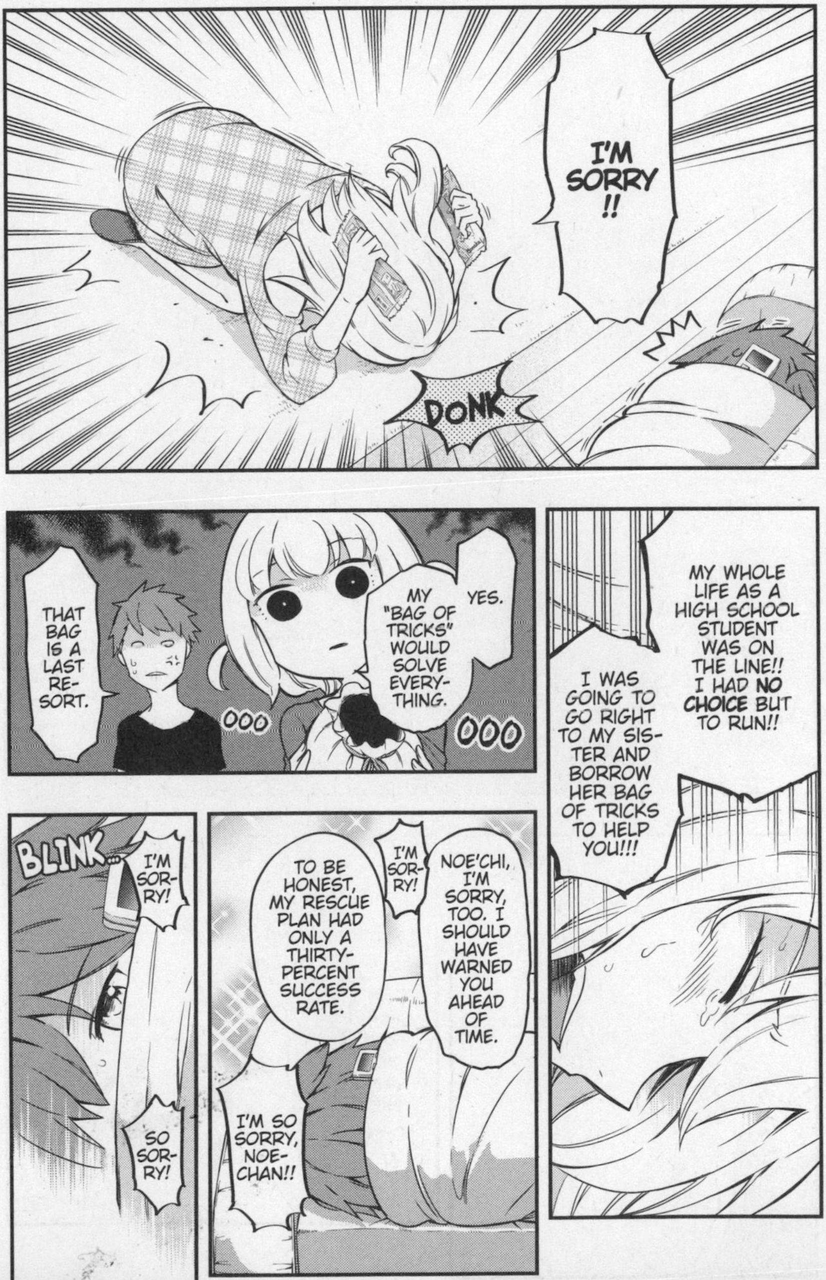
I'M SORRY!!
DONK
MY WHOLE LIFE AS A HIGH SCHOOL STUDENT WAS ON THE LINE!! I HAD NO CHOICE BUT TO RUN!!
I WAS GOING TO GO RIGHT TO MY SISTER AND BORROW HER BAG OF TRICKS TO HELP YOU!!!
YES.
MY "BAG OF TRICKS" WOULD SOLVE EVERYTHING.
OOO
THAT BAG IS A LAST RESORT.
OOO
I'M SORRY!
NOE'CHI, I'M SORRY, TOO. I SHOULD HAVE WARNED YOU AHEAD OF TIME.
TO BE HONEST, MY RESCUE PLAN HAD ONLY A THIRTY-PERCENT SUCCESS RATE.
I'M SO SORRY, NOE-CHAN!!
BLINK...
I'M SORRY!
SO SORRY!

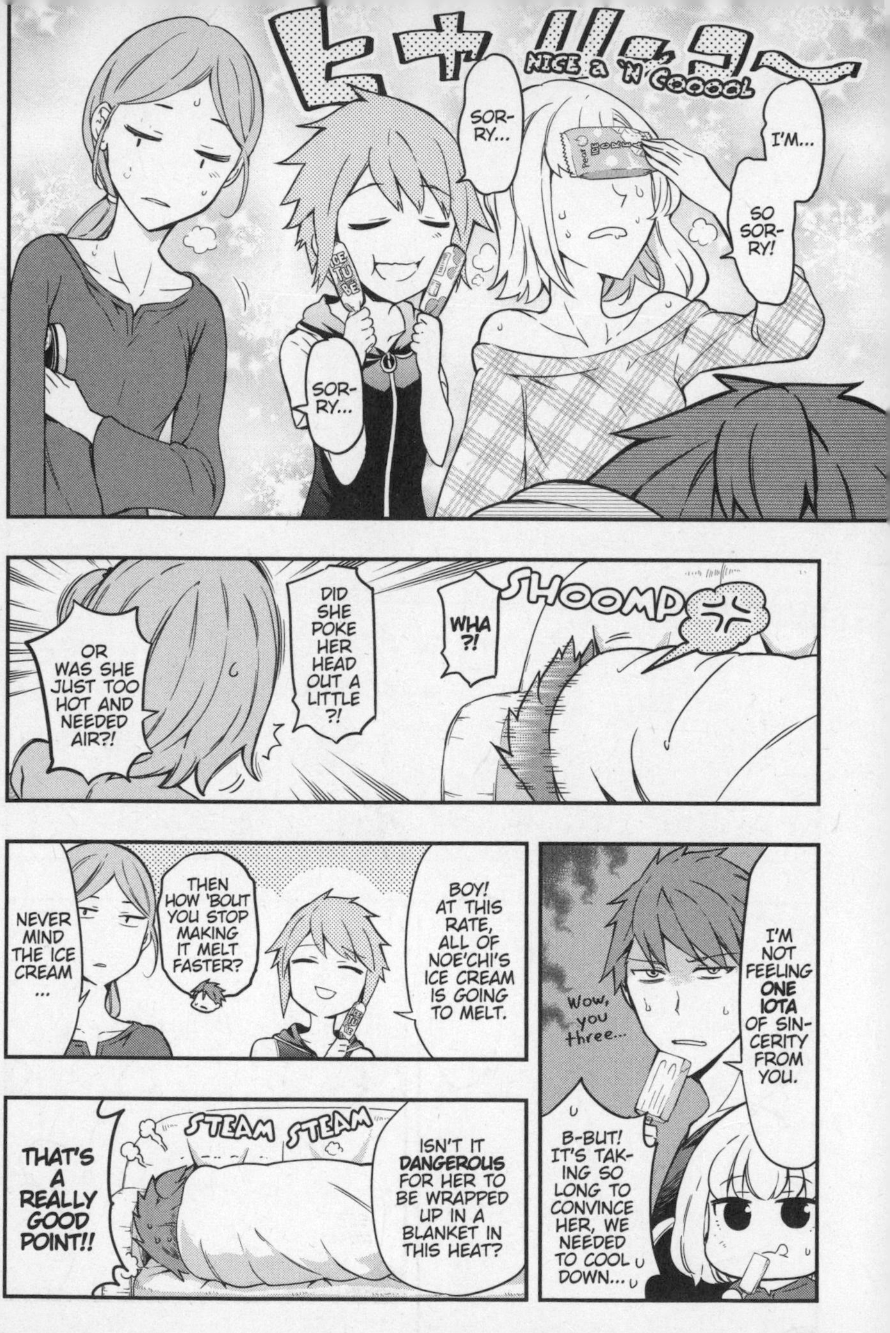
NICE a 'N COOOOL
I'M...
SO SORRY!
SORRY...
ICE TUBE
SORRY...
SHOOMP
WHA?!
DID SHE POKE HER HEAD OUT A LITTLE?!
OR WAS SHE JUST TOO HOT AND NEEDED AIR?!
I'M NOT FEELING **ONE IOTA** OF SINCERITY FROM YOU.
Wow, you three...
B-BUT! IT'S TAKING SO LONG TO CONVINCE HER, WE NEEDED TO COOL DOWN...
BOY! AT THIS RATE, ALL OF NOE'CHI'S ICE CREAM IS GOING TO MELT.
THEN HOW 'BOUT YOU STOP MAKING IT MELT FASTER?
NEVER MIND THE ICE CREAM ...
ISN'T IT **DANGEROUS** FOR HER TO BE WRAPPED UP IN A BLANKET IN THIS HEAT?
STEAM STEAM
THAT'S A REALLY GOOD POINT!!

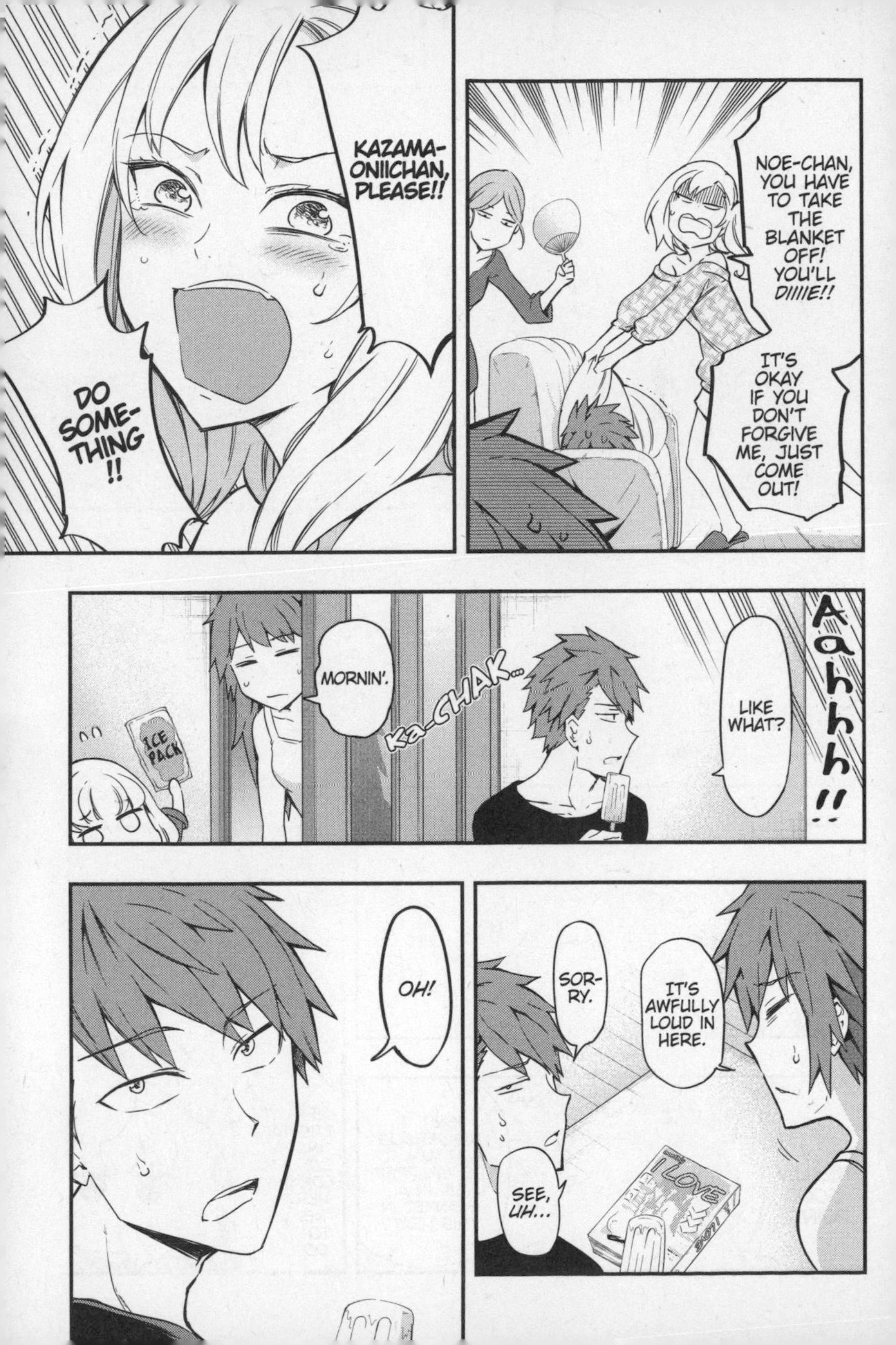
NOE-CHAN, YOU HAVE TO TAKE THE BLANKET OFF! YOU'LL DIIIIE!!
IT'S OKAY IF YOU DON'T FORGIVE ME, JUST COME OUT!
KAZAMA-ONIICHAN, PLEASE!!
DO SOME-THING!!
Aahhh!!
LIKE WHAT?
Ka-CHAK...
MORNIN'.
ICE PACK
IT'S AWFULLY LOUD IN HERE.
SOR-RY.
SEE, UH...
I LOVE
OH!

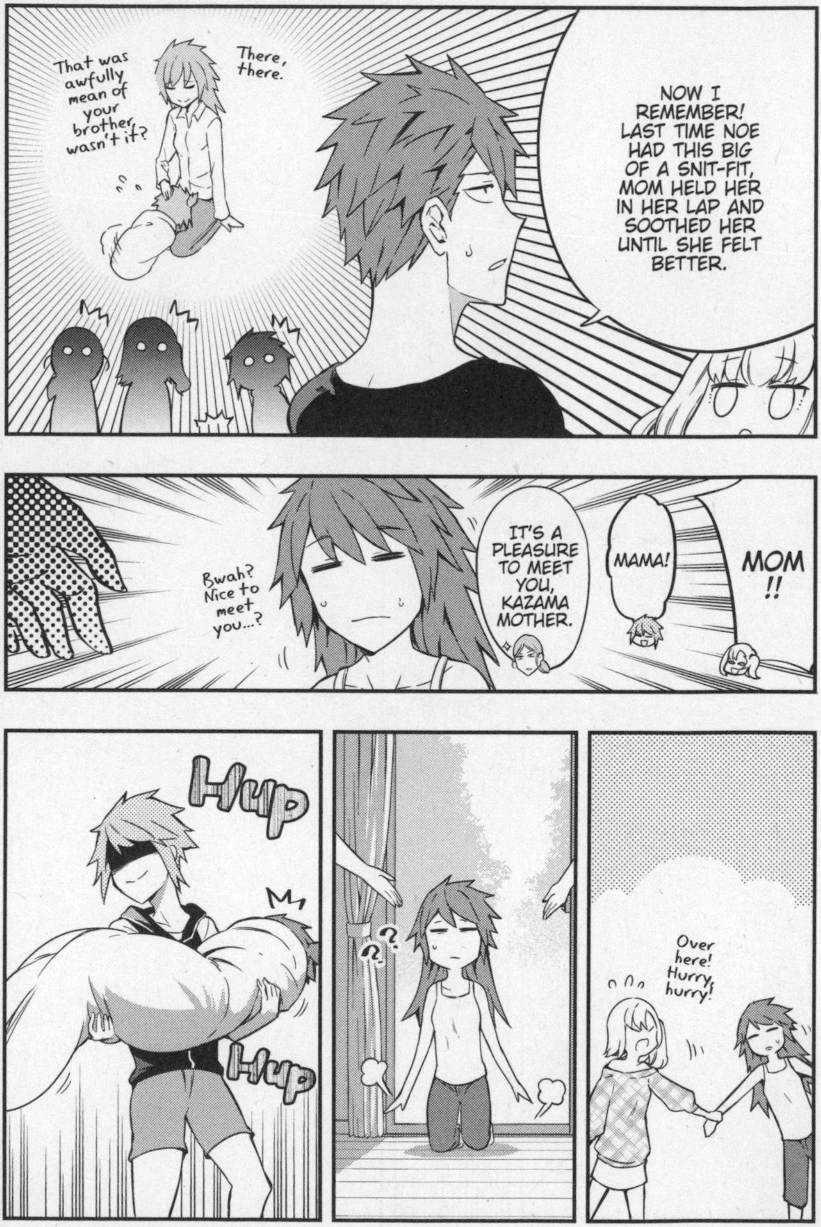
NOW I REMEMBER! LAST TIME NOE HAD THIS BIG OF A SNIT-FIT, MOM HELD HER IN HER LAP AND SOOTHED HER UNTIL SHE FELT BETTER.
There, there.
That was awfully mean of your brother, wasn't it?
MOM !!
MAMA!
IT'S A PLEASURE TO MEET YOU, KAZAMA MOTHER.
Bwah? Nice to meet you...?
Over here! Hurry, hurry!
Hup
Hup

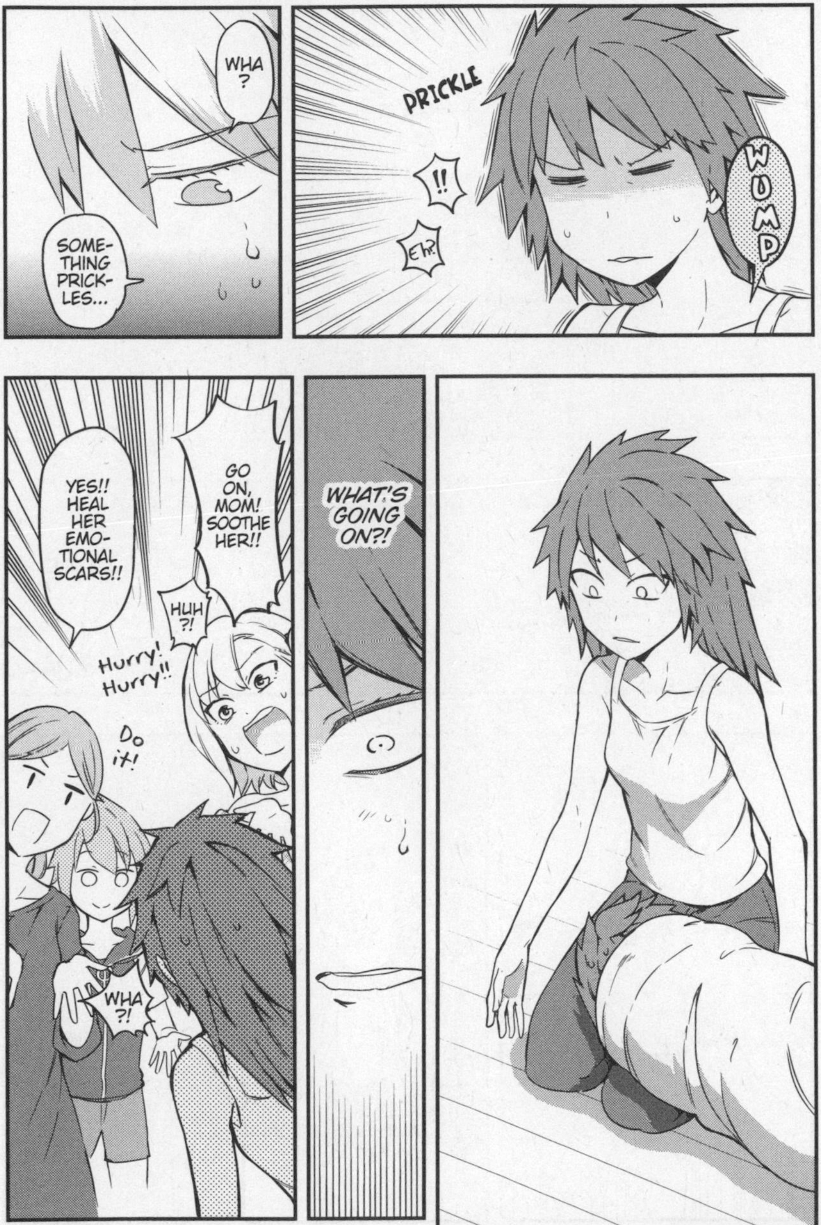
WUMP
PRICKLE
!!
Eh?
WHA?
SOME-THING PRICK-LES...
WHAT'S GOING ON?!
GO ON, MOM! SOOTHE HER!!
YES!! HEAL HER EMO-TIONAL SCARS!!
HUH?!
Hurry! Hurry!!
Do it!
WHA?!

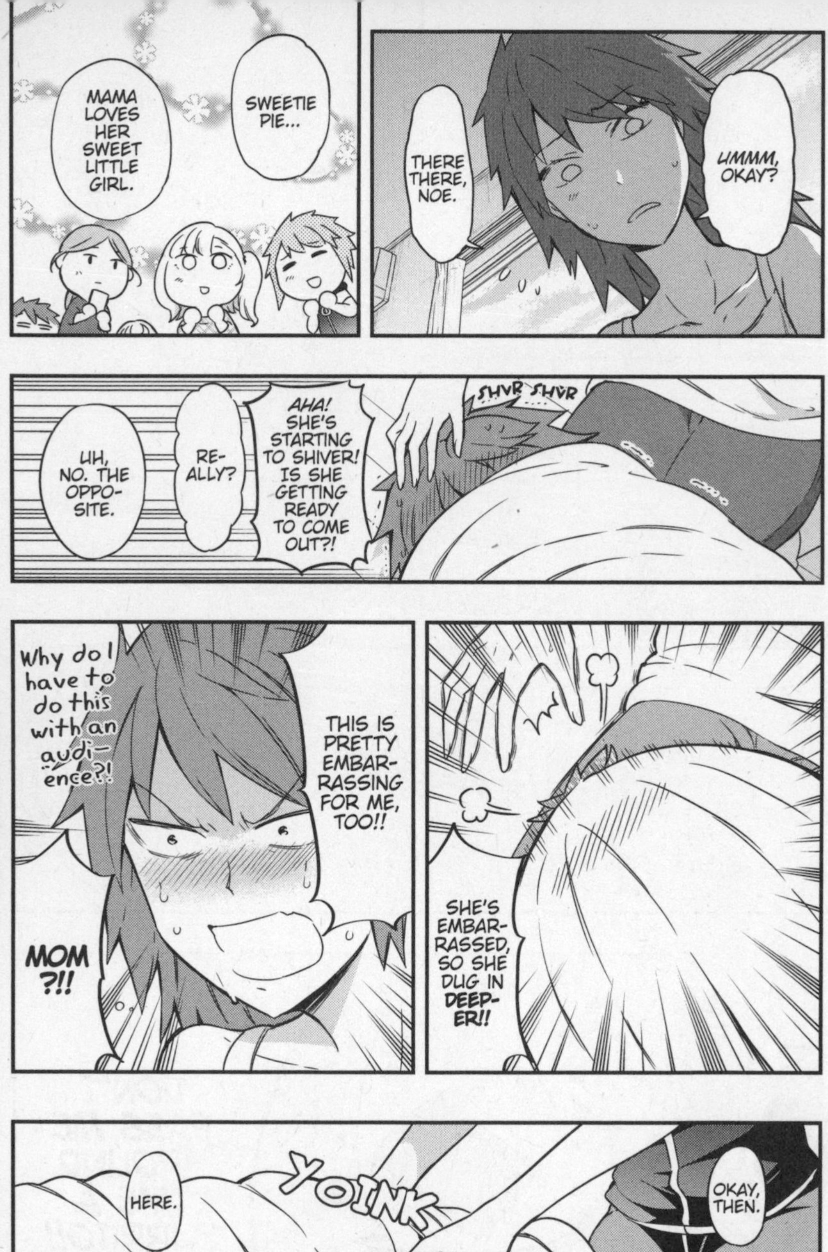
UMMM, OKAY?
THERE THERE, NOE.
SWEETIE PIE...
MAMA LOVES HER SWEET LITTLE GIRL.
SHVR SHVR
AHA! SHE'S STARTING TO SHIVER! IS SHE GETTING READY TO COME OUT?!
RE-ALLY?
UH, NO. THE OPPO-SITE.
SHE'S EMBAR-RASSED, SO SHE DUG IN DEEP-ER!!
THIS IS PRETTY EMBAR-RASSING FOR ME, TOO!!
Why do I have to do this with an audi-ence?!
MOM ?!!
OKAY, THEN.
YOINK
HERE.

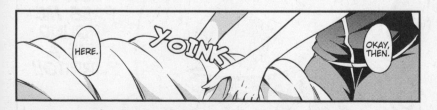

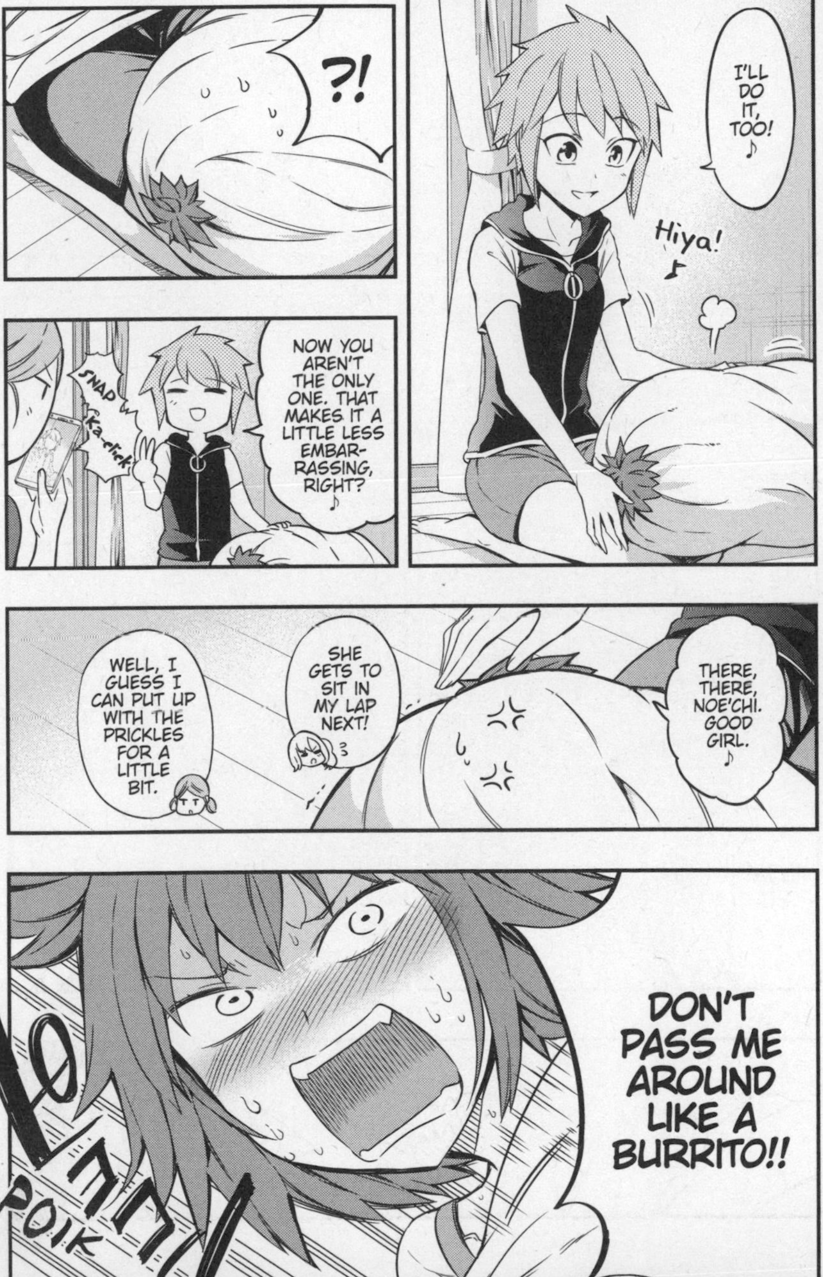
I'LL DO IT, TOO! ♪
Hiya! ♪
?!
NOW YOU AREN'T THE ONLY ONE. THAT MAKES IT A LITTLE LESS EMBARRASSING, RIGHT? ♪
SNAP
ka-click
THERE, THERE, NOE'CHI. GOOD GIRL. ♪
SHE GETS TO SIT IN MY LAP NEXT!
WELL, I GUESS I CAN PUT UP WITH THE PRICKLES FOR A LITTLE BIT.
DON'T PASS ME AROUND LIKE A BURRITO!!
POIK

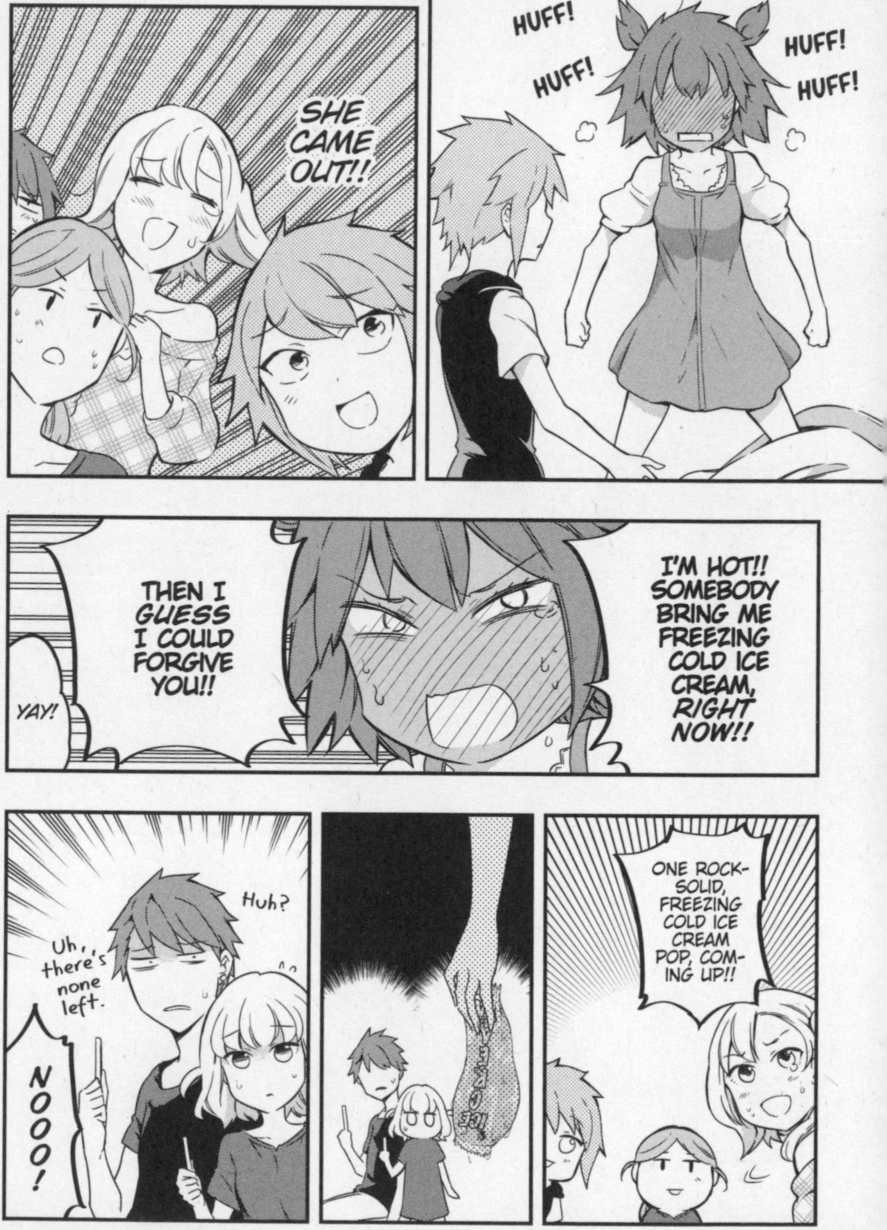
HUFF!
HUFF!
HUFF!
HUFF!
SHE CAME OUT!!
I'M HOT!! SOMEBODY BRING ME FREEZING COLD ICE CREAM, RIGHT NOW!!
THEN I GUESS I COULD FORGIVE YOU!!
YAY!
ONE ROCK-SOLID, FREEZING COLD ICE CREAM POP, COMING UP!!
Huh?
Uh, there's none left.
NOOOO!

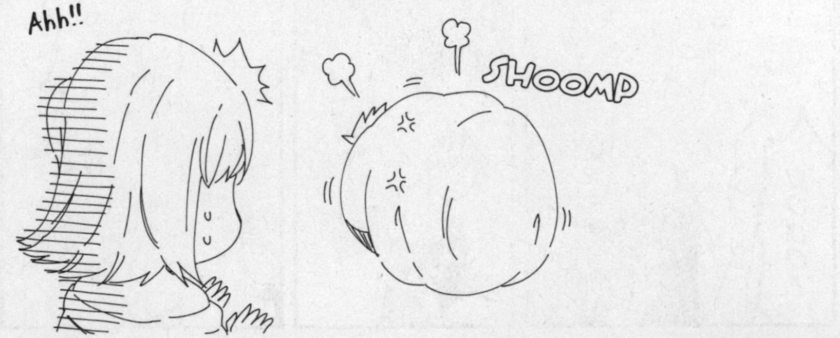
SHOOMP
Ahh!!

D-FRAGMENTS

ディーふらぐ!

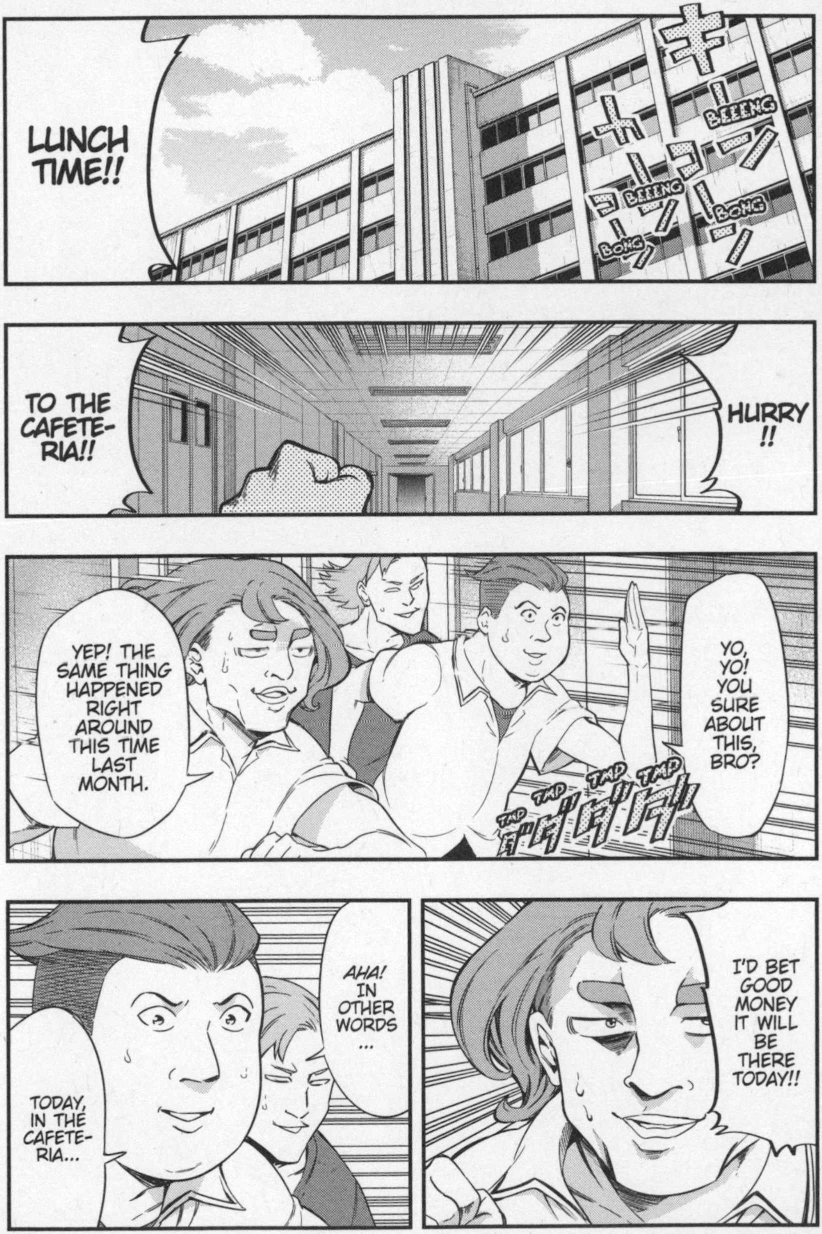
BEEENG
BONG
BEEENG
BONG
LUNCH TIME!!
HURRY !!
TO THE CAFETERIA!!
YO, YO! YOU SURE ABOUT THIS, BRO?
TMP TMP TMP TMP
YEP! THE SAME THING HAPPENED RIGHT AROUND THIS TIME LAST MONTH.
I'D BET GOOD MONEY IT WILL BE THERE TODAY!!
AHA! IN OTHER WORDS ...
TODAY, IN THE CAFETERIA...

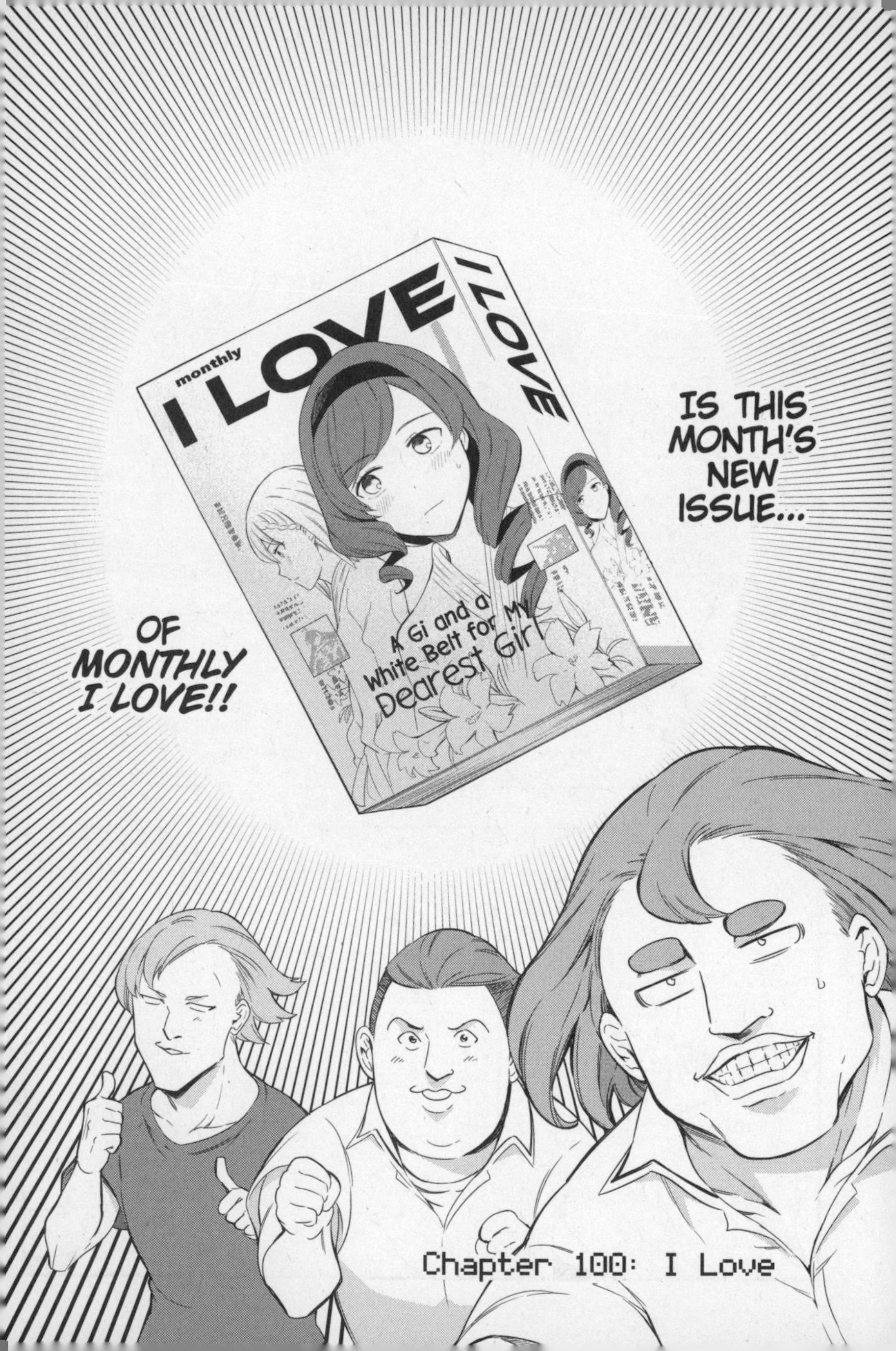
IS THIS MONTH'S NEW ISSUE...
monthly
I LOVE
I LOVE
A Gi and a White Belt for My Dearest Girl
OF MONTHLY I LOVE!!
Chapter 100: I Love

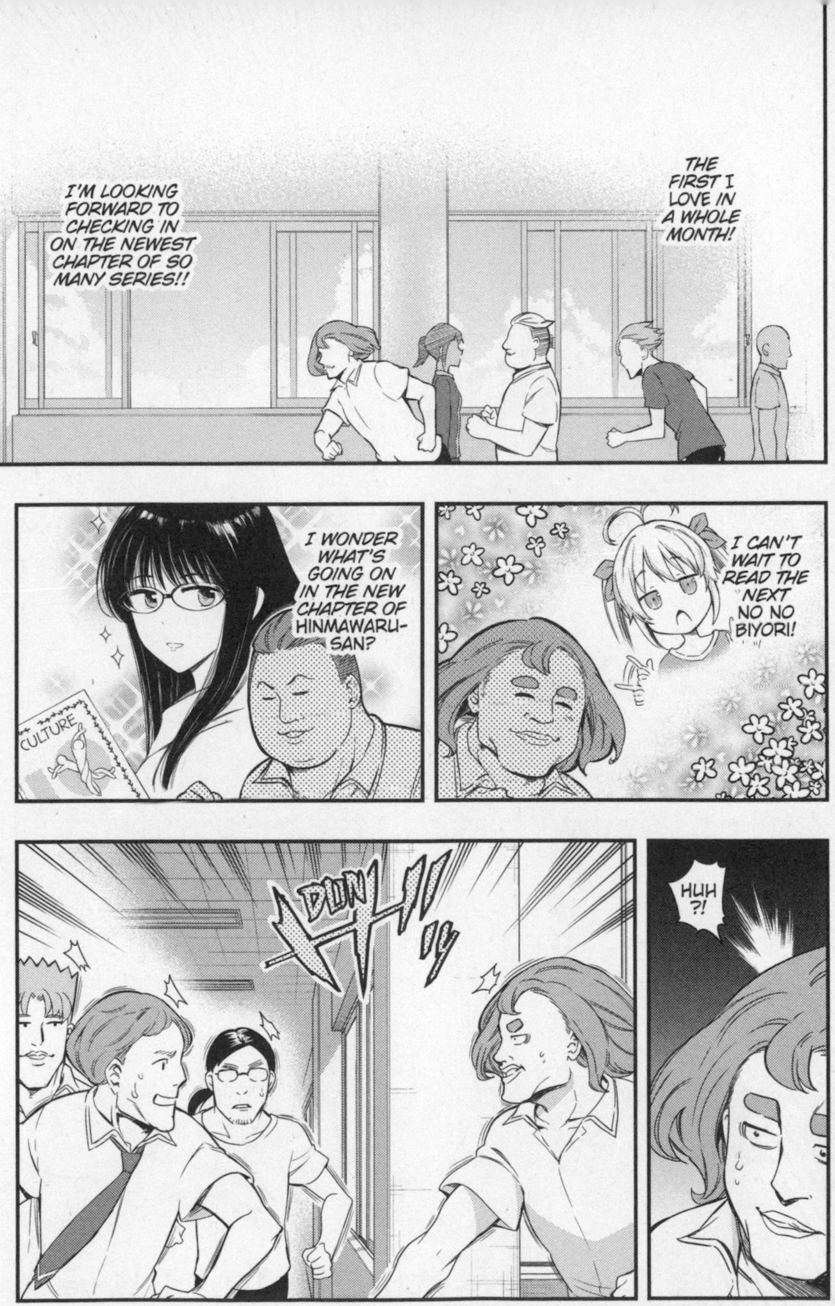
THE FIRST I LOVE IN A WHOLE MONTH!
I'M LOOKING FORWARD TO CHECKING IN ON THE NEWEST CHAPTER OF SO MANY SERIES!!
I CAN'T WAIT TO READ THE NEXT NO NO BIYORI!
I WONDER WHAT'S GOING ON IN THE NEW CHAPTER OF HINMAWARU-SAN?
CULTURE
HUH ?!
DUN

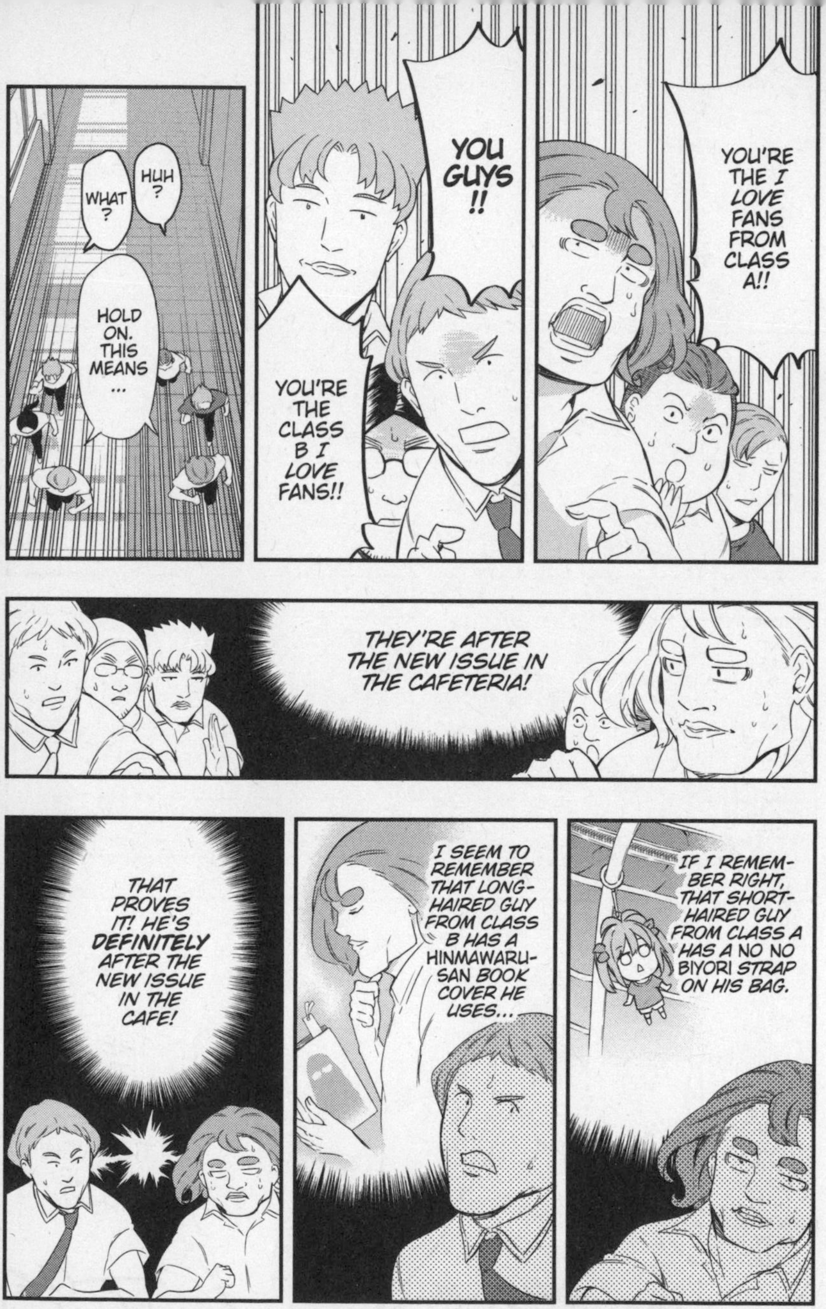
YOU'RE THE I LOVE FANS FROM CLASS A!!
YOU GUYS!!
YOU'RE THE CLASS B I LOVE FANS!!
HUH?
WHAT?
HOLD ON. THIS MEANS...
THEY'RE AFTER THE NEW ISSUE IN THE CAFETERIA!
IF I REMEMBER RIGHT, THAT SHORT-HAIRED GUY FROM CLASS A HAS A NO NO BIYORI STRAP ON HIS BAG.
I SEEM TO REMEMBER THAT LONG-HAIRED GUY FROM CLASS B HAS A HINMAWARU-SAN BOOK COVER HE USES...
THAT PROVES IT! HE'S DEFINITELY AFTER THE NEW ISSUE IN THE CAFE!

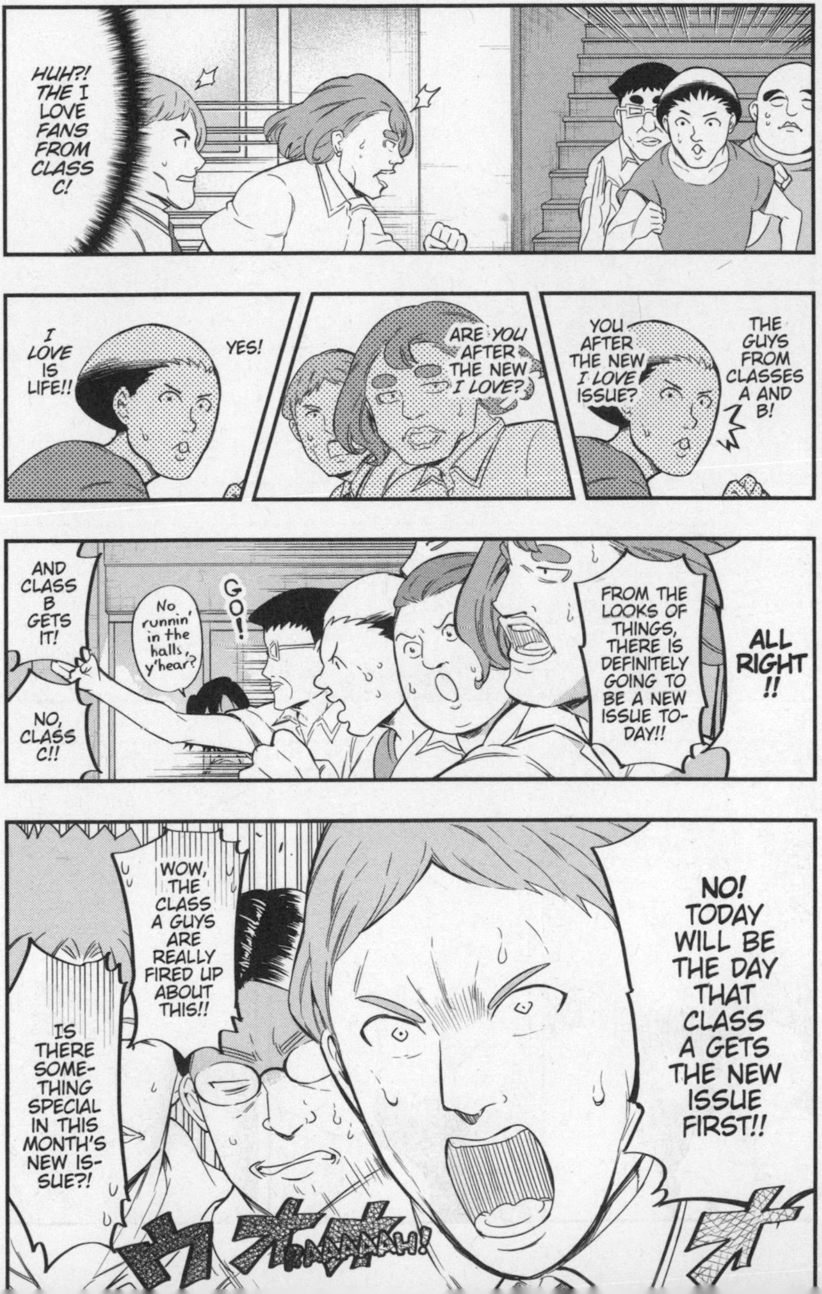
HUH?! THE I LOVE FANS FROM CLASS C!
THE GUYS FROM CLASSES A AND B!
YOU AFTER THE NEW I LOVE ISSUE?
ARE YOU AFTER THE NEW I LOVE?
YES!
I LOVE IS LIFE!!
ALL RIGHT!!
FROM THE LOOKS OF THINGS, THERE IS DEFINITELY GOING TO BE A NEW ISSUE TO-DAY!!
GO!
No runnin' in the halls, y'hear?
AND CLASS B GETS IT!
NO, CLASS C!!
NO! TODAY WILL BE THE DAY THAT CLASS A GETS THE NEW ISSUE FIRST!!
WOW, THE CLASS A GUYS ARE REALLY FIRED UP ABOUT THIS!!
IS THERE SOMETHING SPECIAL IN THIS MONTH'S NEW IS-SUE?!
BWAAAAH!

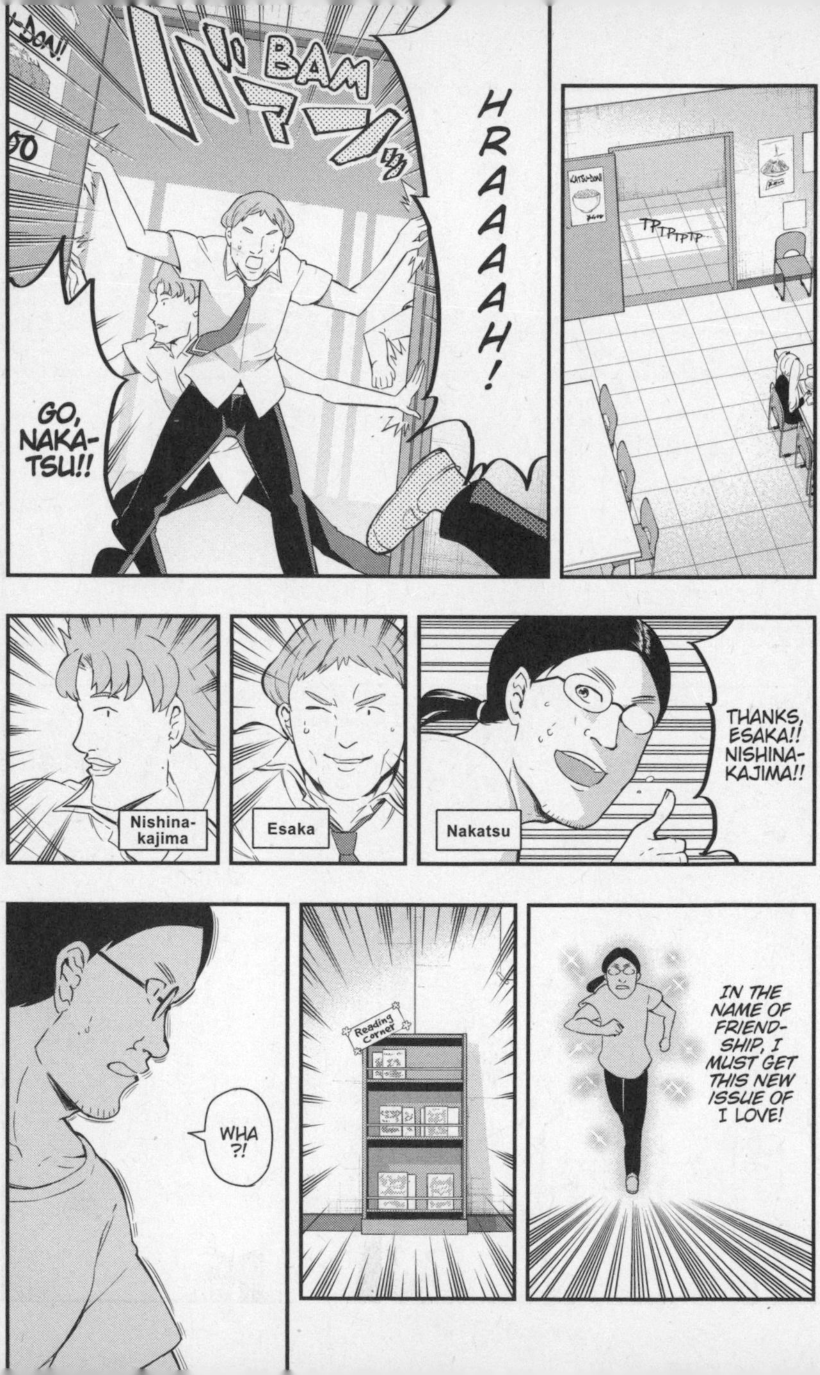

KATSU-DON!
TPTPTPTP
HRAAAAAH!
BAM
GO, NAKA-TSU!!
THANKS, ESAKA!! NISHINA-KAJIMA!!
Nakatsu
Esaka
Nishina-kajima
IN THE NAME OF FRIEND-SHIP, I MUST GET THIS NEW ISSUE OF I LOVE!
Reading Corner
WHA?!

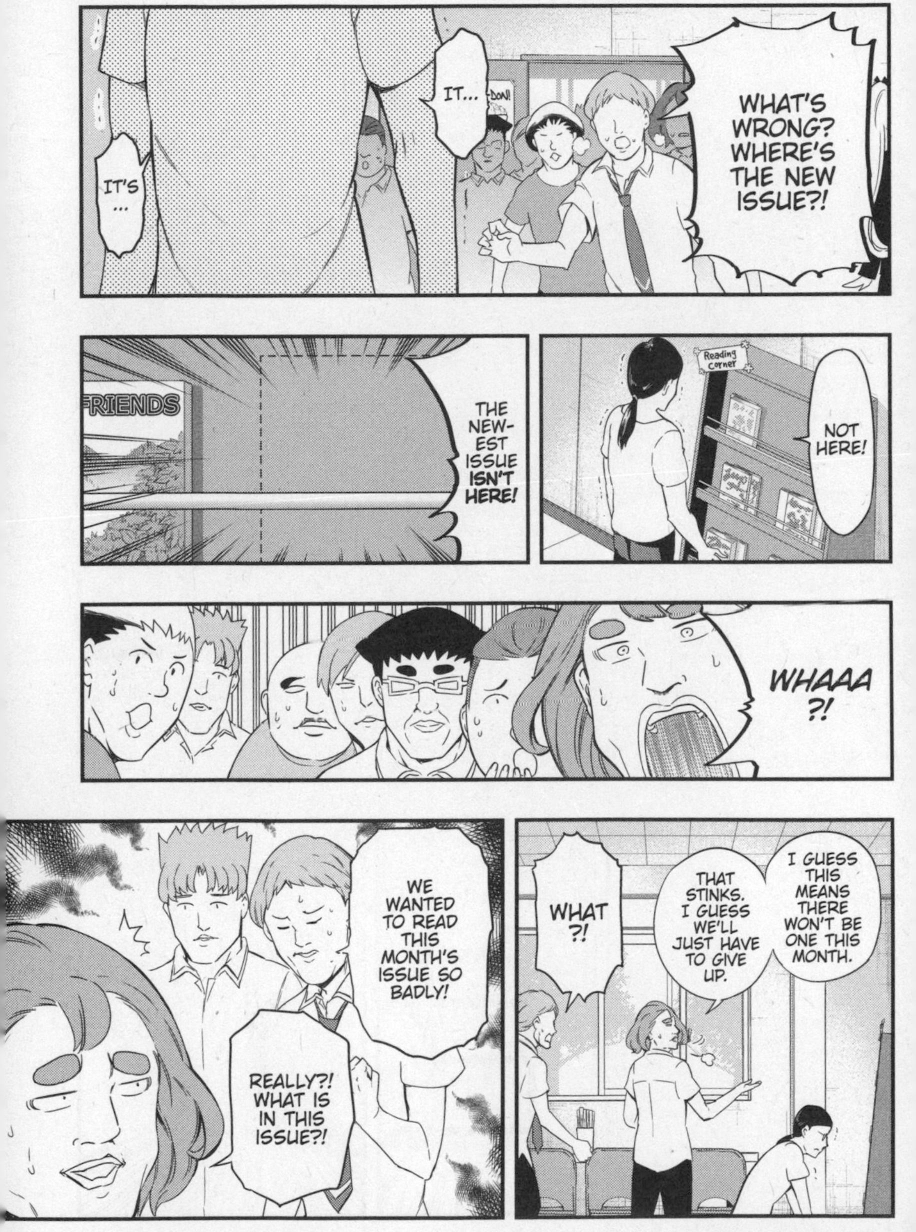
WHAT'S WRONG? WHERE'S THE NEW ISSUE?!
IT...
IT'S ...
Reading corner
NOT HERE!
FRIENDS
THE NEW-EST ISSUE ISN'T HERE!
WHAAA ?!
I GUESS THIS MEANS THERE WON'T BE ONE THIS MONTH.
THAT STINKS. I GUESS WE'LL JUST HAVE TO GIVE UP.
WHAT ?!
WE WANTED TO READ THIS MONTH'S ISSUE SO BADLY!
REALLY?! WHAT IS IN THIS ISSUE?!

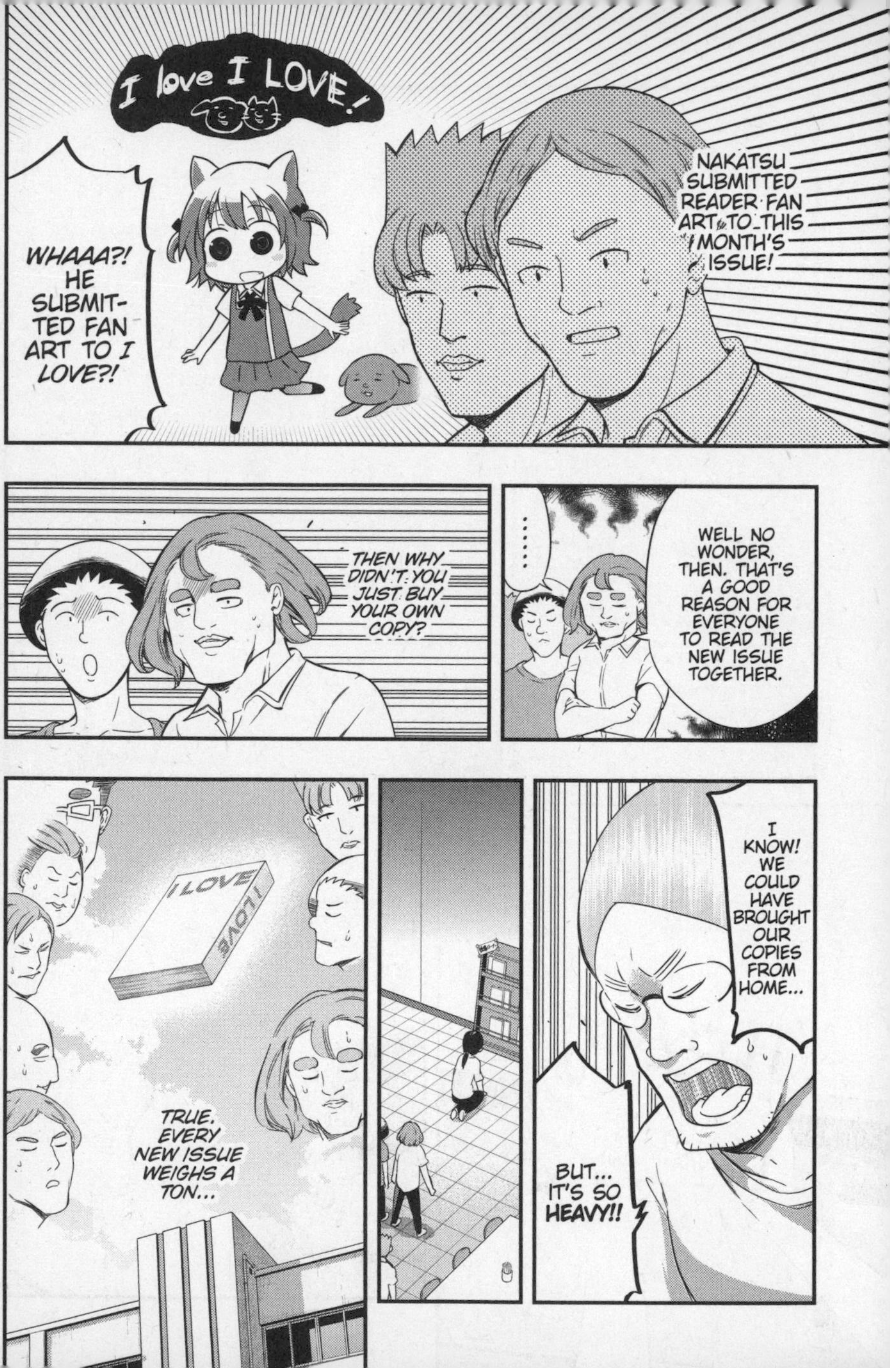
NAKATSU SUBMITTED READER FAN ART TO THIS MONTH'S ISSUE!
I love I LOVE!
WHAAA?! HE SUBMITTED FAN ART TO I LOVE?!
......
WELL NO WONDER, THEN. THAT'S A GOOD REASON FOR EVERYONE TO READ THE NEW ISSUE TOGETHER.
THEN WHY DIDN'T YOU JUST BUY YOUR OWN COPY?
I KNOW! WE COULD HAVE BROUGHT OUR COPIES FROM HOME...
BUT... IT'S SO HEAVY!!
I LOVE
I LOVE
TRUE. EVERY NEW ISSUE WEIGHS A TON...

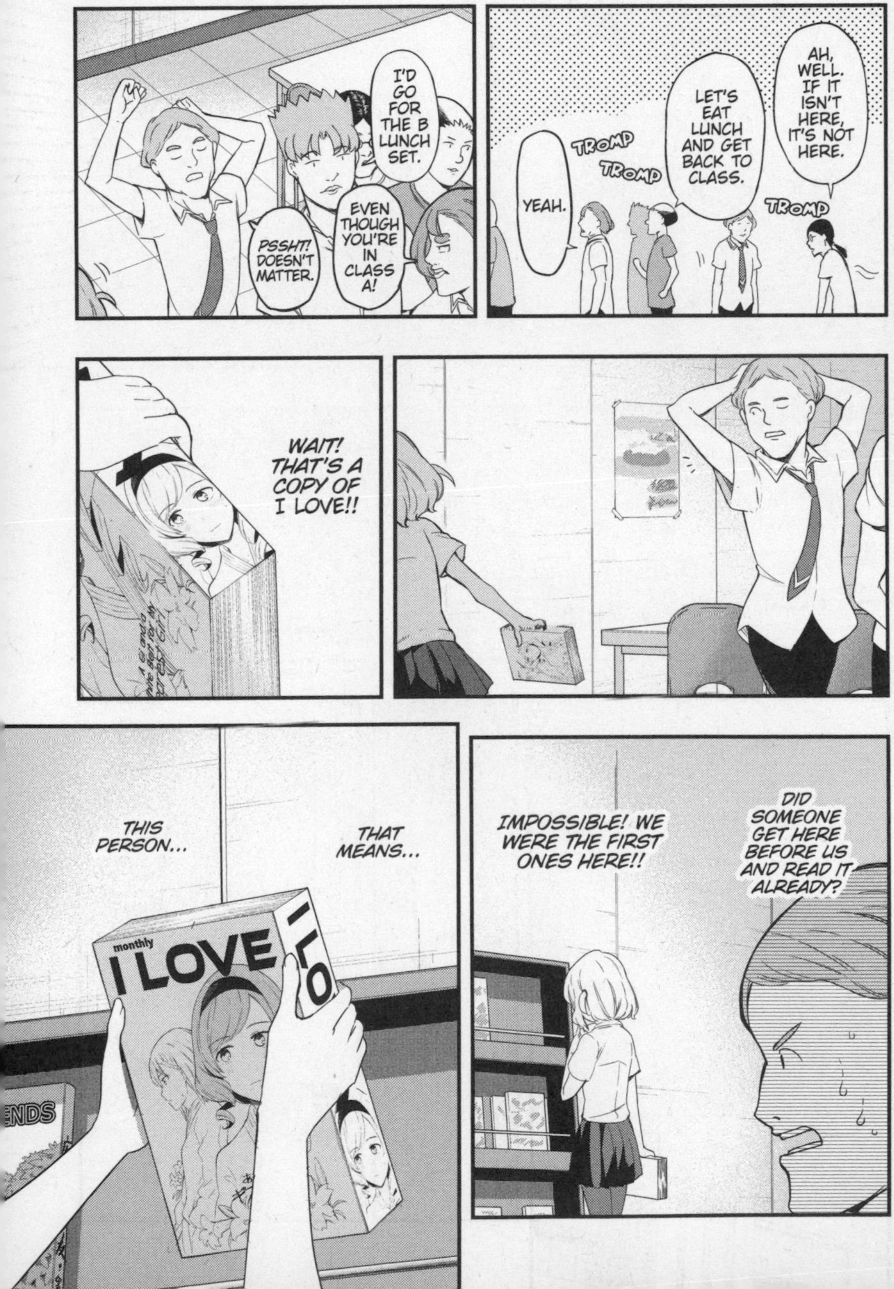
AH, WELL. IF IT ISN'T HERE, IT'S NOT HERE.
TROMP
LET'S EAT LUNCH AND GET BACK TO CLASS.
TROMP
TROMP
YEAH.
I'D GO FOR THE B LUNCH SET.
EVEN THOUGH YOU'RE IN CLASS A!
PSSHT! DOESN'T MATTER.
WAIT! THAT'S A COPY OF I LOVE!!
DID SOMEONE GET HERE BEFORE US AND READ IT ALREADY?
IMPOSSIBLE! WE WERE THE FIRST ONES HERE!!
THAT MEANS...
THIS PERSON...
monthly
I LOVE
I LO
ENDS

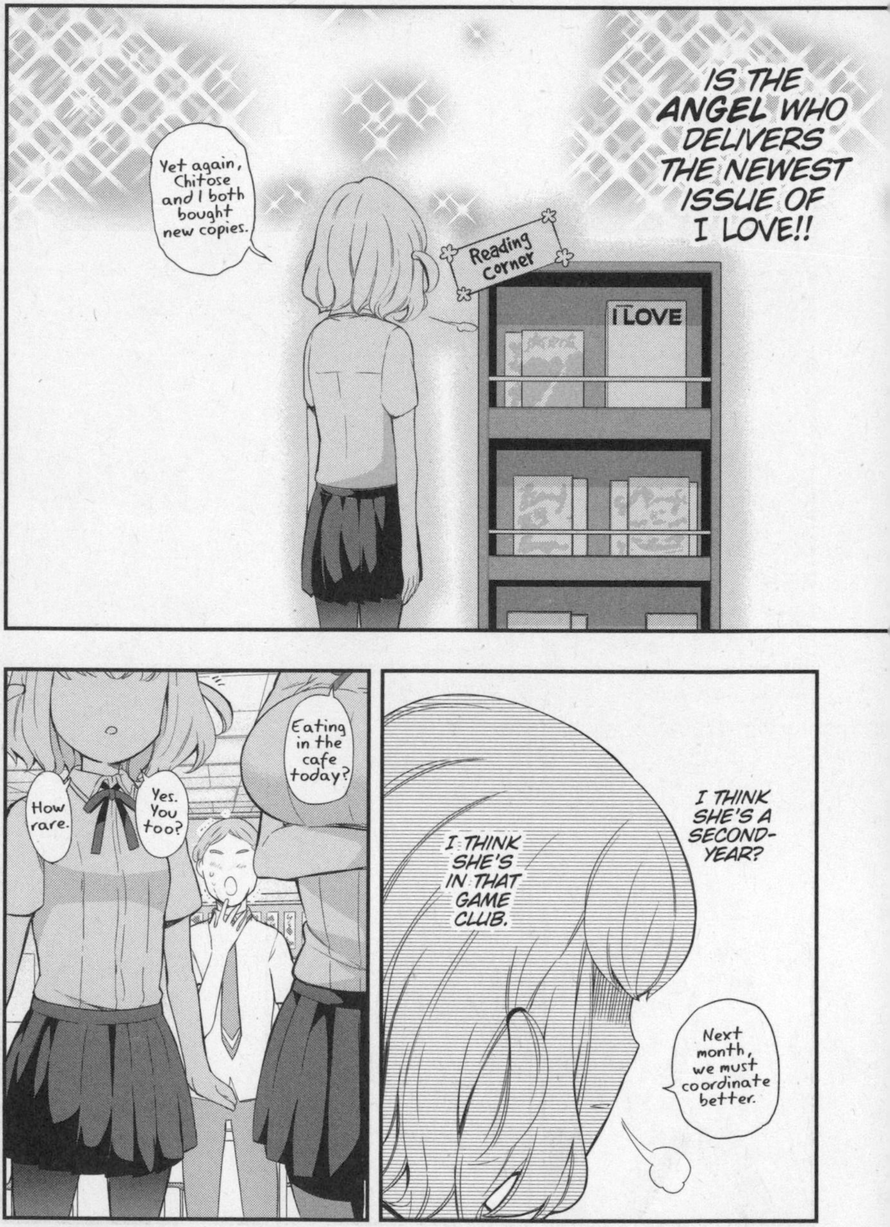
IS THE ANGEL WHO DELIVERS THE NEWEST ISSUE OF I LOVE!!
Reading corner
I LOVE
Yet again, Chitose and I both bought new copies.
I THINK SHE'S A SECOND-YEAR?
I THINK SHE'S IN THAT GAME CLUB.
Next month, we must coordinate better.
Eating in the cafe today?
Yes. You too?
How rare.

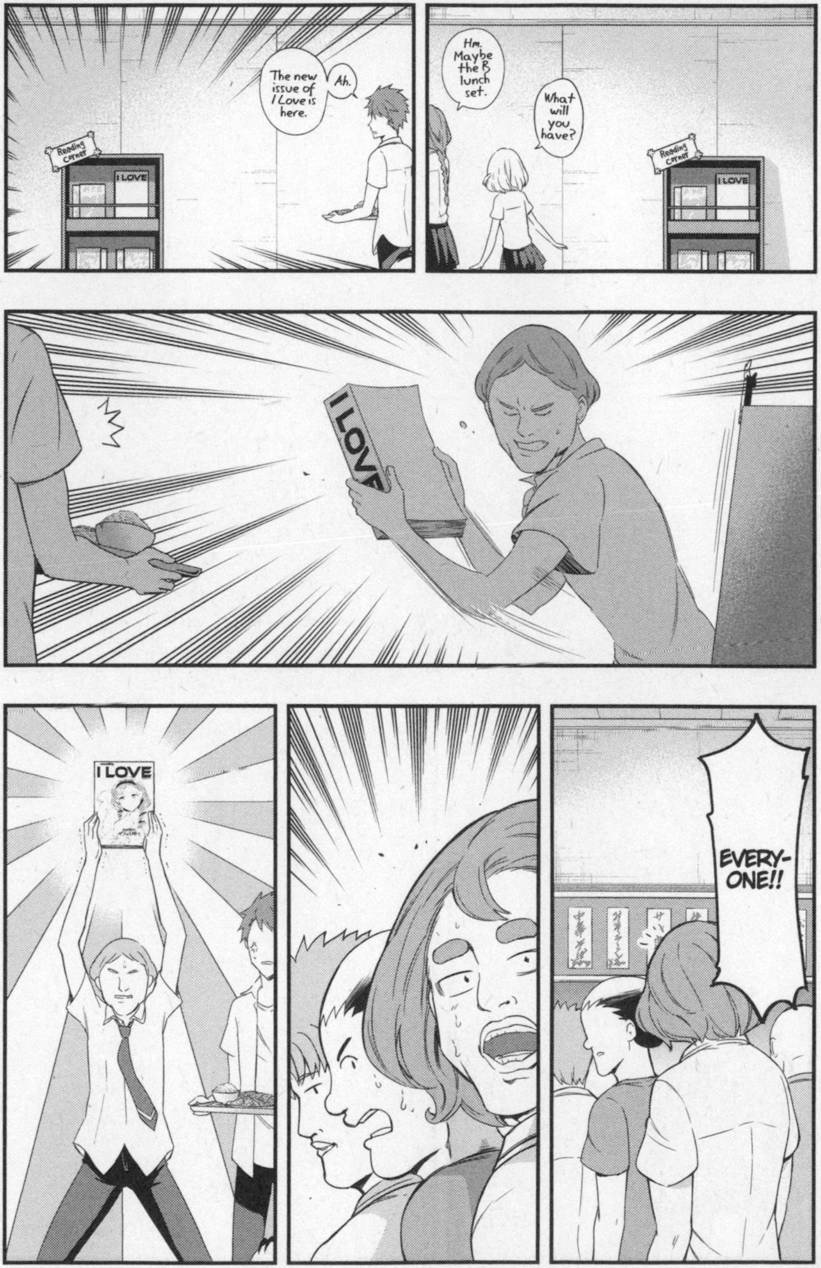

Reading Corner
I LOVE
What will you have?
Hm. Maybe the B lunch set.
Ah.
The new issue of I Love is here.
Reading Corner
I LOVE
I LOVE
EVERY-ONE!!
I LOVE

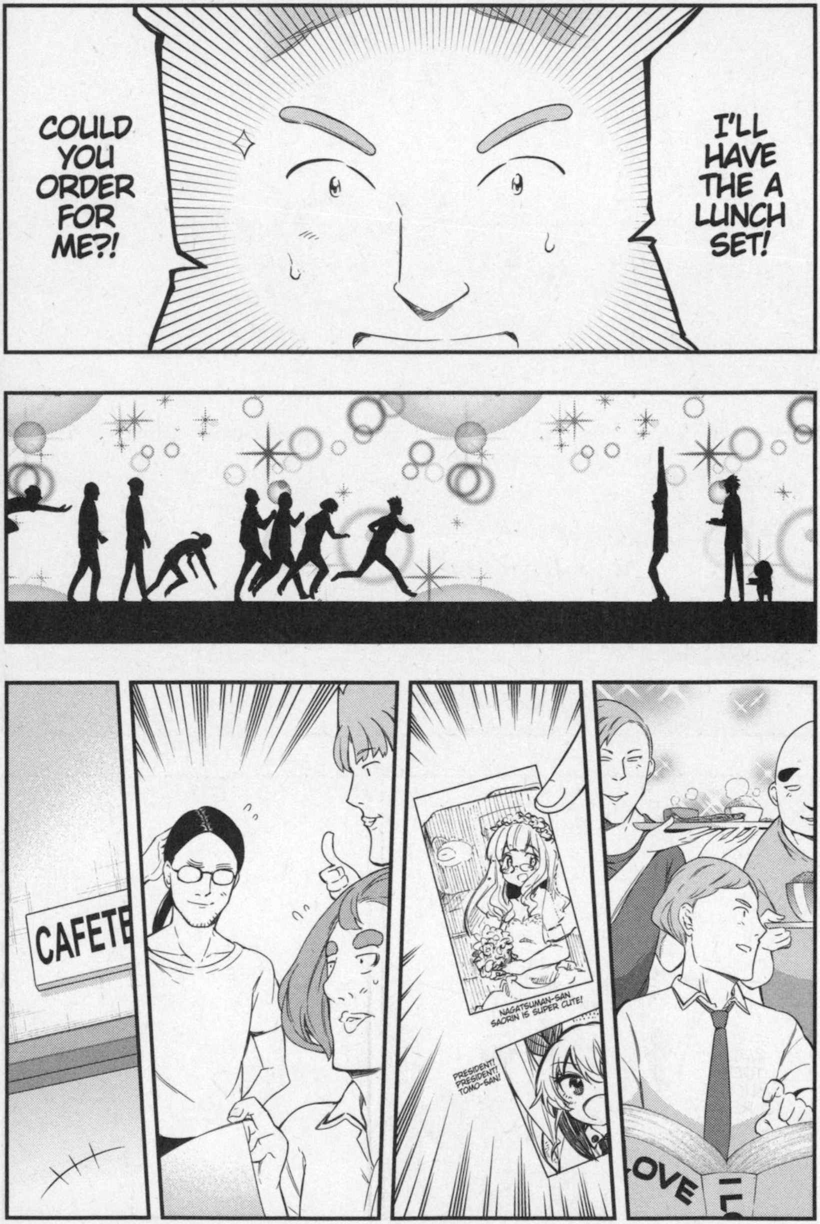
I'LL HAVE THE A LUNCH SET!
COULD YOU ORDER FOR ME?!
LOVE
NAGATSUMAN-SAN SAORIN IS SUPER CUTE!
PRESIDENT! PRESIDENT! TOMO-SAN!

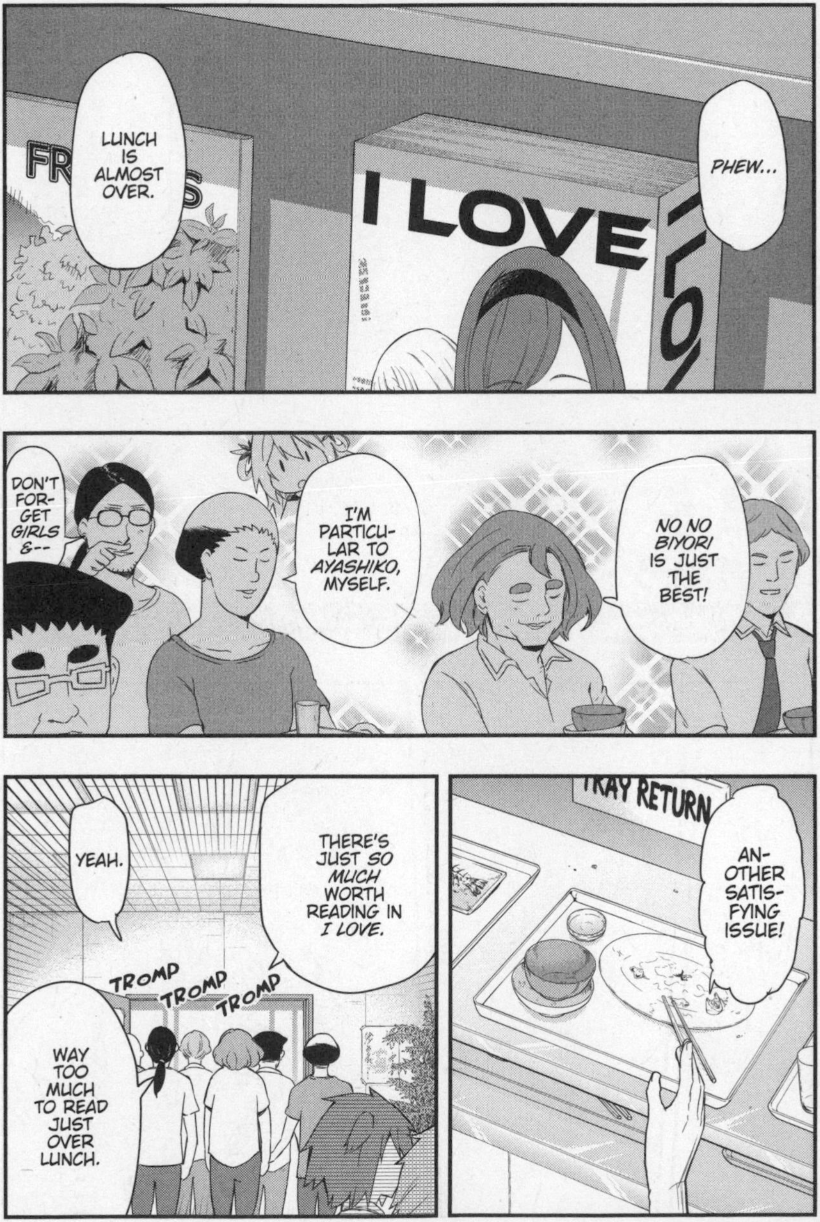
PHEW...
I LOVE
LUNCH IS ALMOST OVER.
NO NO BIYORI IS JUST THE BEST!
I'M PARTICULAR TO AYASHIKO, MYSELF.
DON'T FORGET GIRLS &--
TRAY RETURN
ANOTHER SATISFYING ISSUE!
THERE'S JUST SO MUCH WORTH READING IN I LOVE.
YEAH.
TROMP TROMP TROMP
WAY TOO MUCH TO READ JUST OVER LUNCH.

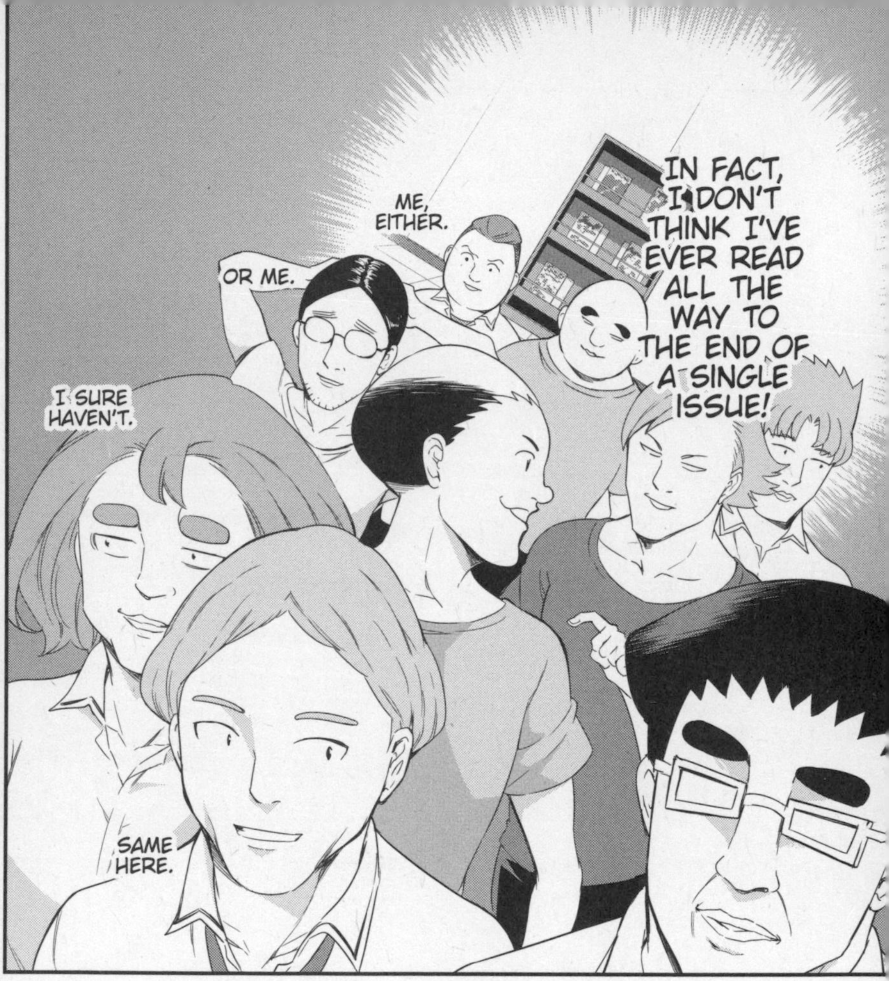
IN FACT, I DON'T THINK I'VE EVER READ ALL THE WAY TO THE END OF A SINGLE ISSUE!
ME, EITHER.
OR ME.
I SURE HAVEN'T.
SAME HERE.
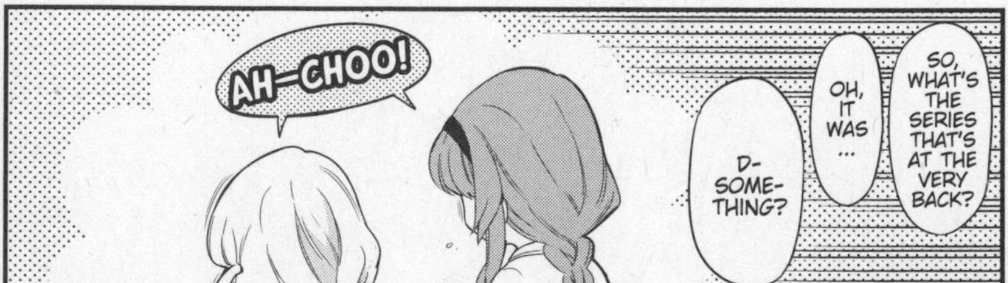
SO, WHAT'S THE SERIES THAT'S AT THE VERY BACK?
OH, IT WAS ...
D-SOMETHING?
AH-CHOO!

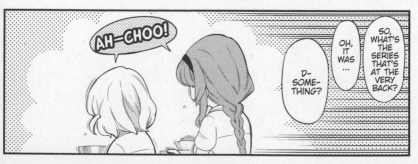

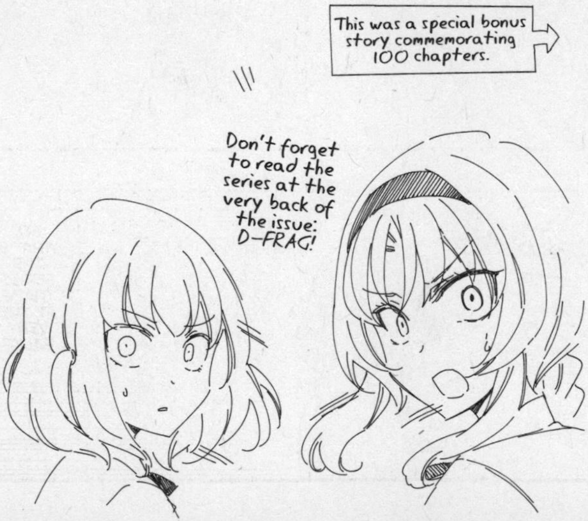
This was a special bonus story commemorating 100 chapters.
Don't forget to read the series at the very back of the issue: D-FRAG!

D-FRAGMENTS
ディーふらぐめんつ!

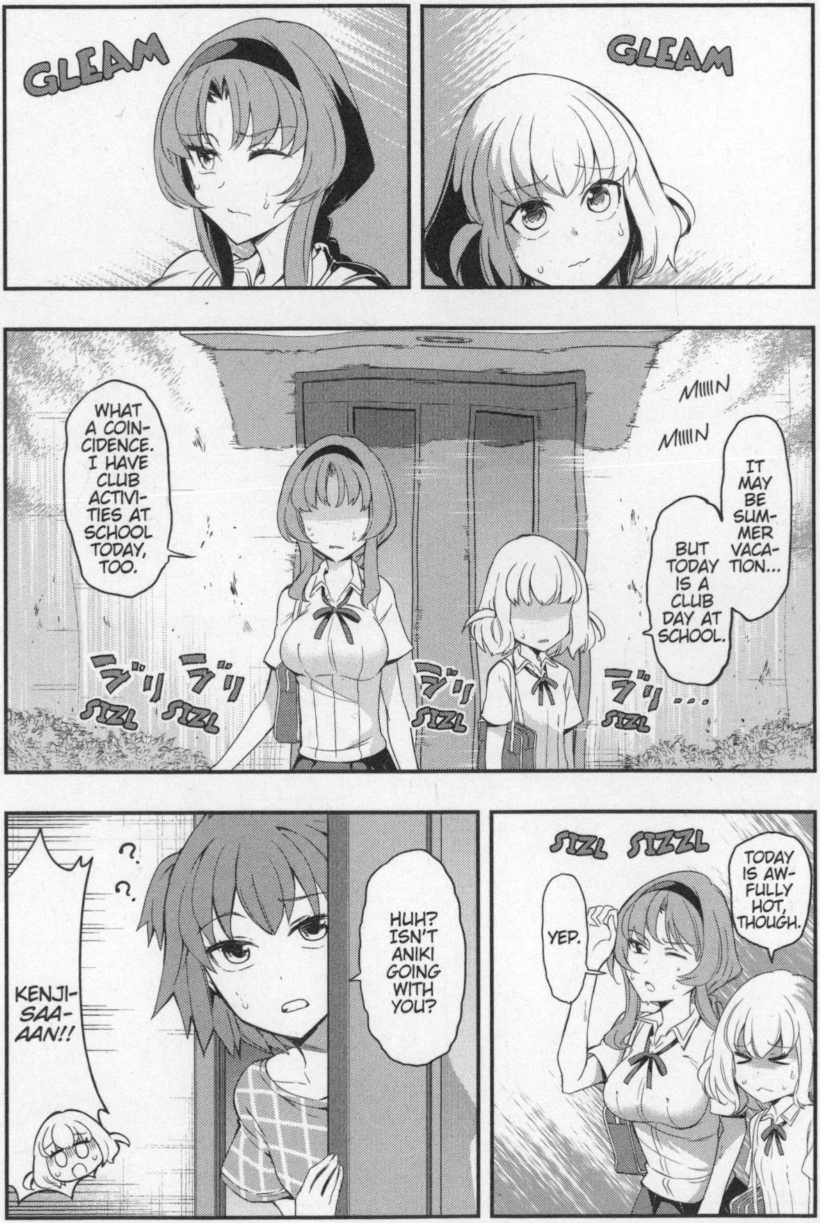
GLEAM
GLEAM
MIIIN
MIIIN
IT MAY BE SUMMER VACATION...
BUT TODAY IS A CLUB DAY AT SCHOOL.
ジリ...
SIZZL
ジリ
SIZZL
ジリ
SIZZL
ジリ
SIZZL
WHAT A COINCIDENCE. I HAVE CLUB ACTIVITIES AT SCHOOL TODAY, TOO.
SIZZL SIZZZL
TODAY IS AWFULLY HOT, THOUGH.
YEP.
HUH? ISN'T ANIKI GOING WITH YOU?
?
?
KENJI-SAAAAN!!

Chapter 101: My Word!

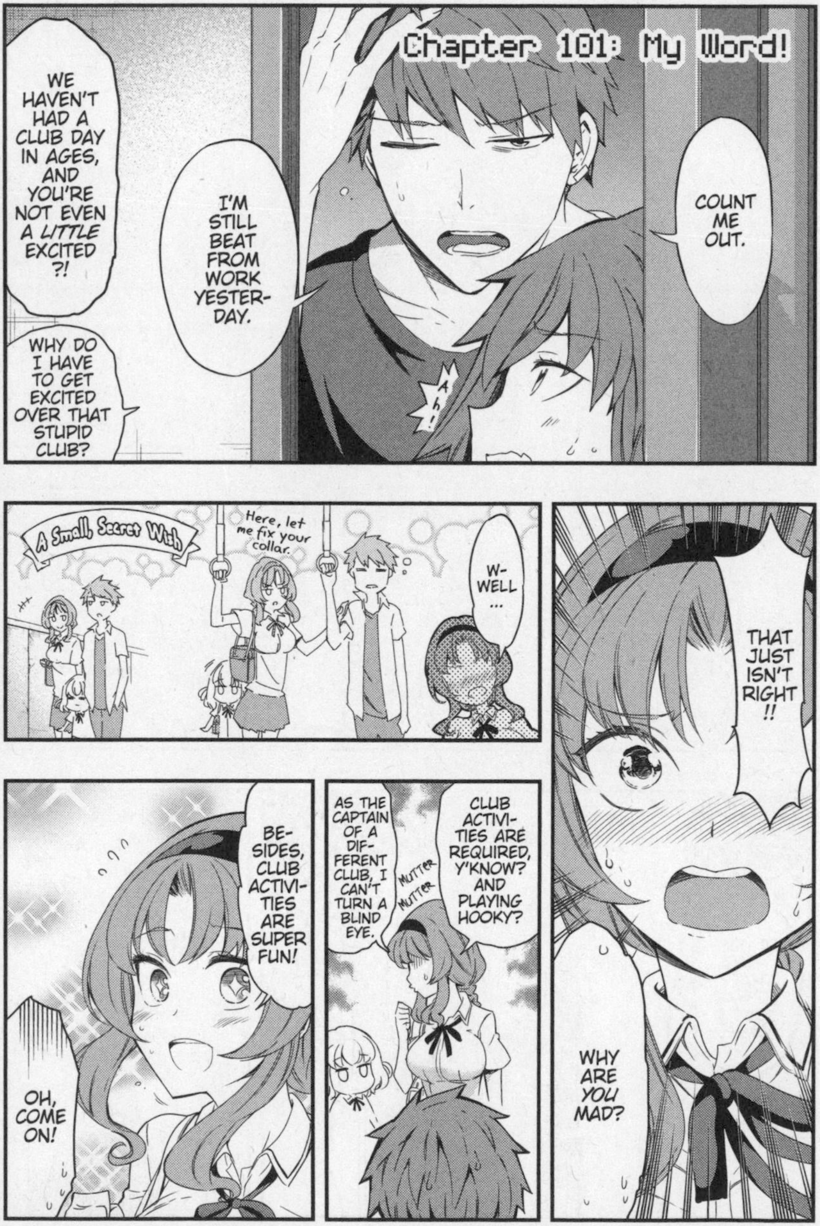
COUNT ME OUT.
I'M STILL BEAT FROM WORK YESTER-DAY.
Ah!
WE HAVEN'T HAD A CLUB DAY IN AGES, AND YOU'RE NOT EVEN A *LITTLE* EXCITED?!
WHY DO I HAVE TO GET EXCITED OVER THAT STUPID CLUB?
THAT JUST ISN'T RIGHT!!
WHY ARE *YOU* MAD?
A Small, Secret Wish
W-WELL...
Here, let me fix your collar.
CLUB ACTIVITIES ARE REQUIRED, Y'KNOW? AND PLAYING HOOKY?
AS THE CAPTAIN OF A DIFFERENT CLUB, I CAN'T TURN A BLIND EYE.
MUTTER MUTTER
BESIDES, CLUB ACTIVITIES ARE SUPER FUN!
OH, COME ON!

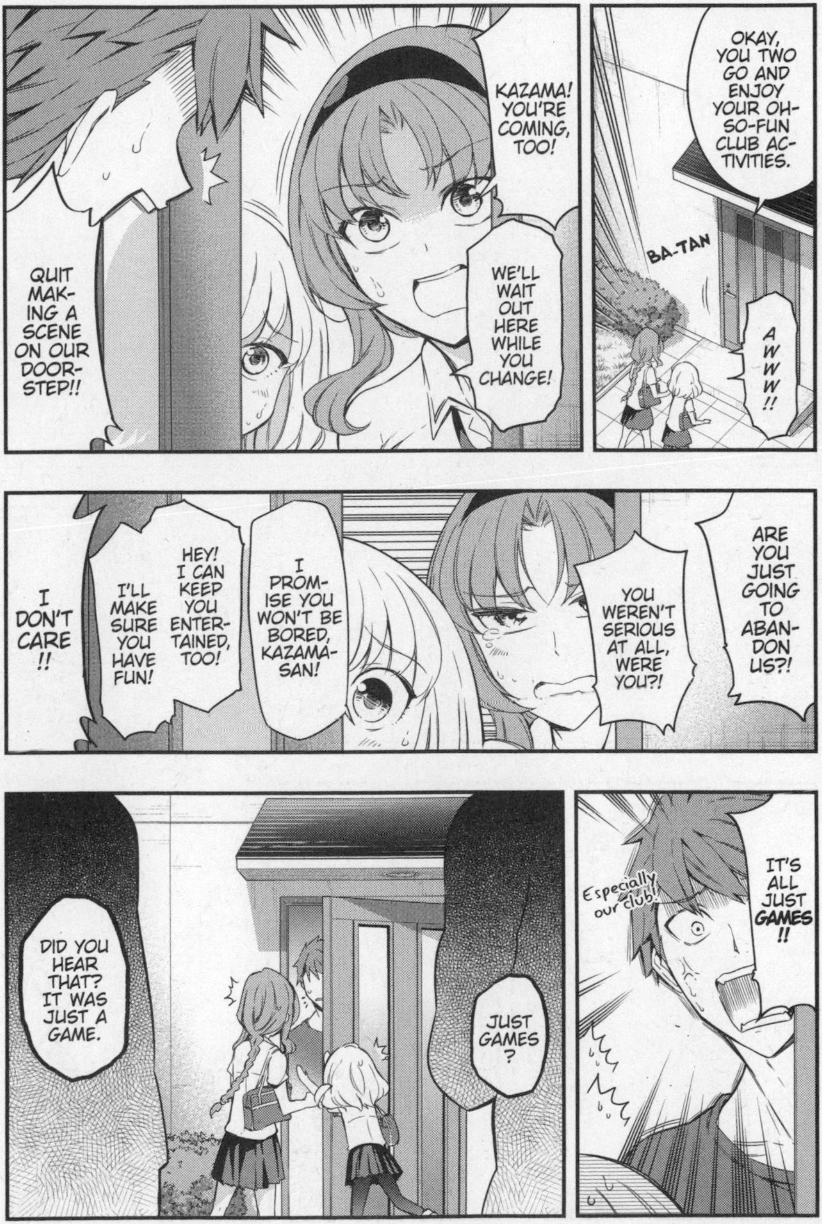
OKAY, YOU TWO GO AND ENJOY YOUR OH-SO-FUN CLUB ACTIVITIES.
BA-TAN
AWWW!!
KAZAMA! YOU'RE COMING, TOO!
WE'LL WAIT OUT HERE WHILE YOU CHANGE!
QUIT MAKING A SCENE ON OUR DOORSTEP!!
ARE YOU JUST GOING TO ABANDON US?!
YOU WEREN'T SERIOUS AT ALL, WERE YOU?!
I PROMISE YOU WON'T BE BORED, KAZAMA-SAN!
HEY! I CAN KEEP YOU ENTERTAINED, TOO!
I'LL MAKE SURE YOU HAVE FUN!
I DON'T CARE!!
IT'S ALL JUST GAMES!!
Especially our club!
JUST GAMES?
DID YOU HEAR THAT? IT WAS JUST A GAME.

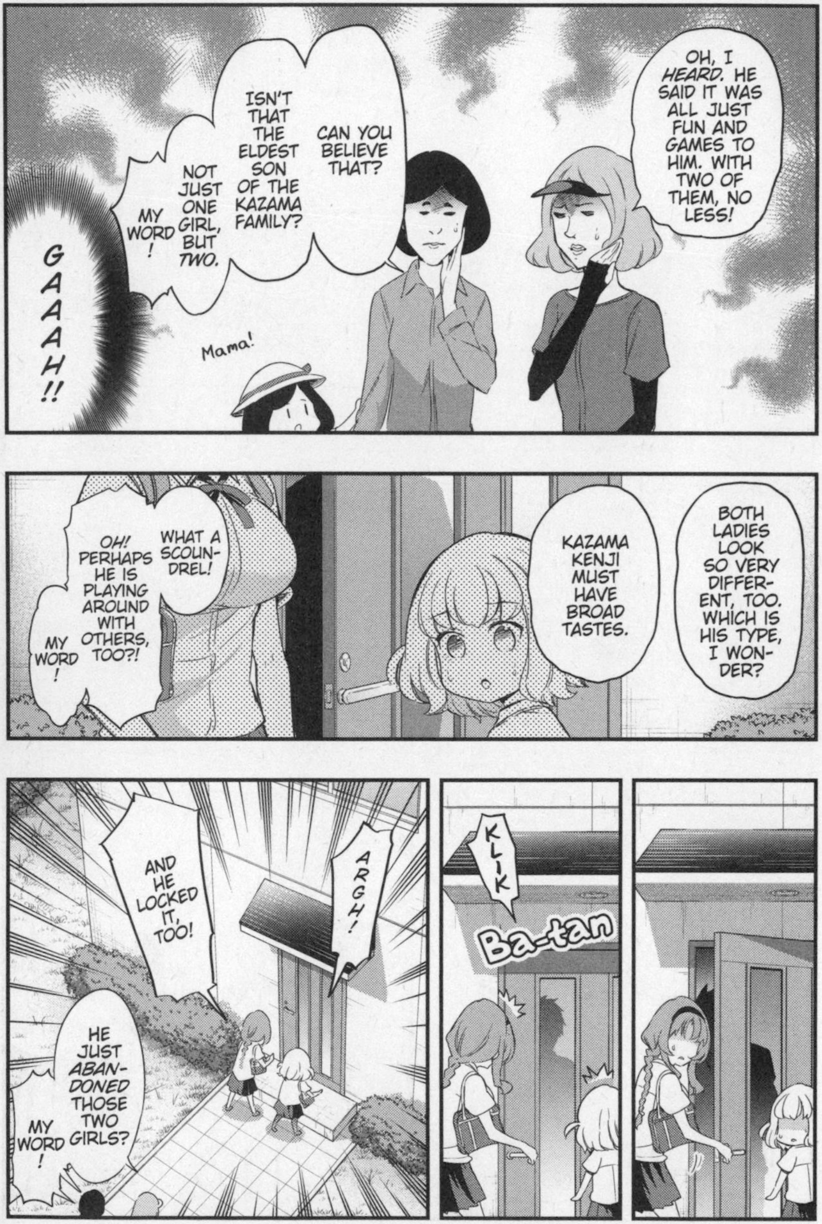
OH, I HEARD. HE SAID IT WAS ALL JUST FUN AND GAMES TO HIM. WITH TWO OF THEM, NO LESS!
CAN YOU BELIEVE THAT?
ISN'T THAT THE ELDEST SON OF THE KAZAMA FAMILY?
NOT JUST ONE GIRL, BUT TWO.
MY WORD!
Mama!
GAAAAH!!
BOTH LADIES LOOK SO VERY DIFFER-ENT, TOO. WHICH IS HIS TYPE, I WON-DER?
KAZAMA KENJI MUST HAVE BROAD TASTES.
WHAT A SCOUN-DREL!
OH! PERHAPS HE IS PLAYING AROUND WITH OTHERS, TOO?!
MY WORD!
KLIK
Ba-tan
ARGH!
AND HE LOCKED IT, TOO!
HE JUST ABAN-DONED THOSE TWO GIRLS?
MY WORD!

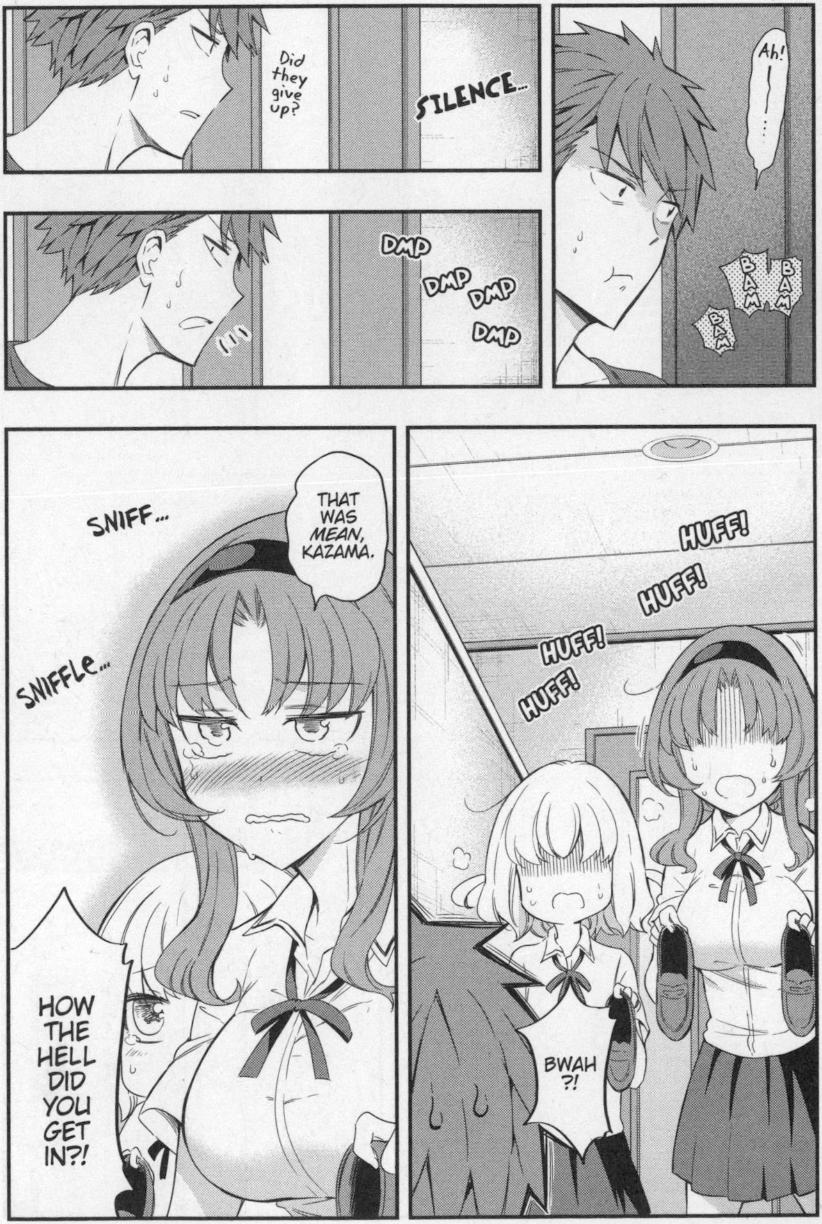
Ah!
—
…
BAM
BAM
BAM
Did they give up?
SILENCE...
DMP
DMP
DMP
DMP
HUFF!
HUFF!
HUFF!
HUFF!
BWAH?!
THAT WAS MEAN, KAZAMA.
SNIFF...
SNIFFLE...
HOW THE HELL DID YOU GET IN?!

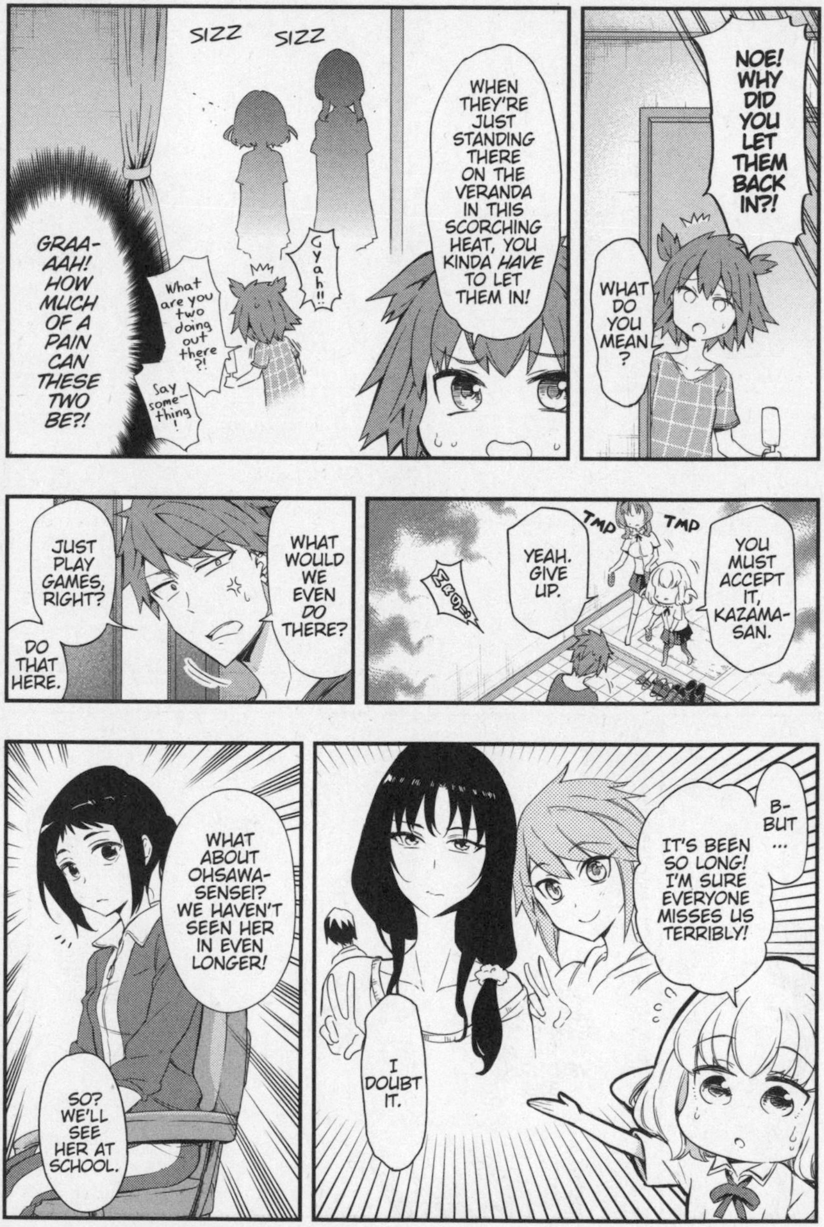
NOE! WHY DID YOU LET THEM BACK IN?!
WHAT DO YOU MEAN?
WHEN THEY'RE JUST STANDING THERE ON THE VERANDA IN THIS SCORCHING HEAT, YOU KINDA *HAVE* TO LET THEM IN!
SIZZ
SIZZ
Gyah!!
What are you two doing out there?!
Say some-thing!
GRAAAAH! HOW MUCH OF A PAIN CAN THESE TWO BE?!
TMP
TMP
YOU MUST ACCEPT IT, KAZAMA-SAN.
YEAH. GIVE UP.
WHAT WOULD WE EVEN *DO* THERE?
JUST PLAY GAMES, RIGHT?
DO THAT HERE.
B-BUT...
IT'S BEEN SO LONG! I'M SURE EVERYONE MISSES US TERRIBLY!
I DOUBT IT.
WHAT ABOUT OHSAWA-SENSEI? WE HAVEN'T SEEN HER IN EVEN LONGER!
SO? WE'LL SEE HER AT SCHOOL.

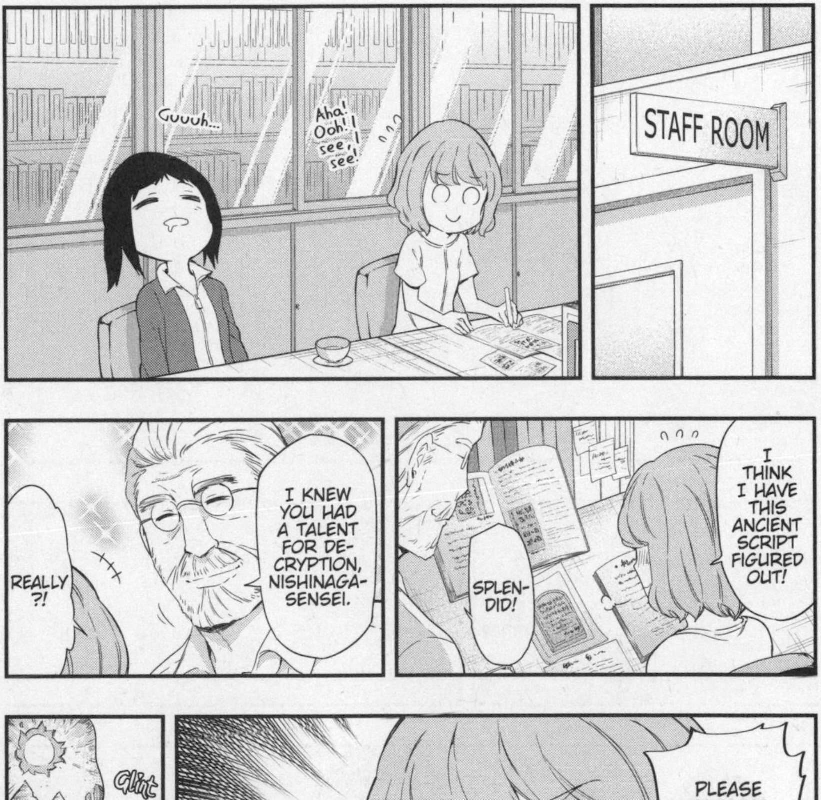
STAFF ROOM
Aha! Ooh! I see, I see!
Guuuh...
I THINK I HAVE THIS ANCIENT SCRIPT FIGURED OUT!
SPLEN-DID!
I KNEW YOU HAD A TALENT FOR DE-CRYPTION, NISHINAGA-SENSEI.
REALLY ?!
PLEASE TAKE ME ALONG ON YOUR NEXT AD-VENTURE, SEAN CONNERY-SENSEI! I PROMISE I'LL BE USEFUL!
GLEAM
HA HA HA! I SEE YOU'VE BEEN BITTEN BY THE AD-VENTURING BUG.
Glint
Urrrgh...
Glint
Glint

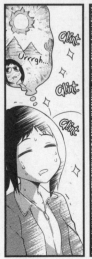

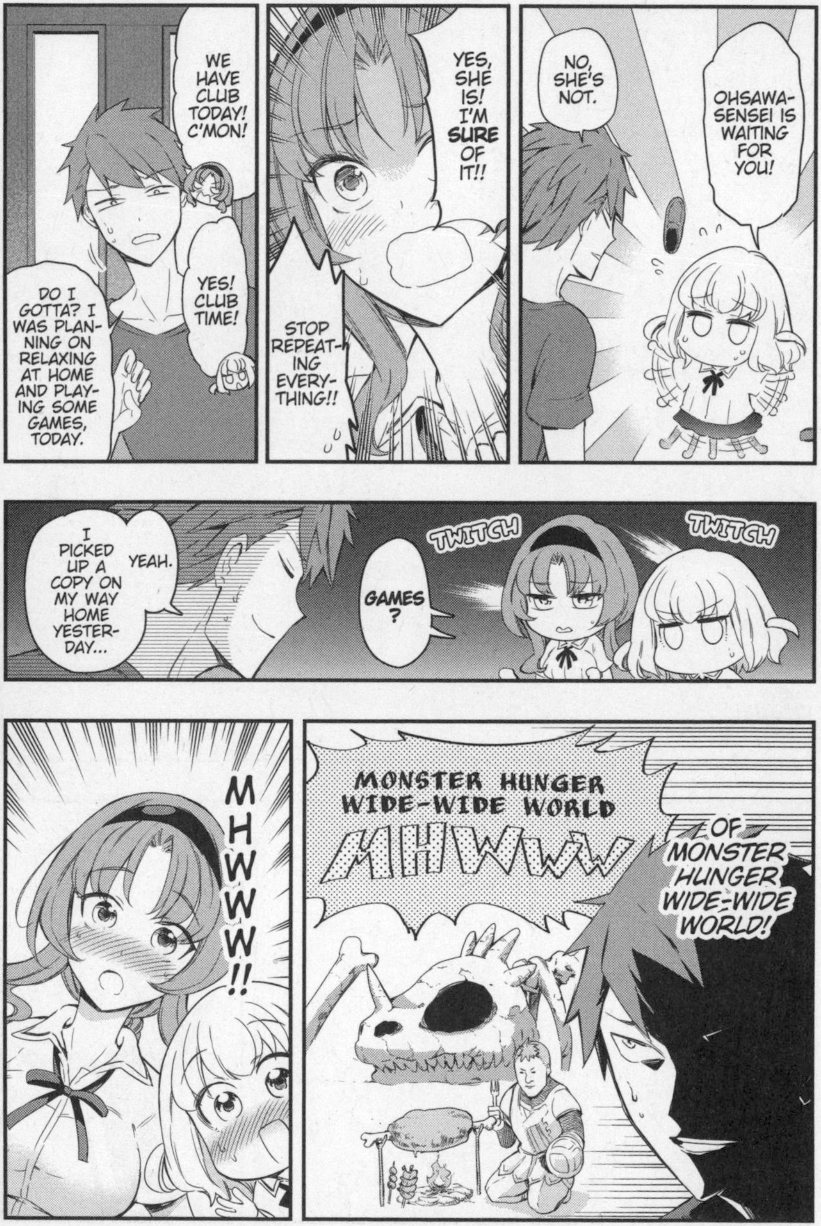
OHSAWA-SENSEI IS WAITING FOR YOU!
NO, SHE'S NOT.
YES, SHE IS! I'M **SURE** OF IT!!
STOP REPEATING EVERYTHING!!
WE HAVE CLUB TODAY! C'MON!
YES! CLUB TIME!
DO I GOTTA? I WAS PLANNING ON RELAXING AT HOME AND PLAYING SOME GAMES, TODAY.
TWITCH
TWITCH
GAMES?
YEAH.
I PICKED UP A COPY ON MY WAY HOME YESTERDAY...
OF MONSTER HUNGER WIDE-WIDE WORLD!
MONSTER HUNGER WIDE-WIDE WORLD
MHWWW
MHWWW!!

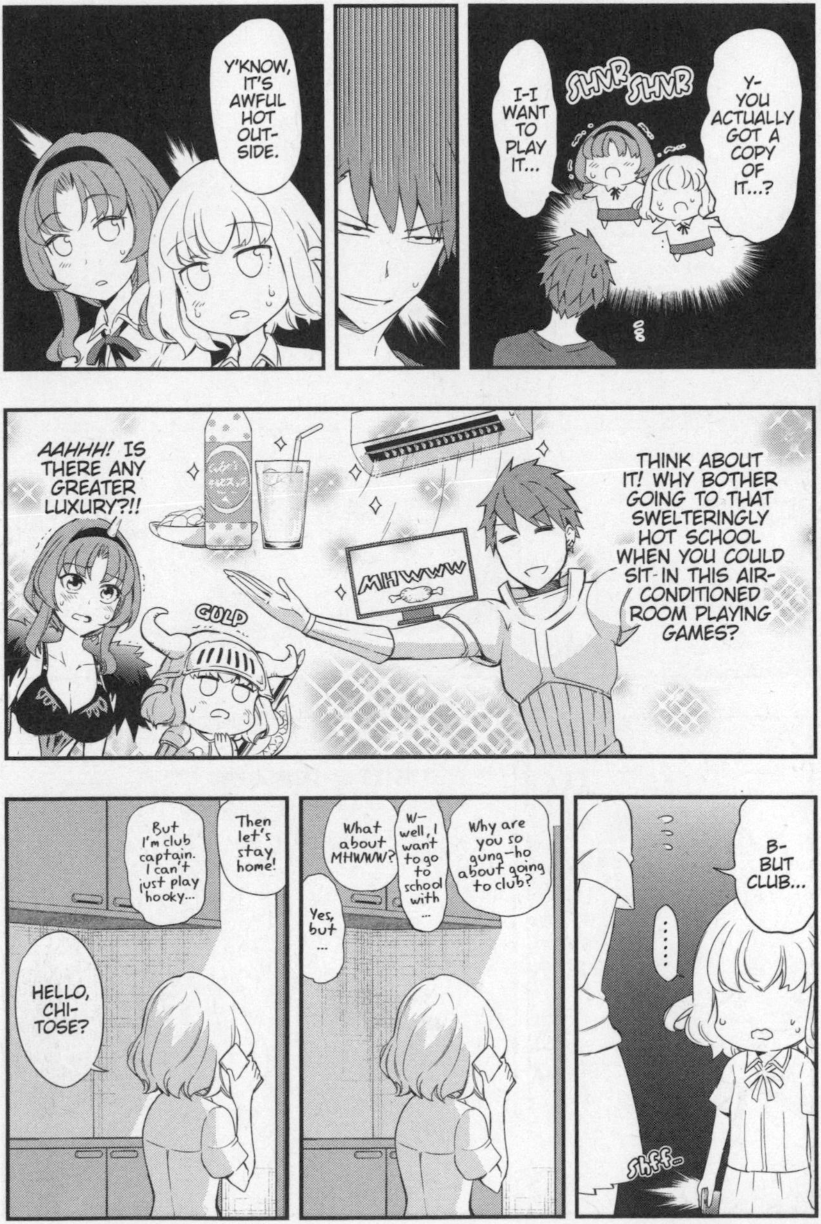
Y-YOU ACTUALLY GOT A COPY OF IT...?
SHVR SHVR
I-I WANT TO PLAY IT...
Y'KNOW, IT'S AWFUL HOT OUT-SIDE.
THINK ABOUT IT! WHY BOTHER GOING TO THAT SWELTERINGLY HOT SCHOOL WHEN YOU COULD SIT IN THIS AIR-CONDITIONED ROOM PLAYING GAMES?
MHWWW
AAHHH! IS THERE ANY GREATER LUXURY?!!
GULP
B-BUT CLUB...
......
Shff..
Why are you so gung-ho about going to club?
W-well, I want to go to school with ...
What about MHWWW?
Yes, but ...
Then let's stay home!
But I'm club captain. I can't just play hooky...
HELLO, CHI-TOSE?

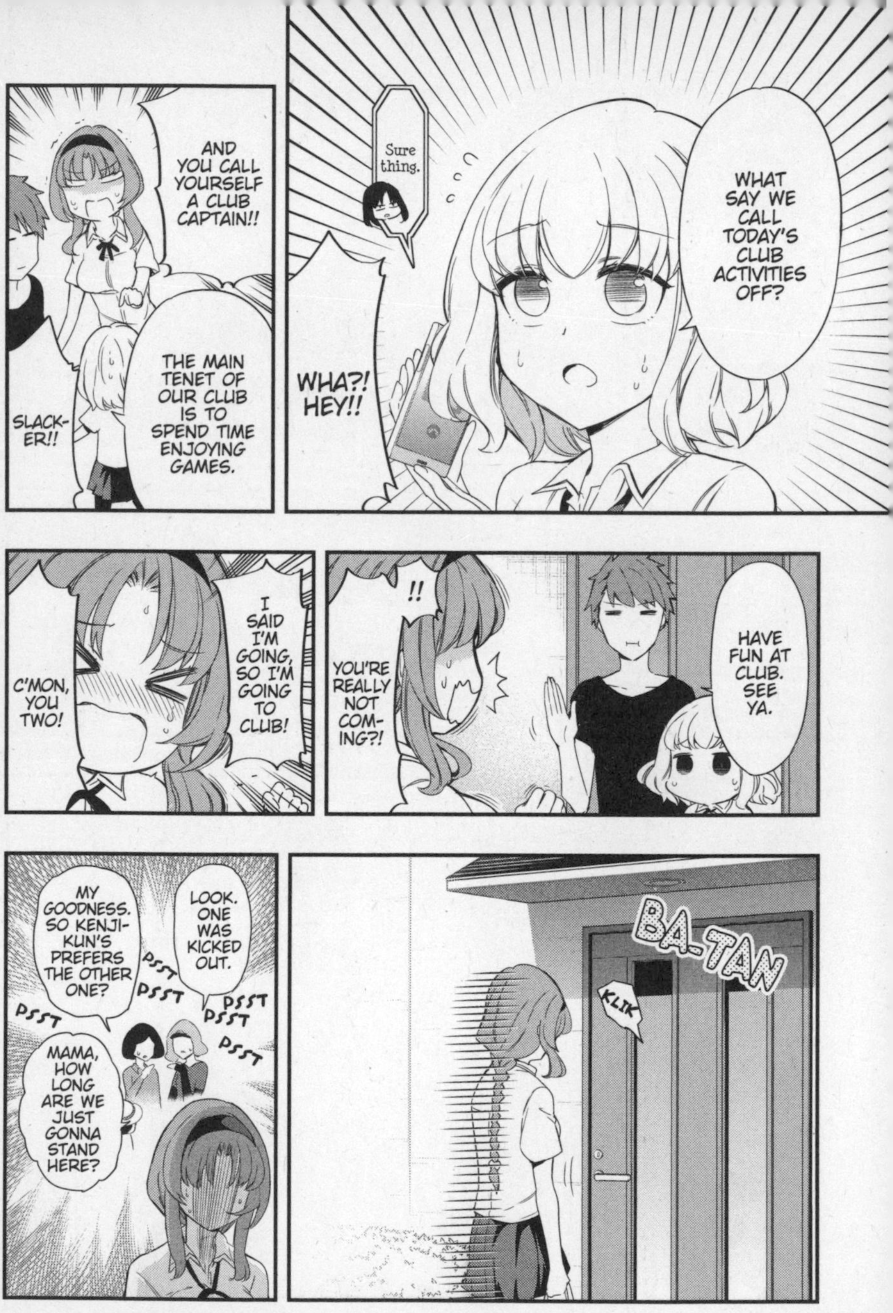
WHAT SAY WE CALL TODAY'S CLUB ACTIVITIES OFF?
Sure thing.
WHA?! HEY!!
AND YOU CALL YOURSELF A CLUB CAPTAIN!!
THE MAIN TENET OF OUR CLUB IS TO SPEND TIME ENJOYING GAMES.
SLACKER!!
HAVE FUN AT CLUB. SEE YA.
!!
YOU'RE REALLY NOT COMING?!
I SAID I'M GOING, SO I'M GOING TO CLUB!
C'MON, YOU TWO!
BA-TAN
KLIK
LOOK. ONE WAS KICKED OUT.
MY GOODNESS. SO KENJI-KUN'S PREFERS THE OTHER ONE?
PSST
PSST
PSST
PSST
PSST
PSST
MAMA, HOW LONG ARE WE JUST GONNA STAND HERE?

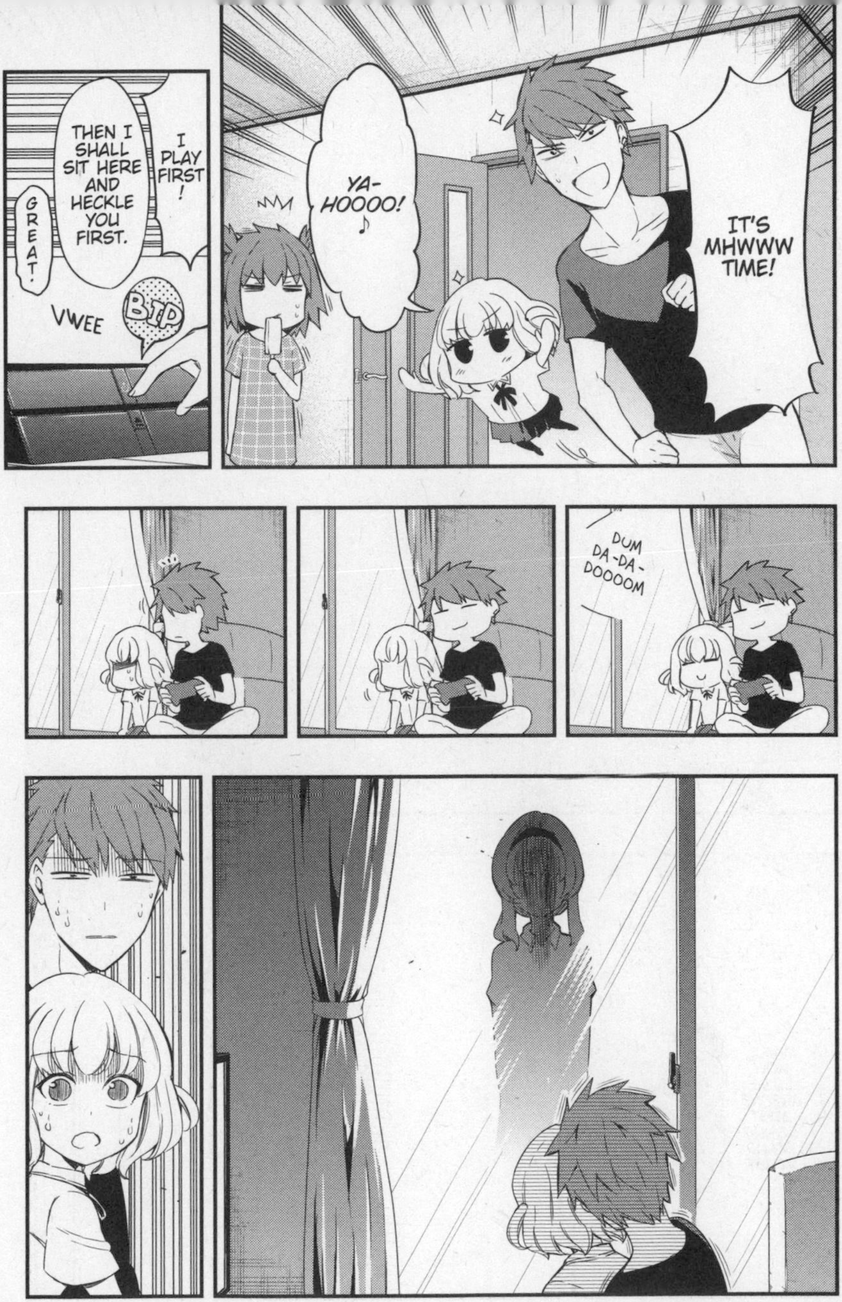
IT'S MHWWW TIME!
YA-HOOOO! ♪
I PLAY FIRST!
THEN I SHALL SIT HERE AND HECKLE YOU FIRST.
GREAT.
BIP
VWEE
DUM DA-DA-DOOOOM

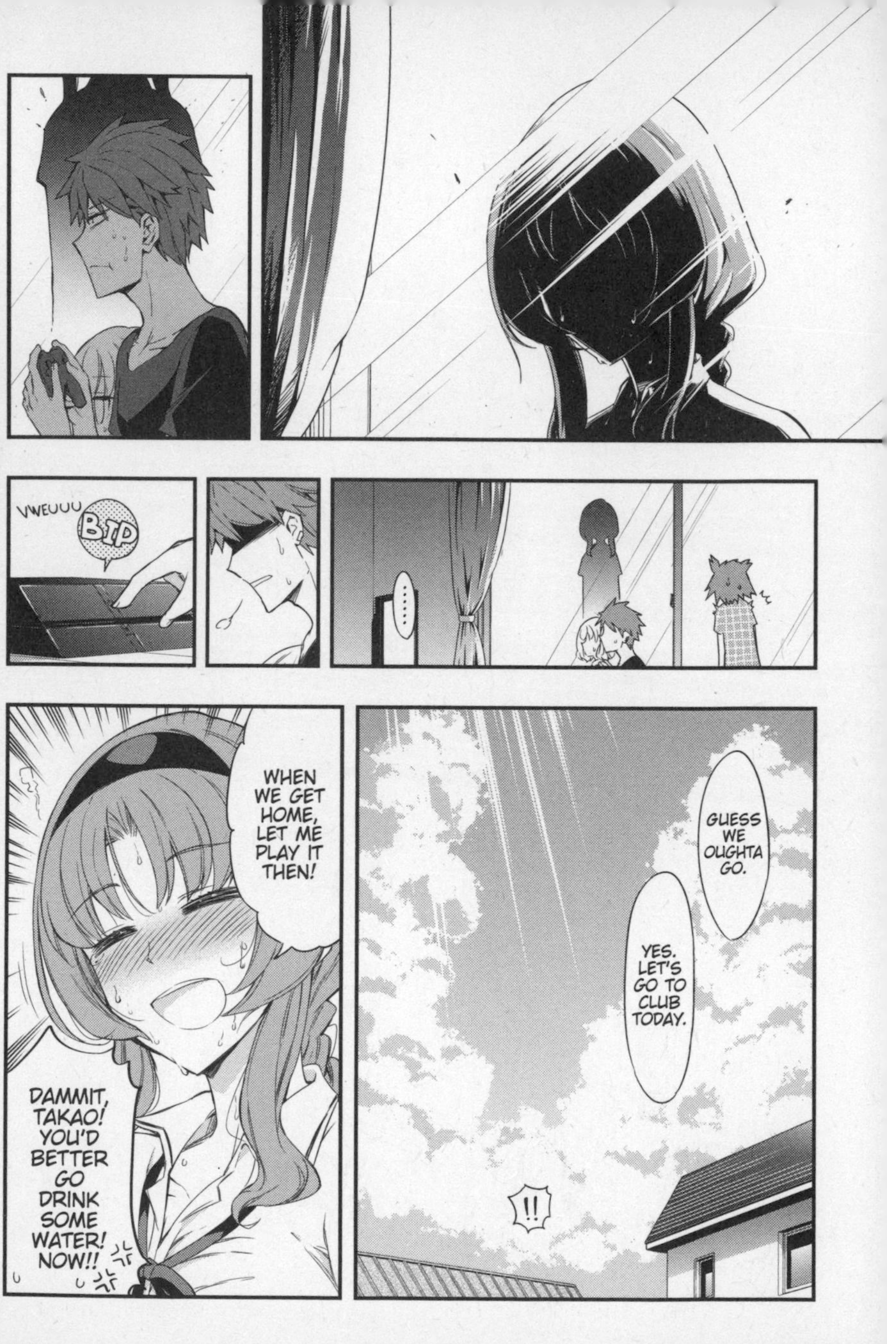
......
VWEUUU
BIP
GUESS WE OUGHTA GO.
YES. LET'S GO TO CLUB TODAY.
!!
WHEN WE GET HOME, LET ME PLAY IT THEN!
DAMMIT, TAKAO! YOU'D BETTER GO DRINK SOME WATER! NOW!!

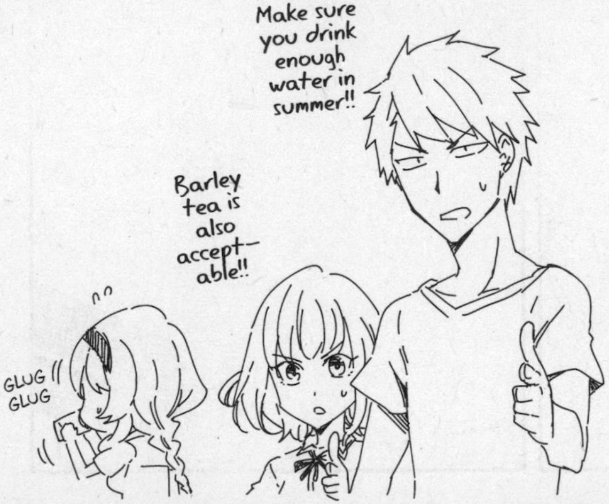
Make sure you drink enough water in summer!!
Barley tea is also accept-able!!
GLUG GLUG

D-FRAGMENTS
ディーふらぐ！

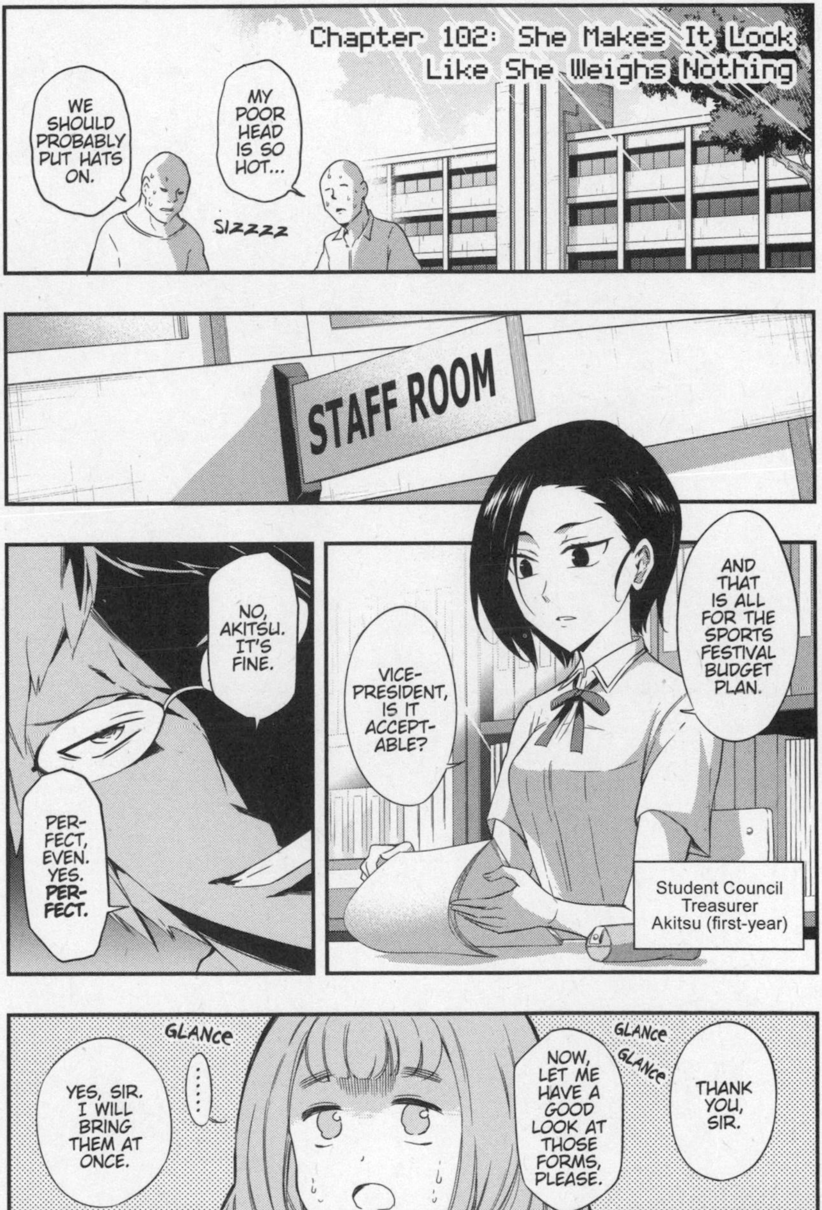
Chapter 102: She Makes It Look Like She Weighs Nothing
MY POOR HEAD IS SO HOT...
WE SHOULD PROBABLY PUT HATS ON.
SIZZZZ
STAFF ROOM
AND THAT IS ALL FOR THE SPORTS FESTIVAL BUDGET PLAN.
VICE-PRESIDENT, IS IT ACCEPTABLE?
Student Council Treasurer Akitsu (first-year)
NO, AKITSU. IT'S FINE.
PERFECT, EVEN. YES. PERFECT.
THANK YOU, SIR.
GLANCE GLANCE
NOW, LET ME HAVE A GOOD LOOK AT THOSE FORMS, PLEASE.
......
GLANCE
YES, SIR. I WILL BRING THEM AT ONCE.

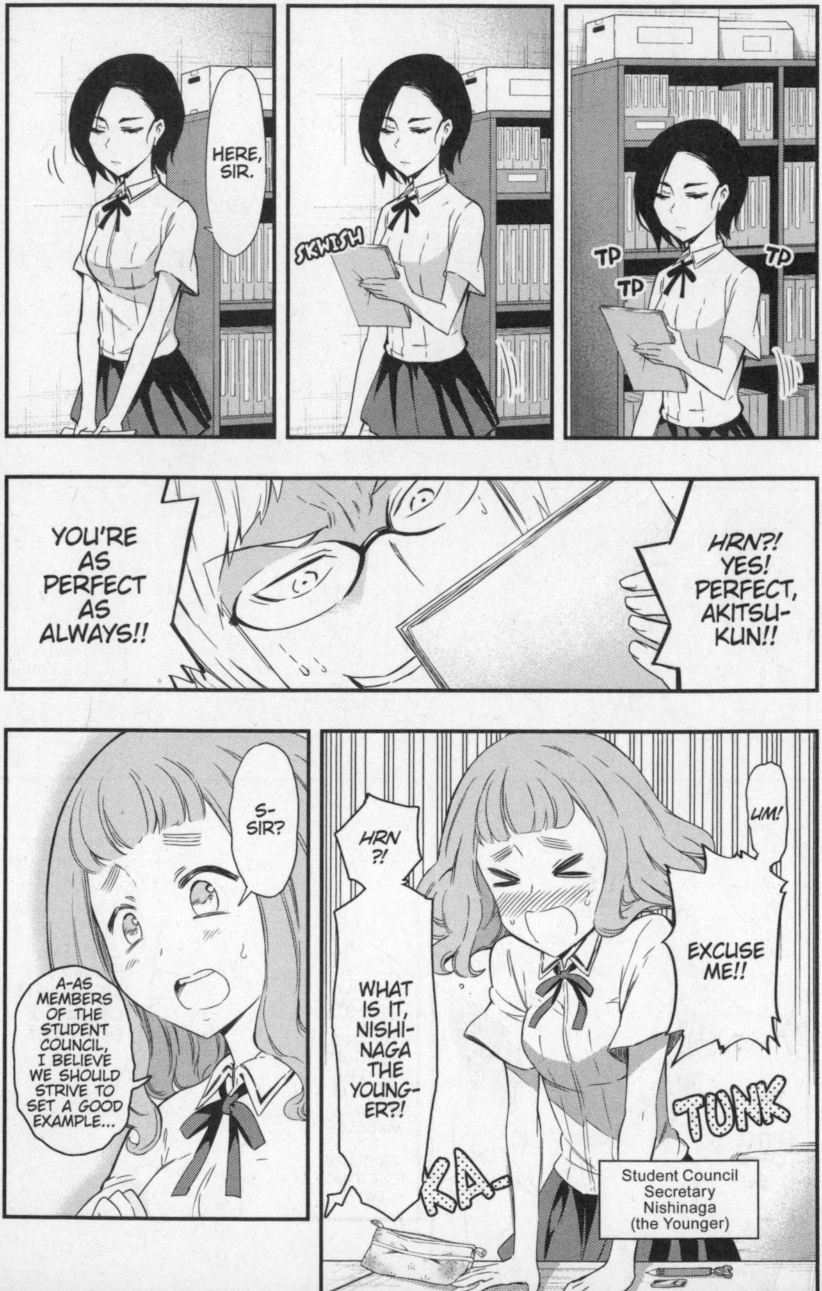
TP
TP
TP
SKWISH
HERE, SIR.
HRN?! YES! PERFECT, AKITSU-KUN!!
YOU'RE AS PERFECT AS ALWAYS!!
UM!
EXCUSE ME!!
HRN ?!
WHAT IS IT, NISHI-NAGA THE YOUNG-ER?!
TUNK
KA-
Student Council Secretary Nishinaga (the Younger)
S-SIR?
A-AS MEMBERS OF THE STUDENT COUNCIL, I BELIEVE WE SHOULD STRIVE TO SET A GOOD EXAMPLE...

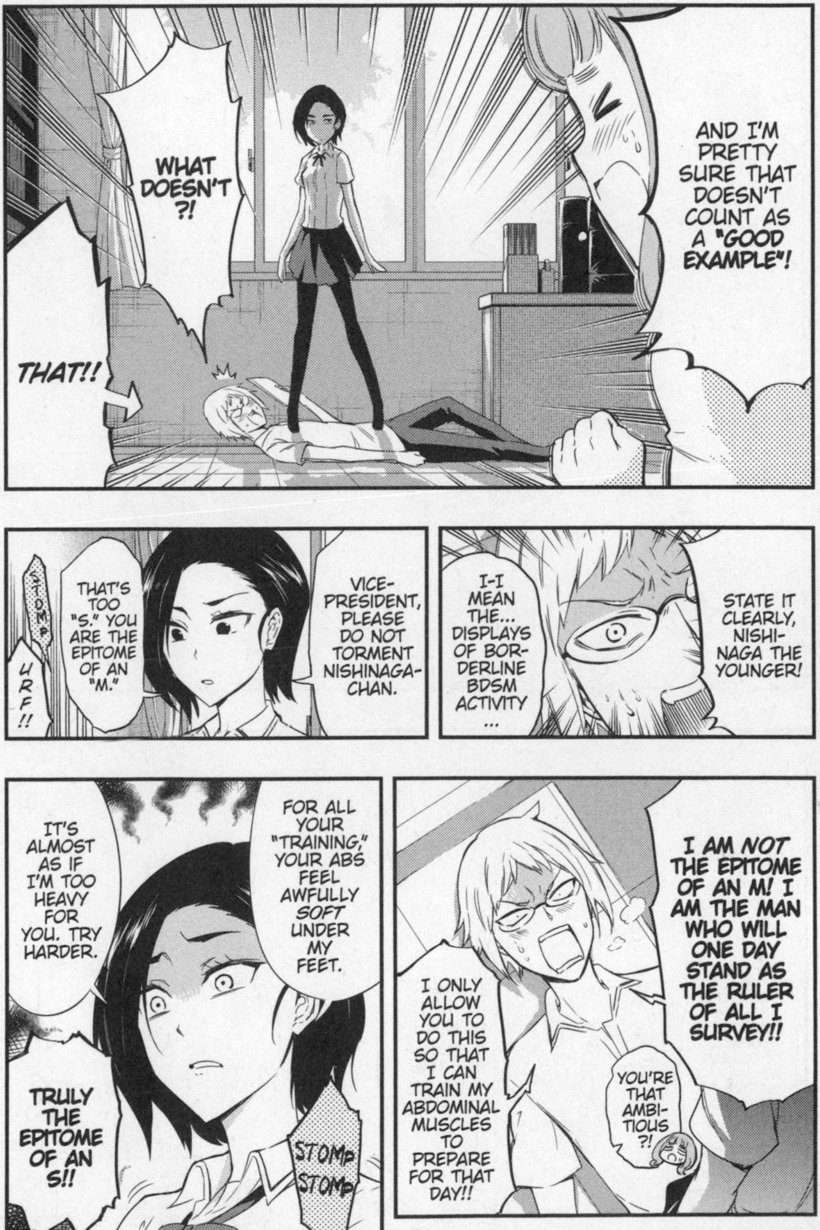
AND I'M PRETTY SURE THAT DOESN'T COUNT AS A "GOOD EXAMPLE"!
WHAT DOESN'T ?!
THAT!!
STATE IT CLEARLY, NISHI-NAGA THE YOUNGER!
I-I MEAN THE... DISPLAYS OF BOR-DERLINE BDSM ACTIVITY ...
VICE-PRESIDENT, PLEASE DO NOT TORMENT NISHINAGA-CHAN.
THAT'S TOO "S." YOU ARE THE EPITOME OF AN "M."
STOMP
URF!!
I AM NOT THE EPITOME OF AN M! I AM THE MAN WHO WILL ONE DAY STAND AS THE RULER OF ALL I SURVEY!!
I ONLY ALLOW YOU TO DO THIS SO THAT I CAN TRAIN MY ABDOMINAL MUSCLES TO PREPARE FOR THAT DAY!!
YOU'RE THAT AMBI-TIOUS ?!
FOR ALL YOUR "TRAINING," YOUR ABS FEEL AWFULLY SOFT UNDER MY FEET.
IT'S ALMOST AS IF I'M TOO HEAVY FOR YOU. TRY HARDER.
TRULY THE EPITOME OF AN S!!
STOMP
STOMP

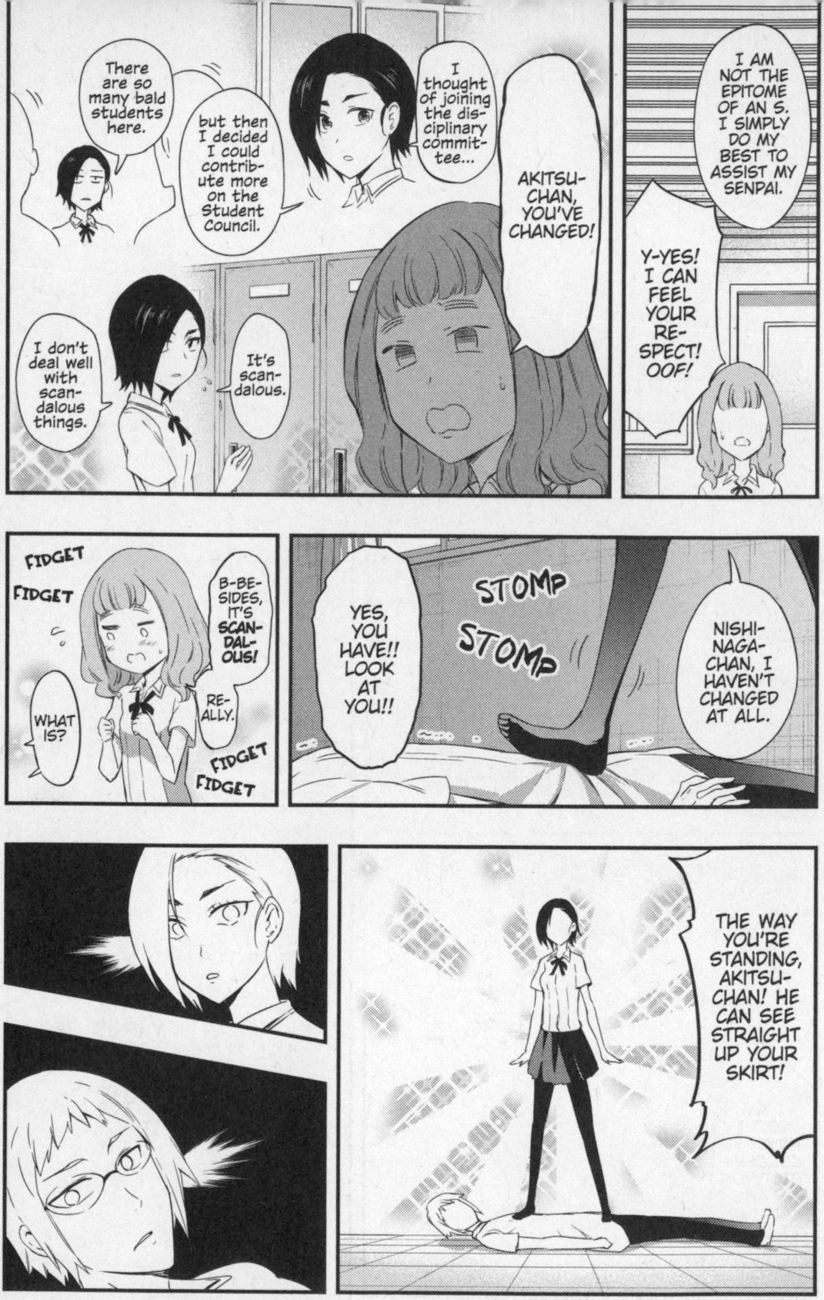
I AM NOT THE EPITOME OF AN S. I SIMPLY DO MY BEST TO ASSIST MY SENPAI.
Y-YES! I CAN FEEL YOUR RE-SPECT! OOF!
AKITSU-CHAN, YOU'VE CHANGED!
I thought of joining the dis-ciplinary commit-tee...
but then I decided I could contrib-ute more on the Student Council.
There are so many bald students here.
It's scan-dalous.
I don't deal well with scan-dalous things.
NISHI-NAGA-CHAN, I HAVEN'T CHANGED AT ALL.
STOMP
STOMP
YES, YOU HAVE!! LOOK AT YOU!!
FIDGET
FIDGET
B-BE-SIDES, IT'S SCAN-DAL-OUS!
RE-ALLY.
WHAT IS?
FIDGET
FIDGET
THE WAY YOU'RE STANDING, AKITSU-CHAN! HE CAN SEE STRAIGHT UP YOUR SKIRT!

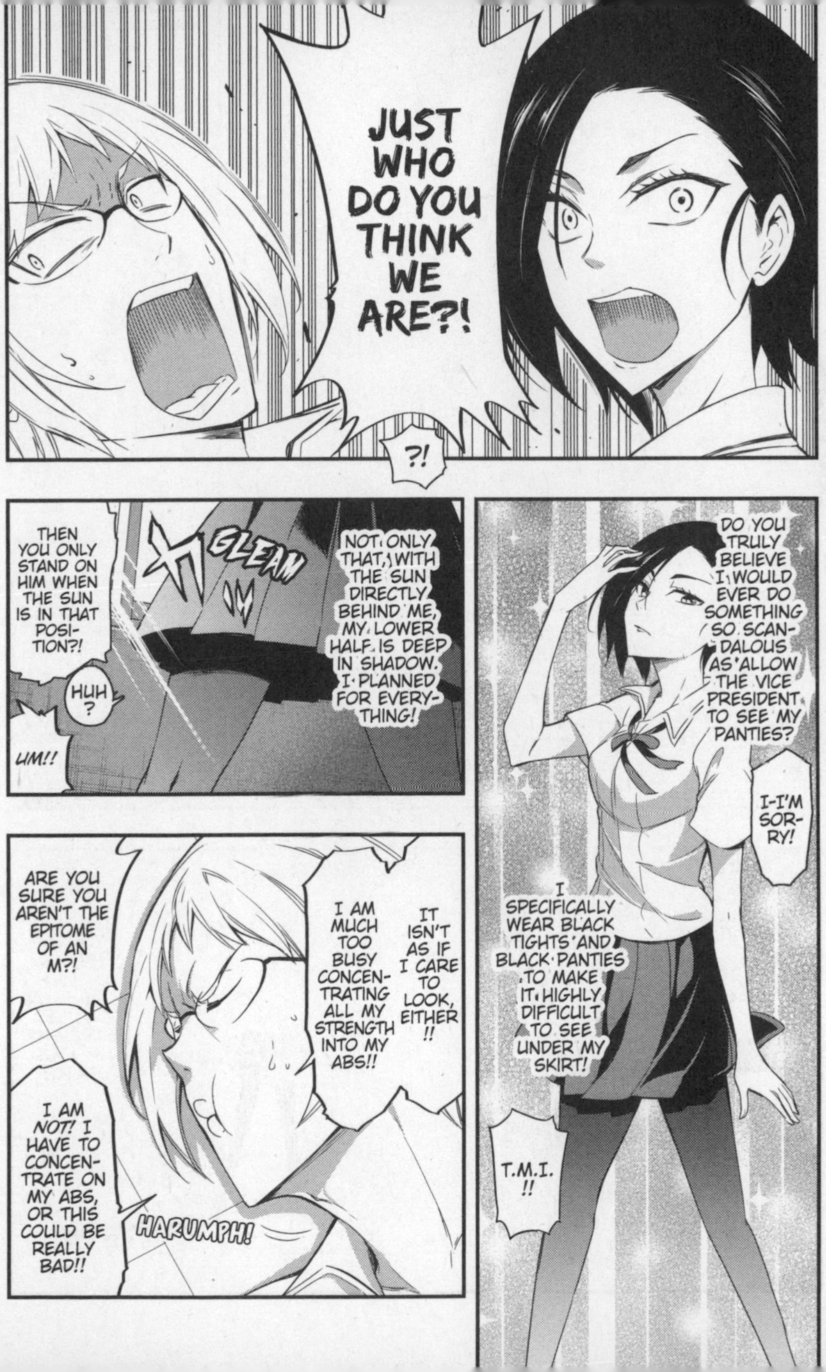

JUST WHO DO YOU THINK WE ARE?!
?!
DO YOU TRULY BELIEVE I WOULD EVER DO SOMETHING SO SCANDALOUS AS ALLOW THE VICE PRESIDENT TO SEE MY PANTIES?
I-I'M SORRY!
I SPECIFICALLY WEAR BLACK TIGHTS AND BLACK PANTIES TO MAKE IT HIGHLY DIFFICULT TO SEE UNDER MY SKIRT!
T.M.I. !!
NOT ONLY THAT, WITH THE SUN DIRECTLY BEHIND ME, MY LOWER HALF IS DEEP IN SHADOW. I PLANNED FOR EVERYTHING!
GLEAM
THEN YOU ONLY STAND ON HIM WHEN THE SUN IS IN THAT POSITION?!
HUH?
UM!!
IT ISN'T AS IF I CARE TO LOOK, EITHER!!
I AM MUCH TOO BUSY CONCENTRATING ALL MY STRENGTH INTO MY ABS!!
ARE YOU SURE YOU AREN'T THE EPITOME OF AN M?!
I AM *NOT!* I HAVE TO CONCENTRATE ON MY ABS, OR THIS COULD BE REALLY BAD!!
HARUMPH!

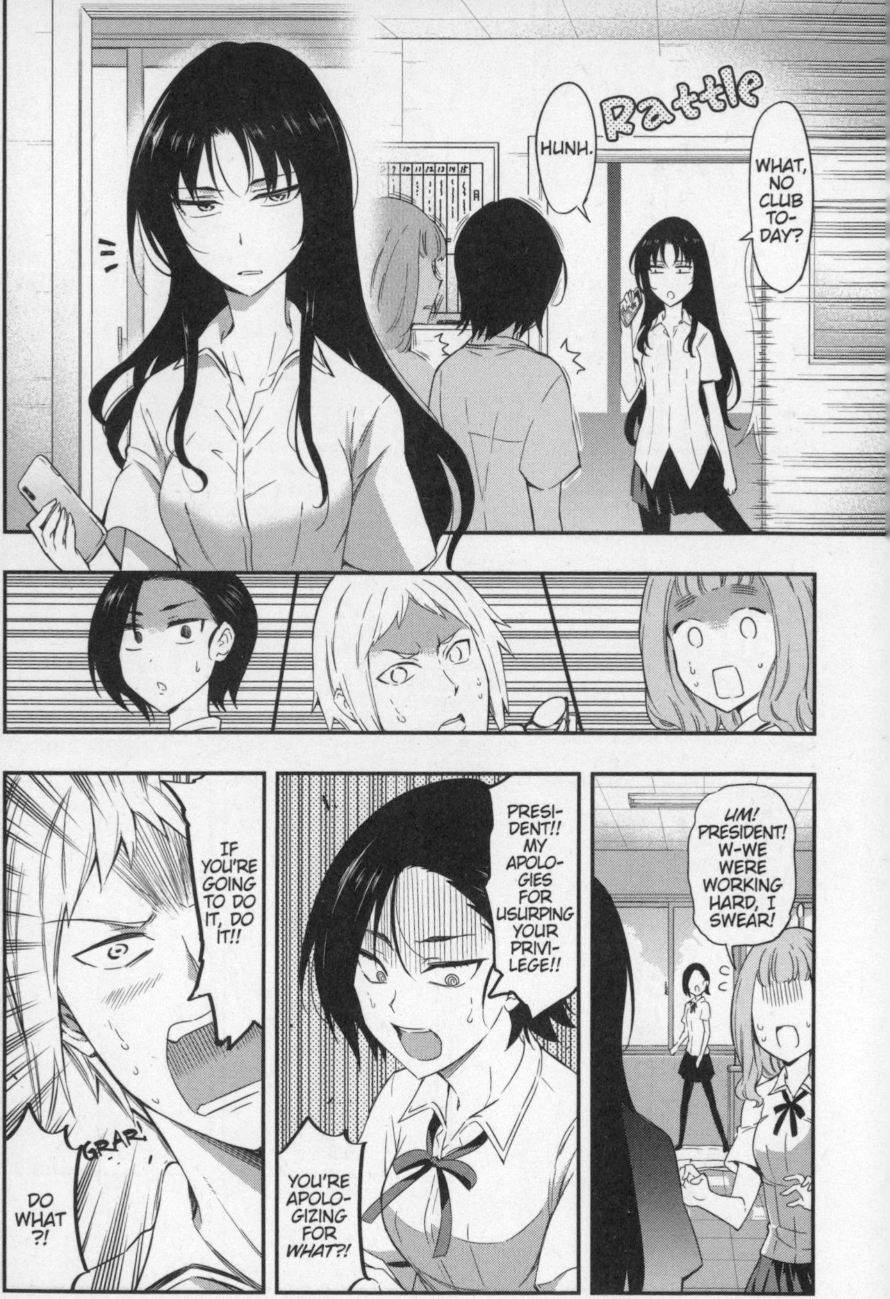
Rattle
WHAT, NO CLUB TO-DAY?
HUNH.
UM! PRESIDENT! W-WE WERE WORKING HARD, I SWEAR!
PRESI-DENT!! MY APOLO-GIES FOR USURPING YOUR PRIVI-LEGE!!
YOU'RE APOLO-GIZING FOR WHAT?!
IF YOU'RE GOING TO DO IT, DO IT!!
GRAR!
DO WHAT ?!

TOSS

STMP

STMP

STMP

STMP

STMP

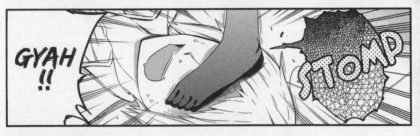

GYAH!!

STOMP

......

Shff

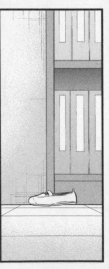

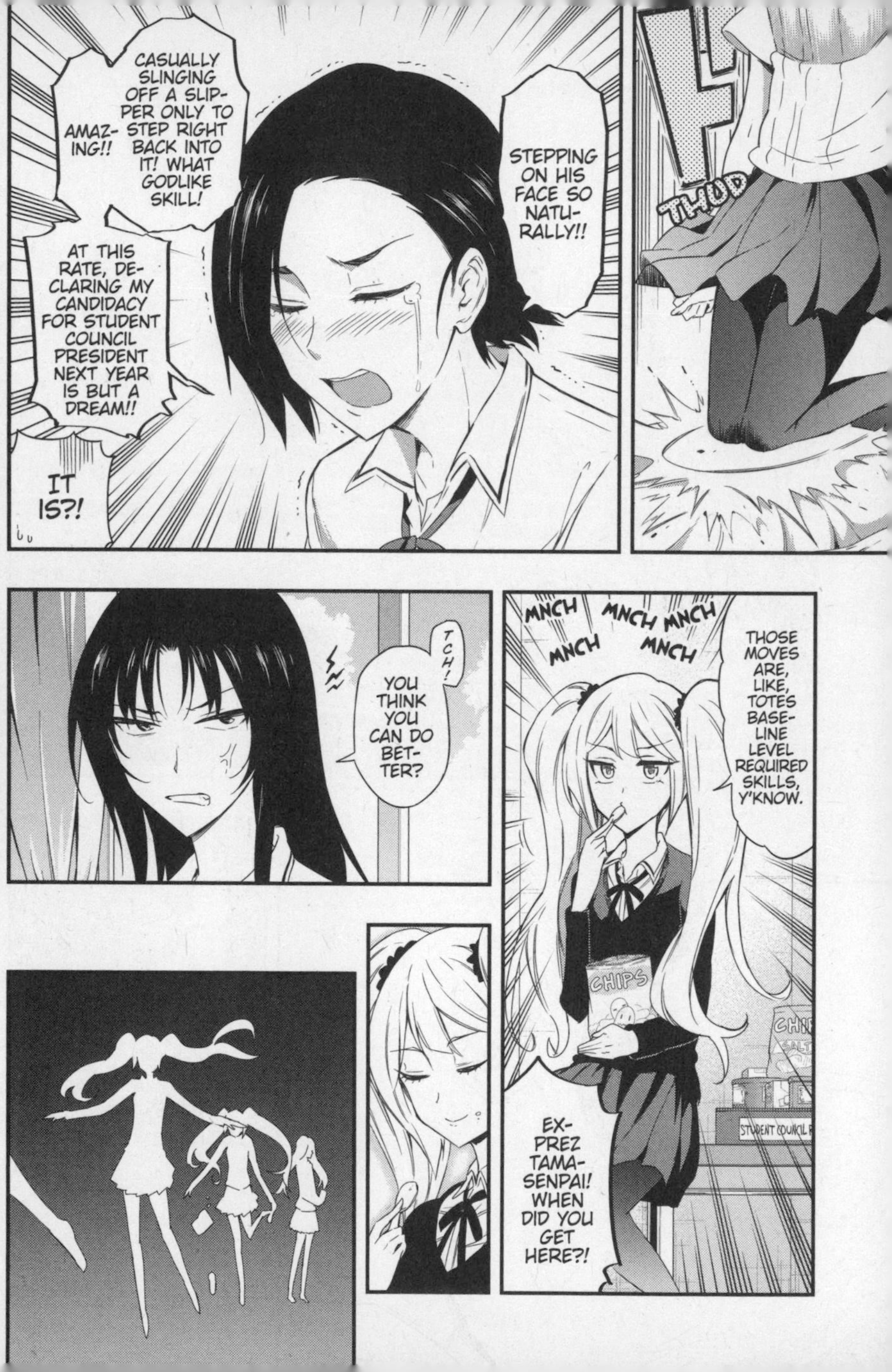
THUD
STEPPING ON HIS FACE SO NATU-RALLY!!
CASUALLY SLINGING OFF A SLIP-PER ONLY TO STEP RIGHT BACK INTO IT! WHAT GODLIKE SKILL!
AMAZ-ING!!
AT THIS RATE, DE-CLARING MY CANDIDACY FOR STUDENT COUNCIL PRESIDENT NEXT YEAR IS BUT A DREAM!!
IT IS?!
MNCH MNCH MNCH MNCH MNCH
THOSE MOVES ARE, LIKE, TOTES BASE-LINE LEVEL REQUIRED SKILLS, Y'KNOW.
CHIPS
EX-PREZ TAMA-SENPAI! WHEN DID YOU GET HERE?!
TCH!
YOU THINK YOU CAN DO BET-TER?

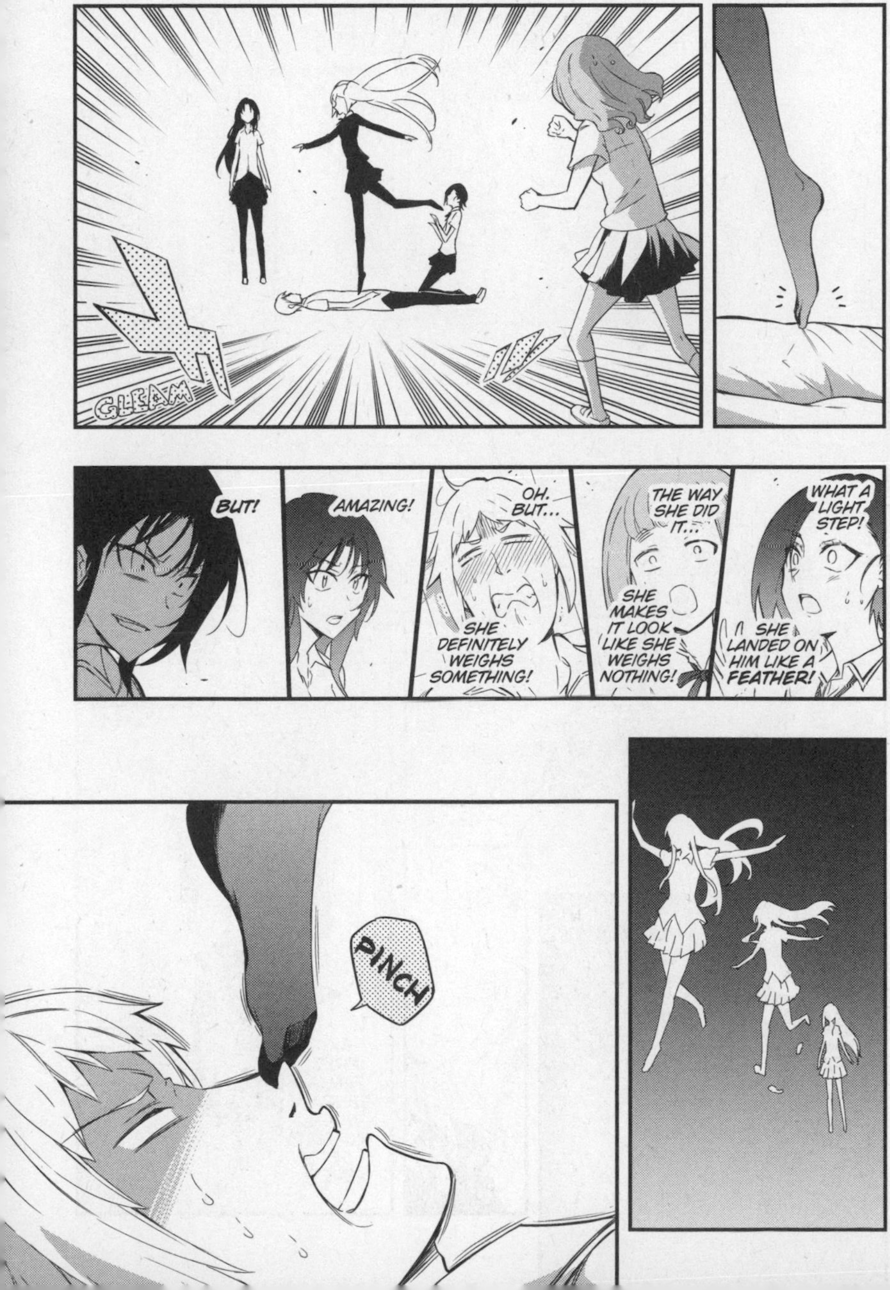
GLEAM
WHAT A LIGHT STEP!
SHE LANDED ON HIM LIKE A FEATHER!
THE WAY SHE DID IT...
SHE MAKES IT LOOK LIKE SHE WEIGHS NOTHING!
OH. BUT...
SHE DEFINITELY WEIGHS SOMETHING!
AMAZING!
BUT!
PINCH

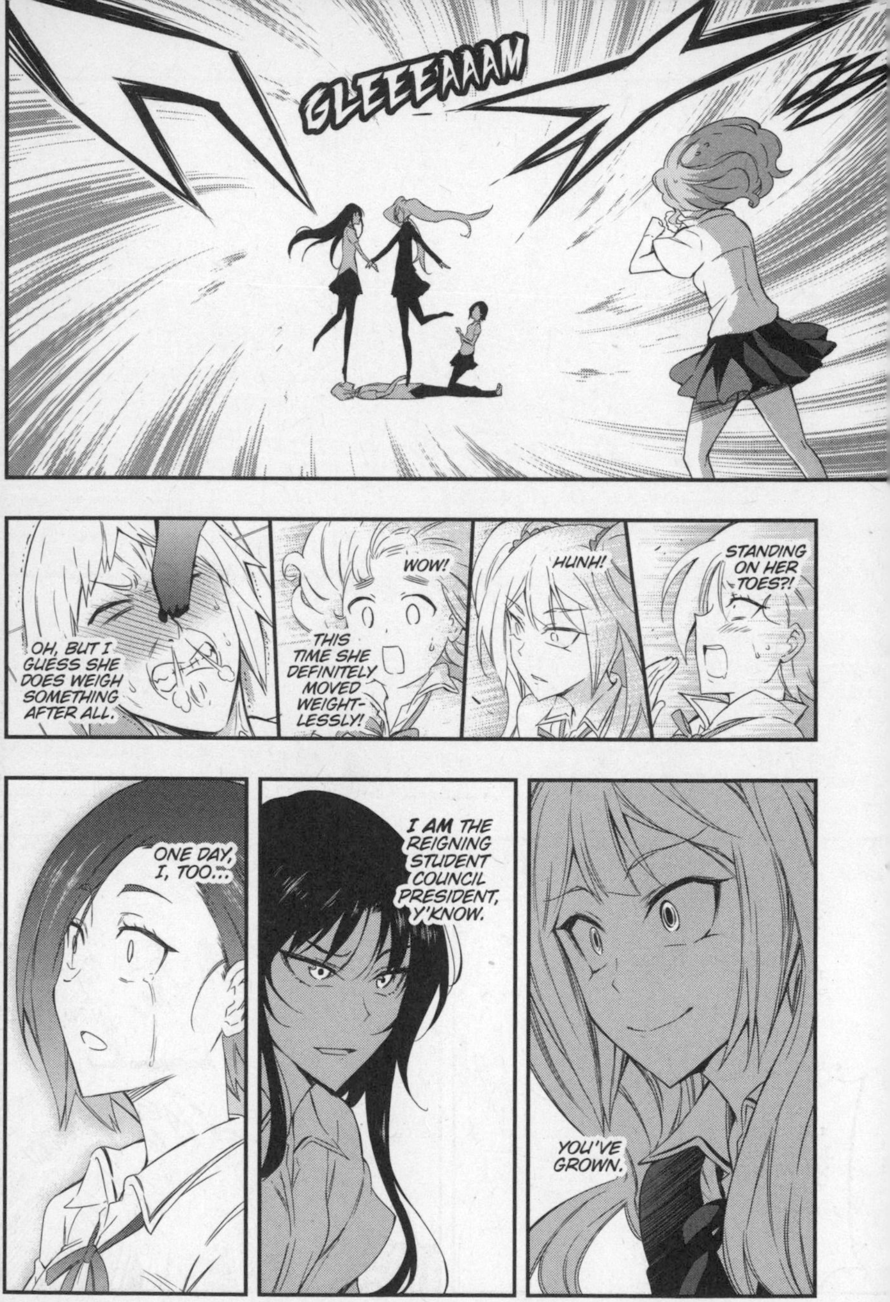
GLEEEAAAM
STANDING ON HER TOES?!
HUNH!
WOW!
THIS TIME SHE DEFINITELY MOVED WEIGHTLESSLY!
OH, BUT I GUESS SHE DOES WEIGH SOMETHING AFTER ALL.
YOU'VE GROWN.
I AM THE REIGNING STUDENT COUNCIL PRESIDENT, Y'KNOW.
ONE DAY, I, TOO...

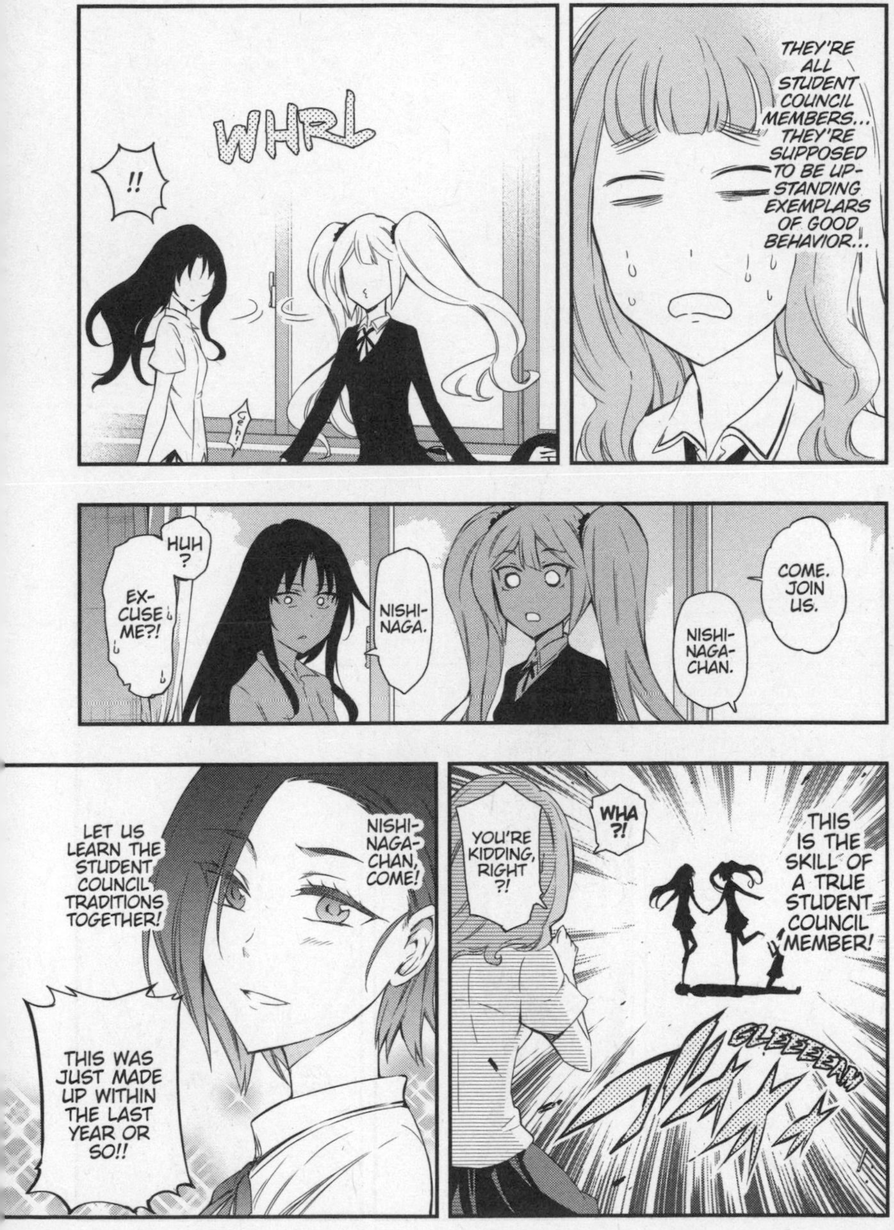
THEY'RE ALL STUDENT COUNCIL MEMBERS... THEY'RE SUPPOSED TO BE UP-STANDING EXEMPLARS OF GOOD BEHAVIOR...
WHRL
!!
COME. JOIN US.
NISHI-NAGA-CHAN.
NISHI-NAGA.
HUH? EX-CUSE ME?!
THIS IS THE SKILL OF A TRUE STUDENT COUNCIL MEMBER!
WHA?!
YOU'RE KIDDING, RIGHT?!
GLEEEEAM
NISHI-NAGA-CHAN, COME!
LET US LEARN THE STUDENT COUNCIL TRADITIONS TOGETHER!
THIS WAS JUST MADE UP WITHIN THE LAST YEAR OR SO!!

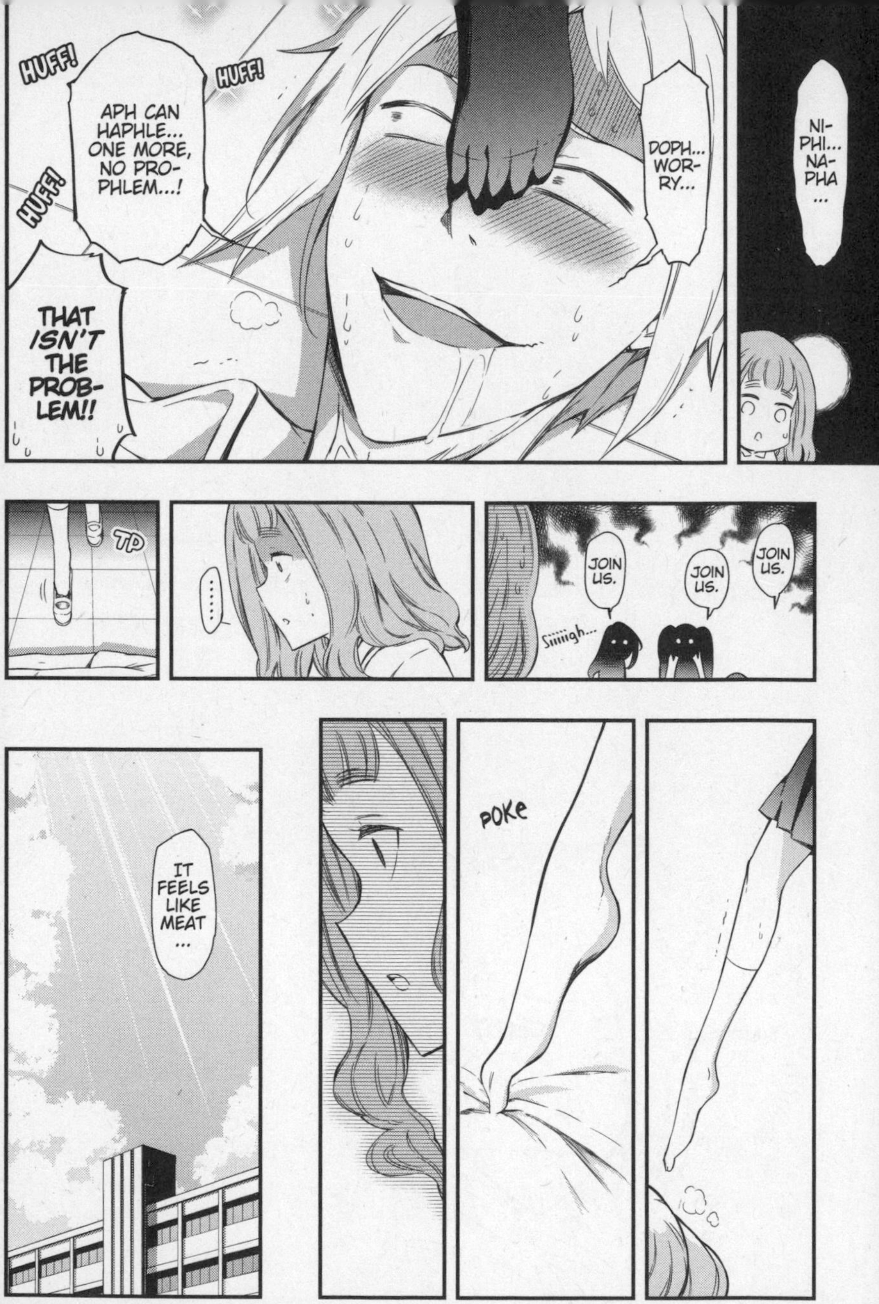
NI-PHI... NA-PHA ...
DOPH... WOR-RY...
HUFF!
HUFF!
APH CAN HAPHLE... ONE MORE, NO PRO-PHLEM...!
HUFF!
THAT ISN'T THE PROB-LEM!!
JOIN US.
JOIN US.
JOIN US.
Siiiigh...
......
TP
POKE
IT FEELS LIKE MEAT ...

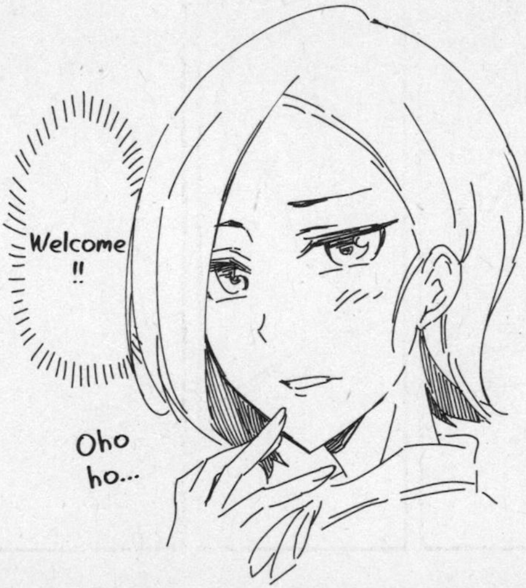
Welcome !!
Oho ho...

D-FRAGMENTS

ディーふらぐ!

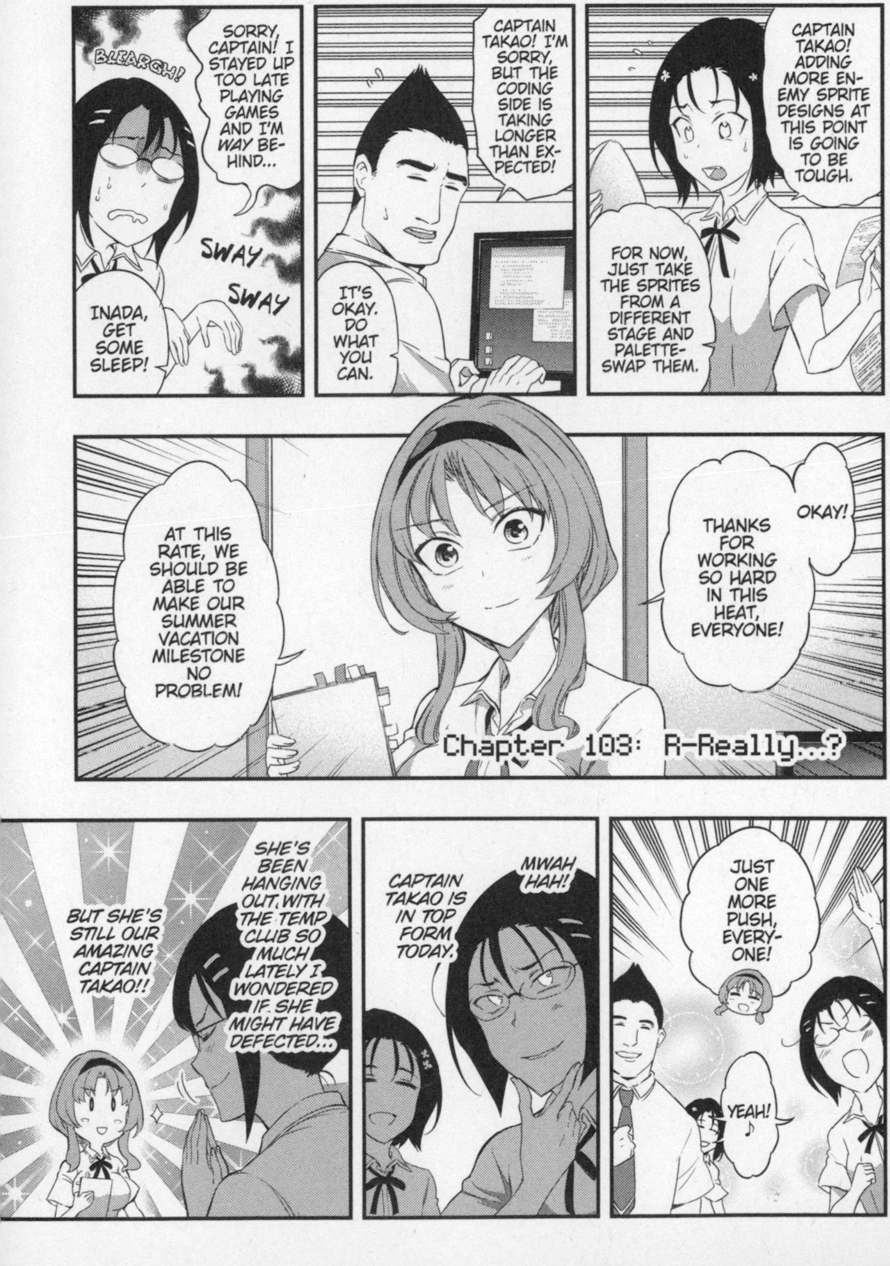
CAPTAIN TAKAO! ADDING MORE EN-EMY SPRITE DESIGNS AT THIS POINT IS GOING TO BE TOUGH.
FOR NOW, JUST TAKE THE SPRITES FROM A DIFFERENT STAGE AND PALETTE-SWAP THEM.
CAPTAIN TAKAO! I'M SORRY, BUT THE CODING SIDE IS TAKING LONGER THAN EX-PECTED!
IT'S OKAY. DO WHAT YOU CAN.
BLEARGH!
SORRY, CAPTAIN! I STAYED UP TOO LATE PLAYING GAMES AND I'M WAY BE-HIND...
SWAY
SWAY
INADA, GET SOME SLEEP!
OKAY!
THANKS FOR WORKING SO HARD IN THIS HEAT, EVERYONE!
AT THIS RATE, WE SHOULD BE ABLE TO MAKE OUR SUMMER VACATION MILESTONE NO PROBLEM!
Chapter 103: R-Really...?
JUST ONE MORE PUSH, EVERY-ONE!
YEAH! ♪
MWAH HAH!
CAPTAIN TAKAO IS IN TOP FORM TODAY.
SHE'S BEEN HANGING OUT WITH THE TEMP CLUB SO MUCH LATELY I WONDERED IF SHE MIGHT HAVE DEFECTED...
BUT SHE'S STILL OUR AMAZING CAPTAIN TAKAO!!

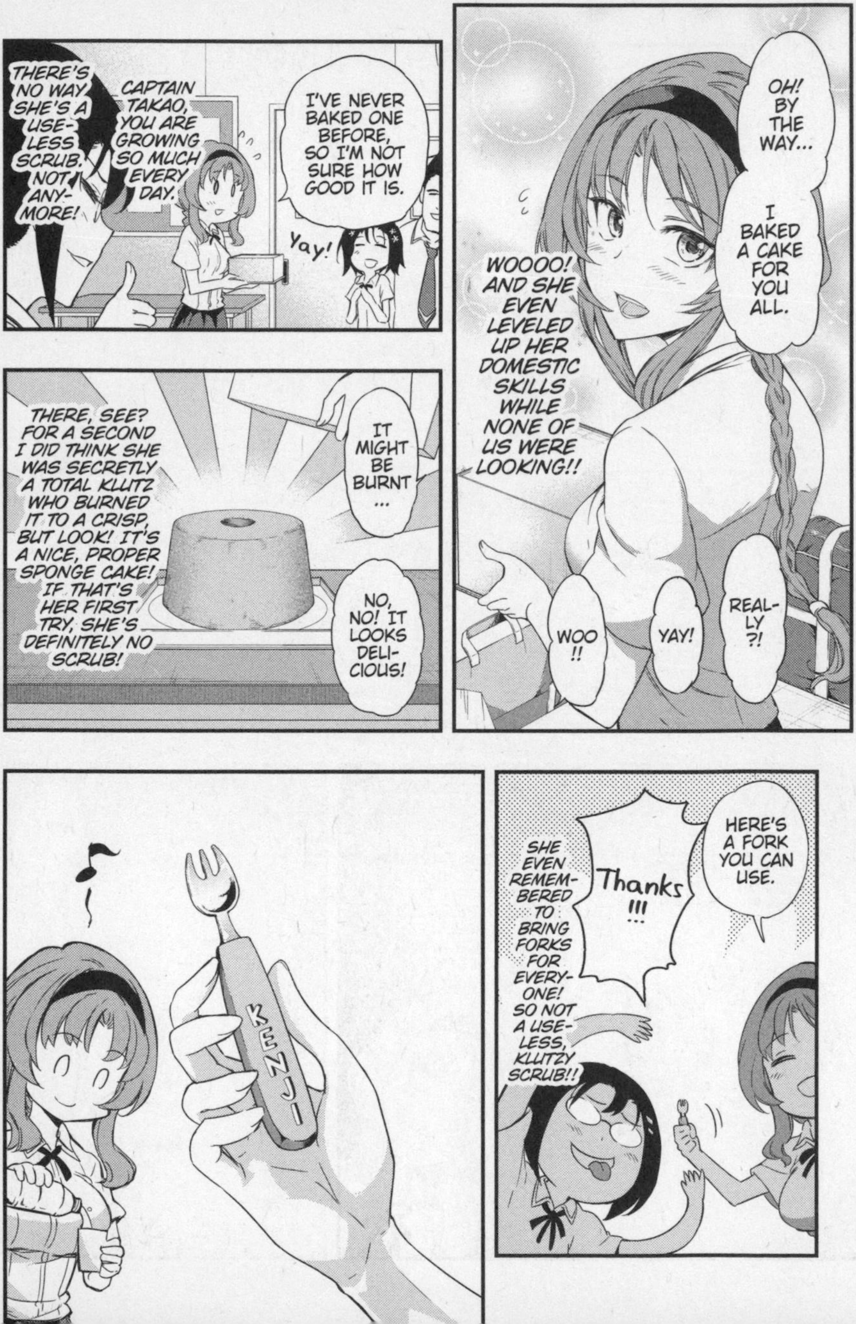
OH! BY THE WAY...
I BAKED A CAKE FOR YOU ALL.
WOOOO! AND SHE EVEN LEVELED UP HER DOMESTIC SKILLS WHILE NONE OF US WERE LOOKING!!
REAL-LY?!
YAY!
WOO!!
I'VE NEVER BAKED ONE BEFORE, SO I'M NOT SURE HOW GOOD IT IS.
Yay!
CAPTAIN TAKAO, YOU ARE GROWING SO MUCH EVERY DAY.
THERE'S NO WAY SHE'S A USE-LESS SCRUB. NOT ANY-MORE!
IT MIGHT BE BURNT...
NO, NO! IT LOOKS DELI-CIOUS!
THERE, SEE? FOR A SECOND I DID THINK SHE WAS SECRETLY A TOTAL KLUTZ WHO BURNED IT TO A CRISP, BUT LOOK! IT'S A NICE, PROPER SPONGE CAKE! IF THAT'S HER FIRST TRY, SHE'S DEFINITELY NO SCRUB!
HERE'S A FORK YOU CAN USE.
Thanks!!!
SHE EVEN REMEM-BERED TO BRING FORKS FOR EVERY-ONE! SO NOT A USE-LESS, KLUTZY SCRUB!!
KENJI

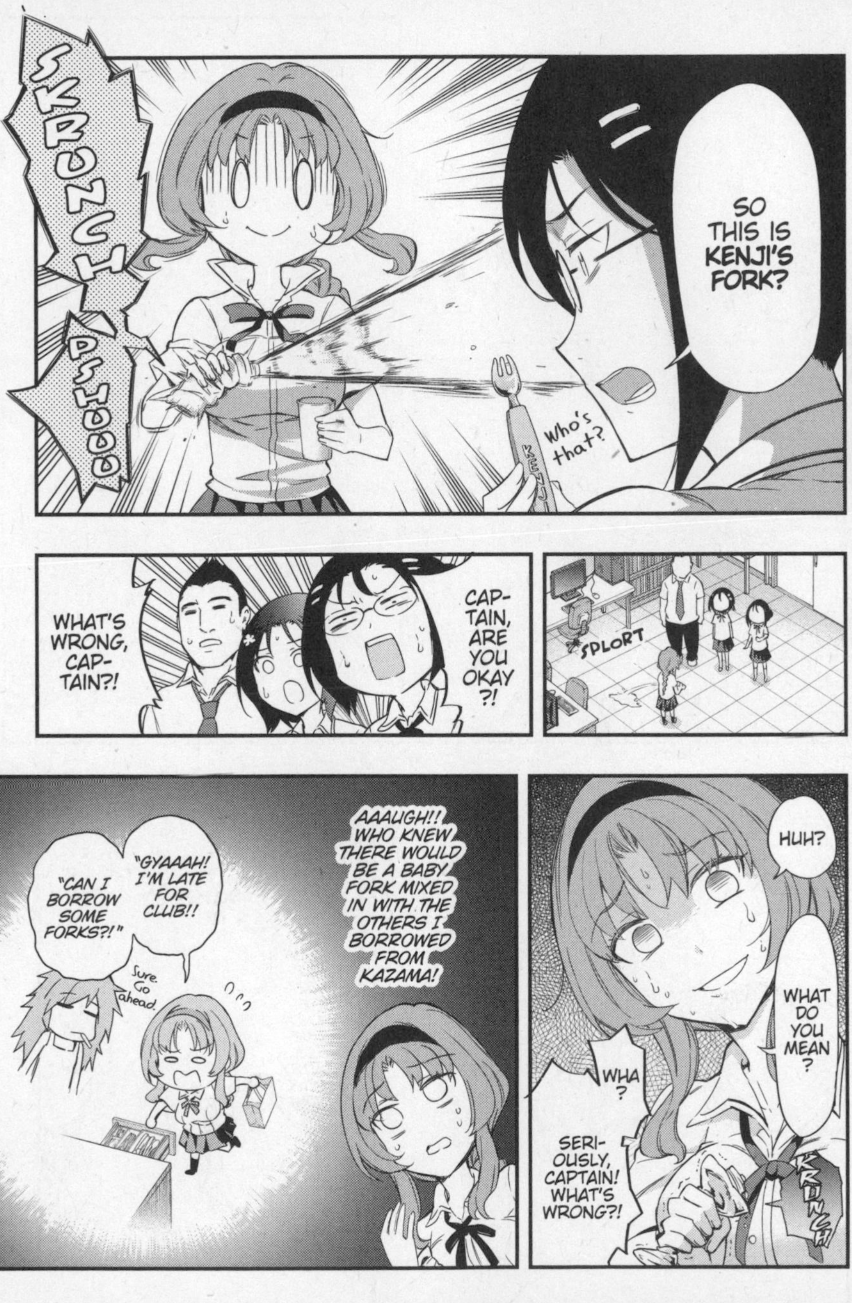
SO THIS IS KENJI'S FORK?
Who's that?
KENJI
SKRUNCH
PSHUUUU
SPLORT
CAP-TAIN, ARE YOU OKAY?!
WHAT'S WRONG, CAP-TAIN?!
HUH?
WHAT DO YOU MEAN?
WHA?
SERI-OUSLY, CAPTAIN! WHAT'S WRONG?!
KRUNCH
AAAUGH!! WHO KNEW THERE WOULD BE A BABY FORK MIXED IN WITH THE OTHERS I BORROWED FROM KAZAMA!
"GYAAAH! I'M LATE FOR CLUB!!
"CAN I BORROW SOME FORKS?!"
Sure. Go ahead.

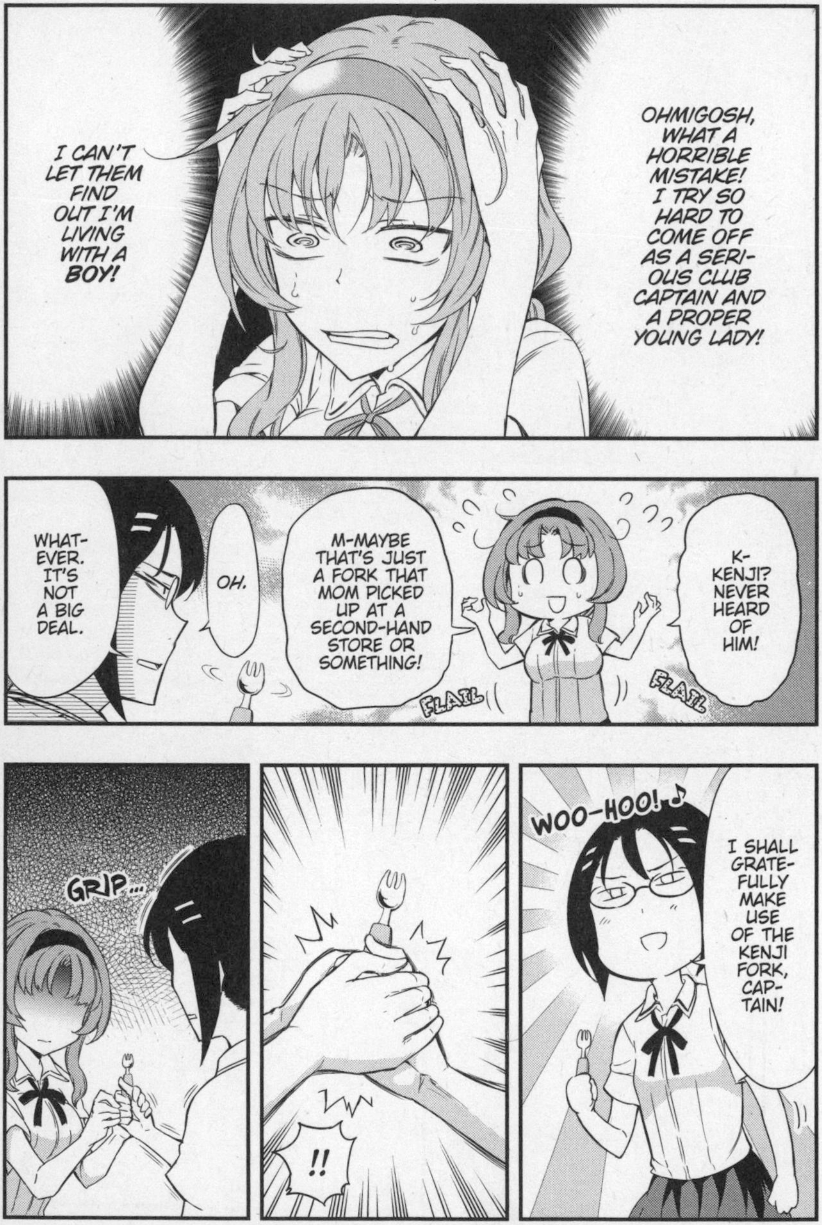
OHMIGOSH, WHAT A HORRIBLE MISTAKE! I TRY SO HARD TO COME OFF AS A SERIOUS CLUB CAPTAIN AND A PROPER YOUNG LADY!
I CAN'T LET THEM FIND OUT I'M LIVING WITH A BOY!
K-KENJI? NEVER HEARD OF HIM!
FLAIL
FLAIL
M-MAYBE THAT'S JUST A FORK THAT MOM PICKED UP AT A SECOND-HAND STORE OR SOMETHING!
OH.
WHATEVER. IT'S NOT A BIG DEAL.
WOO-HOO! ♪
I SHALL GRATEFULLY MAKE USE OF THE KENJI FORK, CAPTAIN!
!!
GRIP...

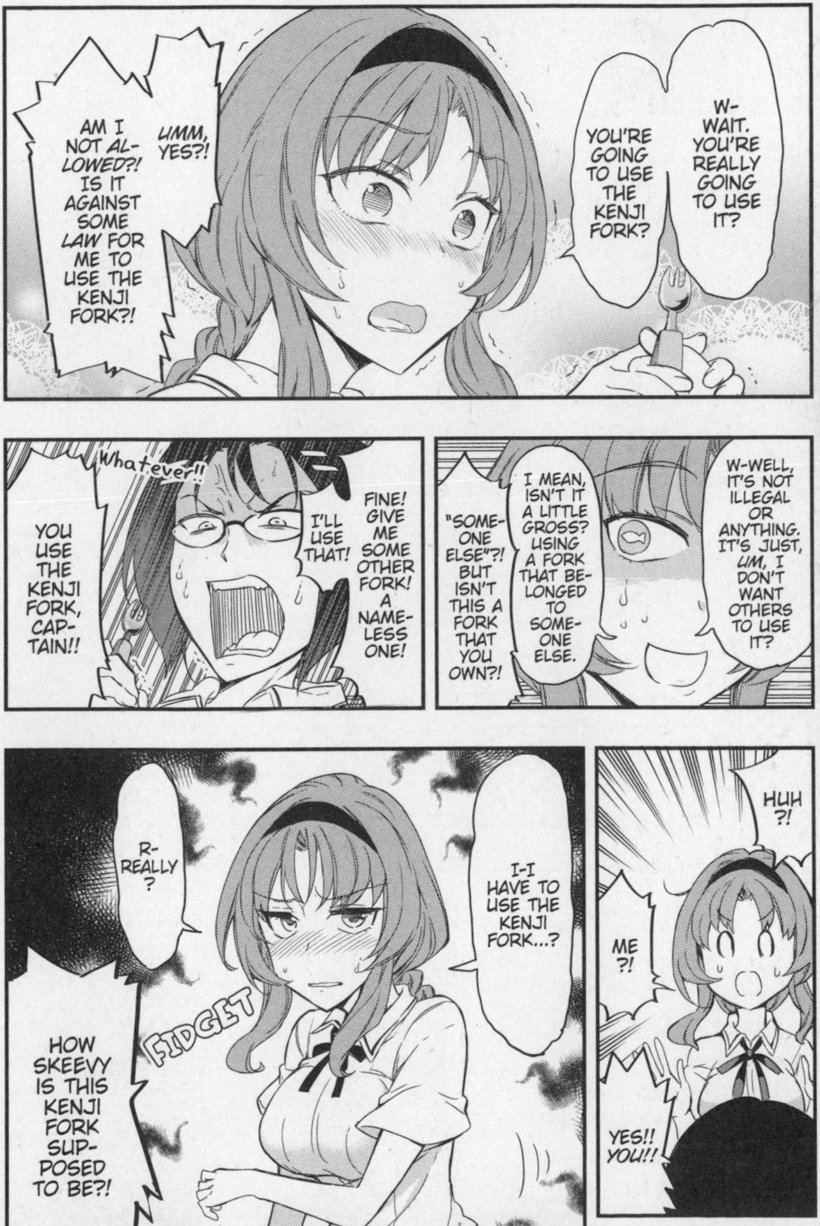
W-WAIT. YOU'RE REALLY GOING TO USE IT?
YOU'RE GOING TO USE THE KENJI FORK?
UMM, YES?!
AM I NOT ALLOWED?! IS IT AGAINST SOME LAW FOR ME TO USE THE KENJI FORK?!
W-WELL, IT'S NOT ILLEGAL OR ANYTHING. IT'S JUST, UM, I DON'T WANT OTHERS TO USE IT?
I MEAN, ISN'T IT A LITTLE GROSS? USING A FORK THAT BELONGED TO SOMEONE ELSE.
"SOMEONE ELSE"?! BUT ISN'T THIS A FORK THAT YOU OWN?!
FINE! GIVE ME SOME OTHER FORK! A NAMELESS ONE!
I'LL USE THAT!
Whatever!!
YOU USE THE KENJI FORK, CAPTAIN!!
HUH ?!
ME ?!
YES!! YOU!!
I-I HAVE TO USE THE KENJI FORK...?
R-REALLY ?
FIDGET
HOW SKEEVY IS THIS KENJI FORK SUPPOSED TO BE?!

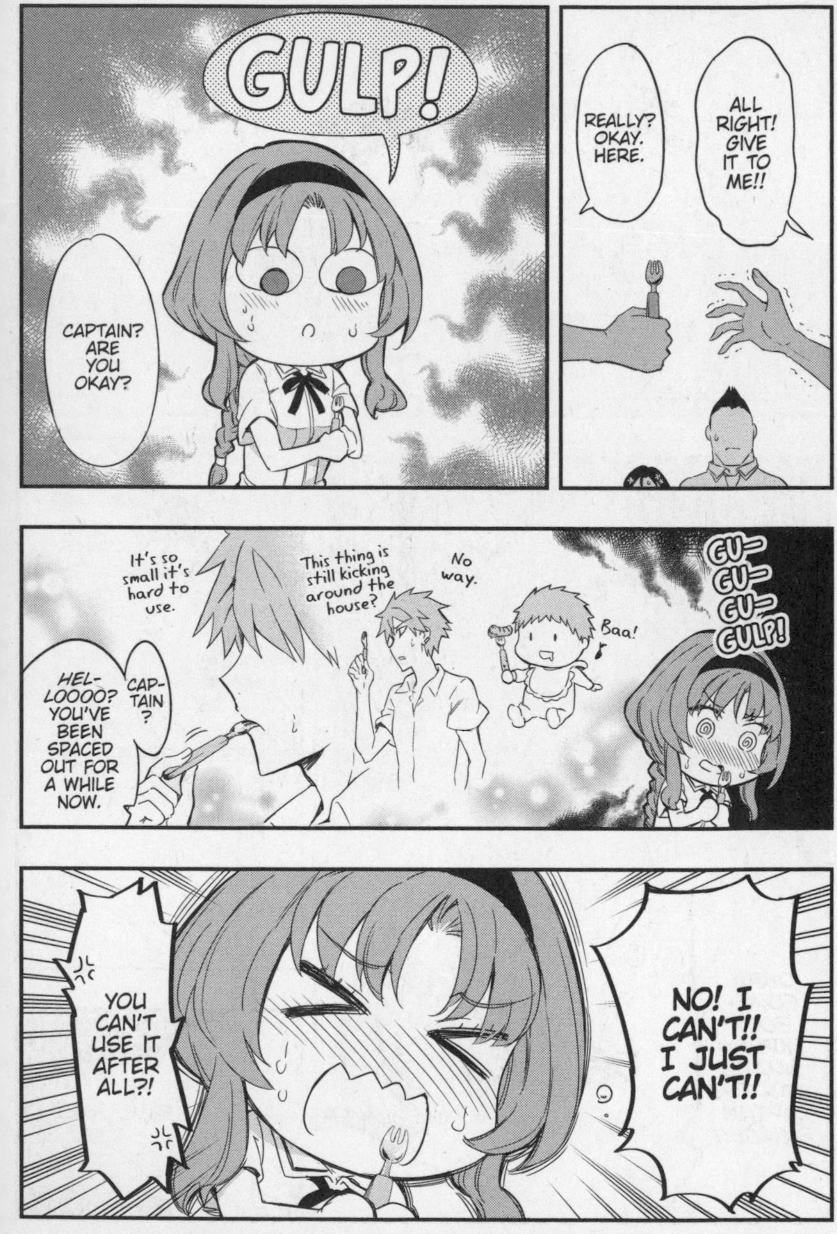
ALL RIGHT! GIVE IT TO ME!!
REALLY? OKAY. HERE.
GULP!
CAPTAIN? ARE YOU OKAY?
GU-GU-GU-GULP!
Baa!
No way.
This thing is still kicking around the house?
It's so small it's hard to use.
CAPTAIN?
HEL-LOOOO? YOU'VE BEEN SPACED OUT FOR A WHILE NOW.
NO! I CAN'T!! I JUST CAN'T!!
YOU CAN'T USE IT AFTER ALL?!

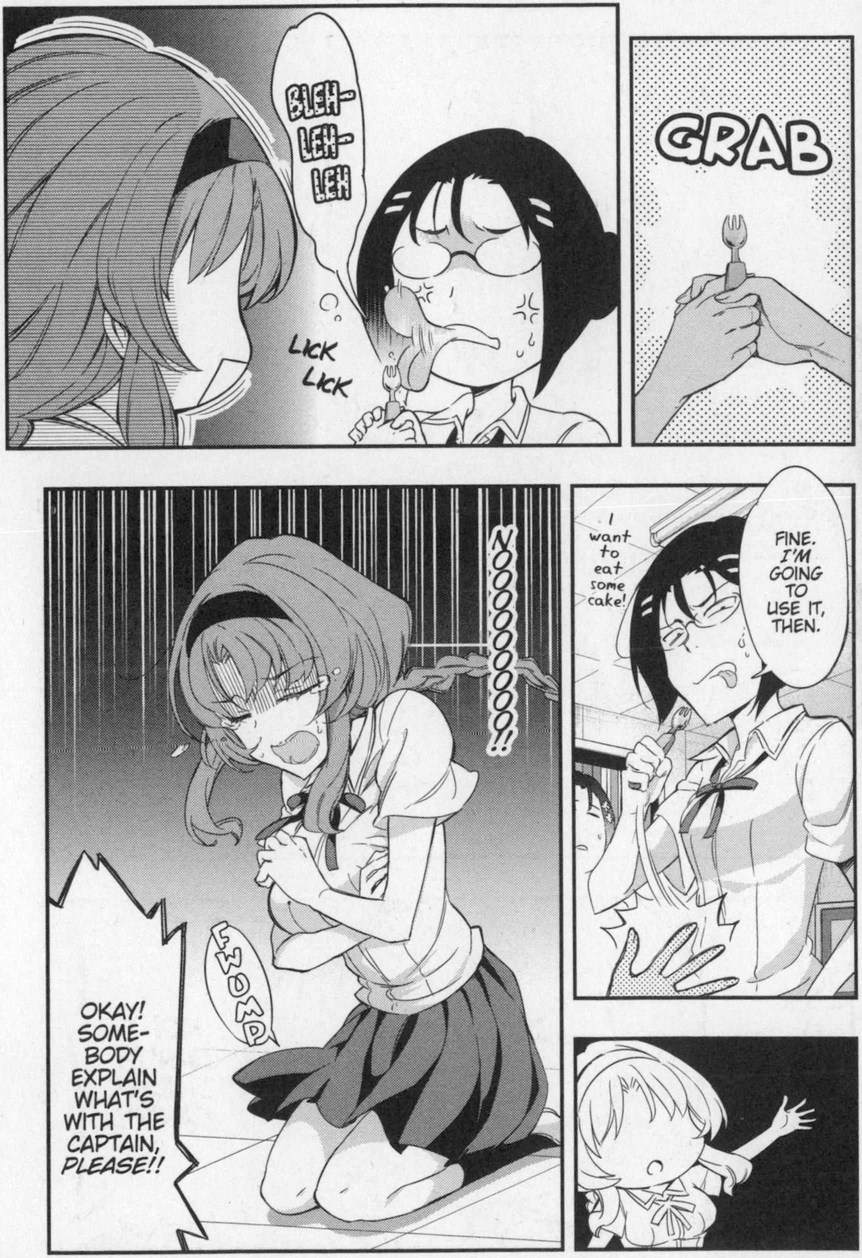
GRAB
BLEH-LEH-LEH
LICK LICK
FINE. I'M GOING TO USE IT, THEN.
I want to eat some cake!
NOOOOOOOOOOOOO!!
FWOMP
OKAY! SOMEBODY EXPLAIN WHAT'S WITH THE CAPTAIN, PLEASE!!

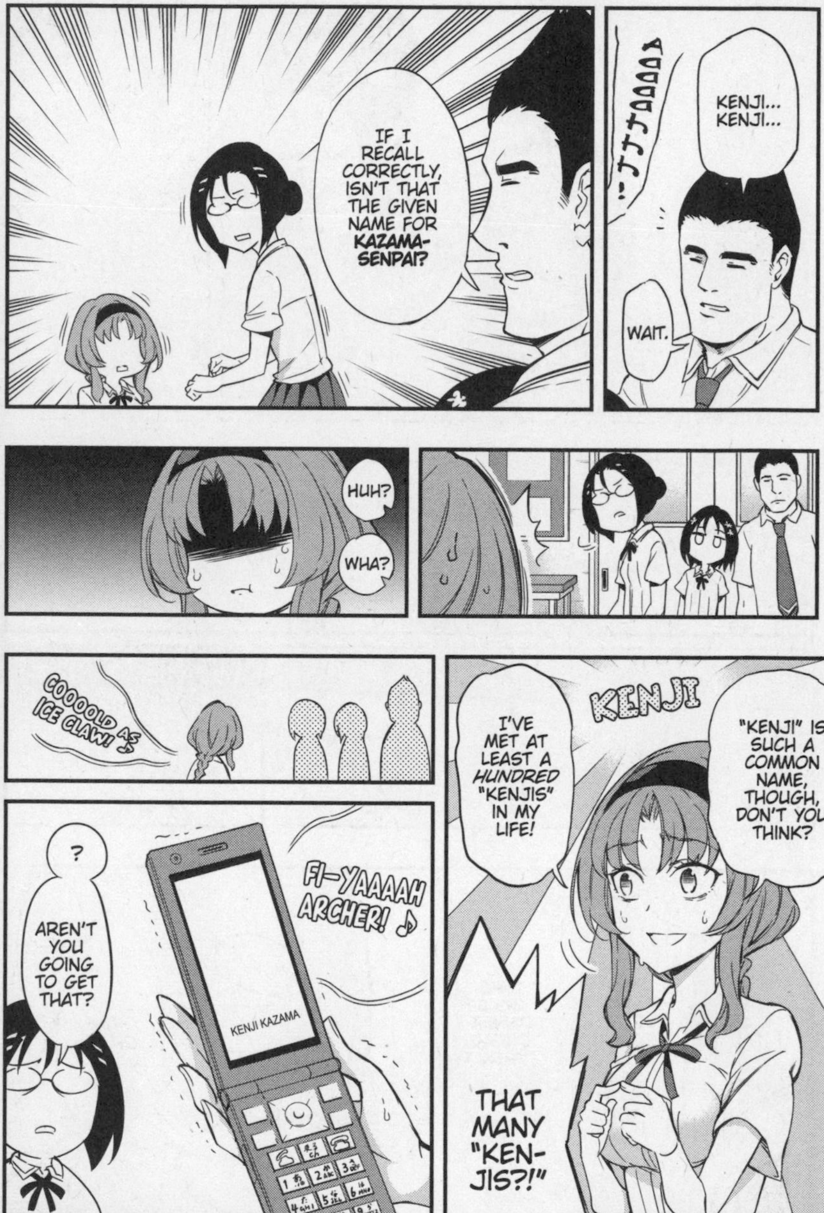
KENJI... KENJI...
WAIT.
IF I RECALL CORRECTLY, ISN'T THAT THE GIVEN NAME FOR **KAZAMA-SENPAI**?
HUH?
WHA?
KENJI
"KENJI" IS SUCH A COMMON NAME, THOUGH, DON'T YOU THINK?
I'VE MET AT LEAST A *HUNDRED* "KENJIS" IN MY LIFE!
THAT MANY "KEN-JIS?!"
COOOOLD AS ICE CLAW! ♪
?
AREN'T YOU GOING TO GET THAT?
FI-YAAAAH ARCHER! ♪
KENJI KAZAMA

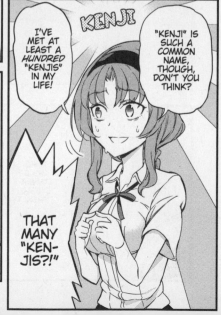

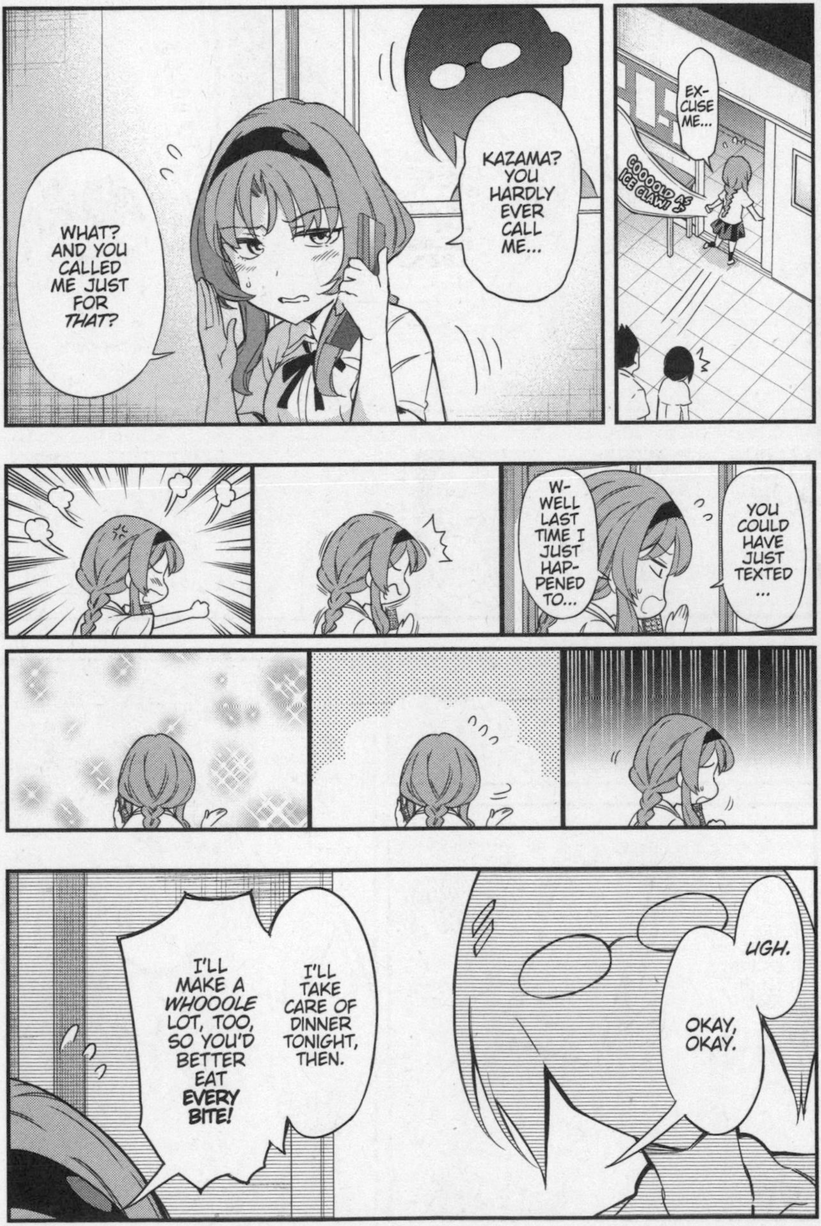
EX-CUSE ME...
GOOOOLD AS ICE CLAW!
KAZAMA? YOU HARDLY EVER CALL ME...
WHAT? AND YOU CALLED ME JUST FOR THAT?
YOU COULD HAVE JUST TEXTED ...
W-WELL LAST TIME I JUST HAP-PENED TO...
UGH.
OKAY, OKAY.
I'LL TAKE CARE OF DINNER TONIGHT, THEN.
I'LL MAKE A WHOOOLE LOT, TOO, SO YOU'D BETTER EAT EVERY BITE!

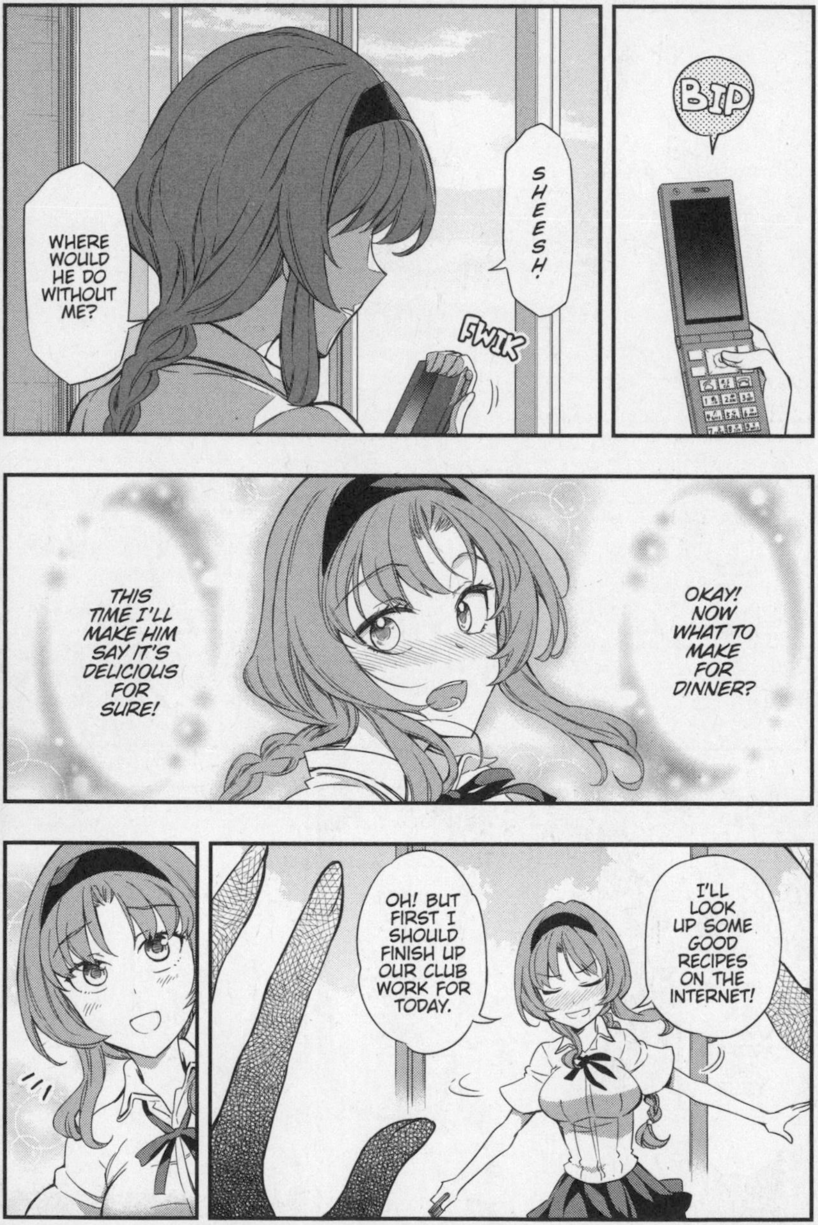
BIP
SHEESH!
FWIK
WHERE WOULD HE DO WITHOUT ME?
OKAY! NOW WHAT TO MAKE FOR DINNER?
THIS TIME I'LL MAKE HIM SAY IT'S DELICIOUS FOR SURE!
I'LL LOOK UP SOME GOOD RECIPES ON THE INTERNET!
OH! BUT FIRST I SHOULD FINISH UP OUR CLUB WORK FOR TODAY.

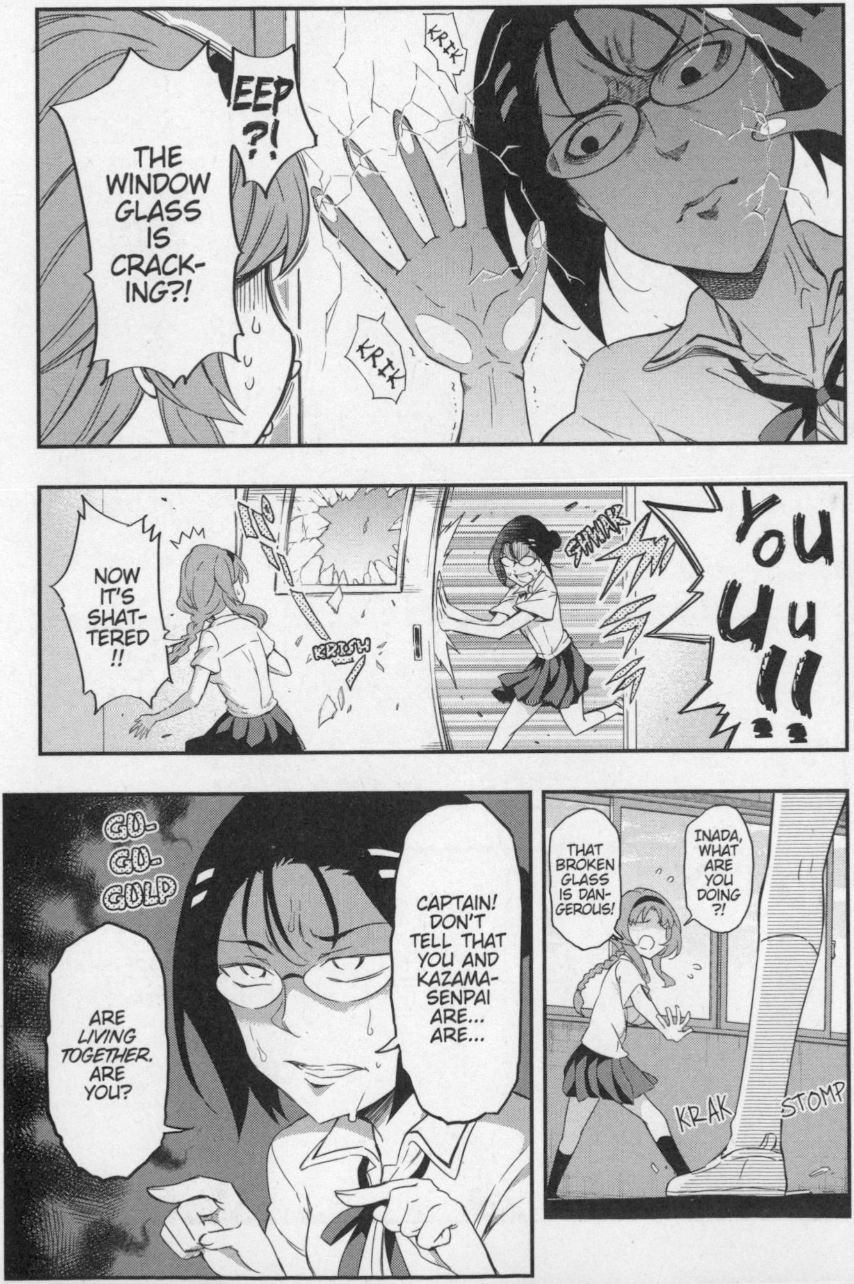
KRIK
EEP?!
THE WINDOW GLASS IS CRACKING?!
KRIK
YOU UUU!!
SHWAK
KRISH
NOW IT'S SHATTERED!!
INADA, WHAT ARE YOU DOING?!
THAT BROKEN GLASS IS DANGEROUS!
STOMP
KRAK
CAPTAIN! DON'T TELL THAT YOU AND KAZAMA-SENPAI ARE... ARE...
GU-GU-GULP
ARE LIVING TOGETHER. ARE YOU?

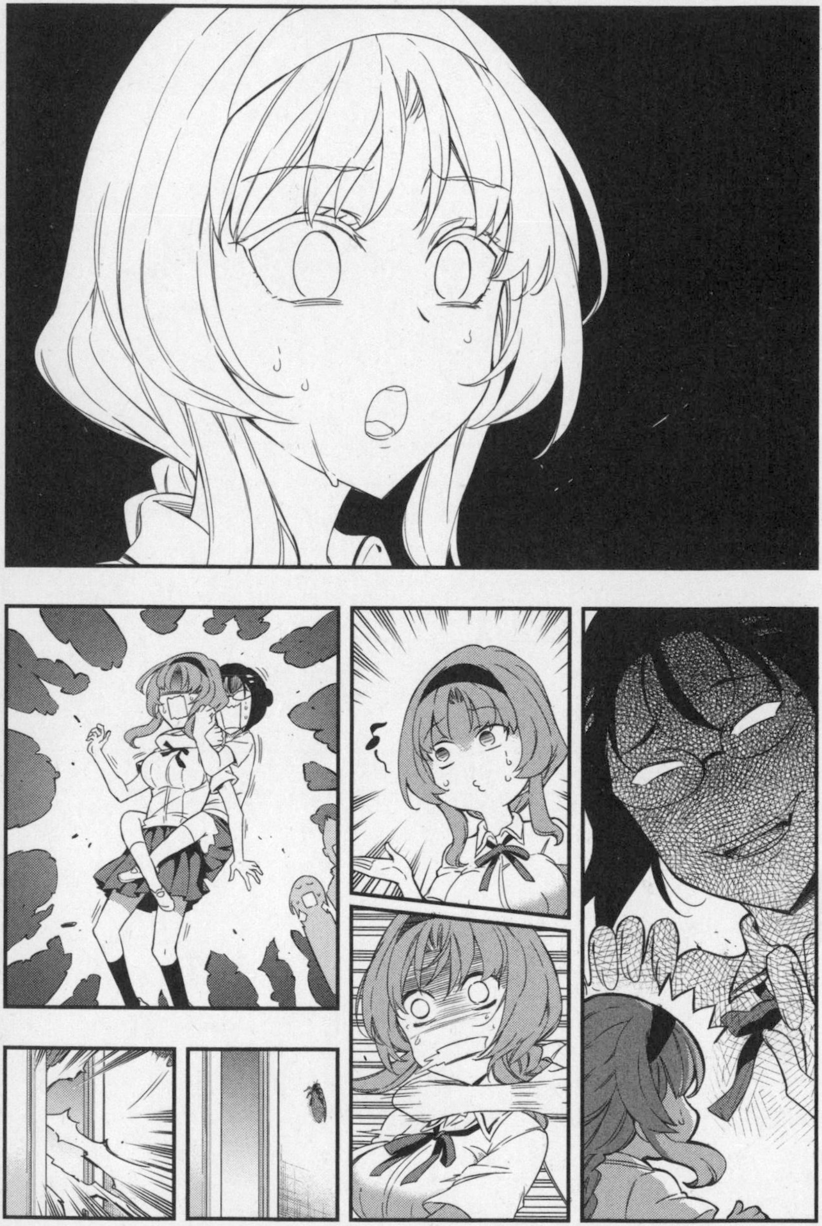

Her Mason phone strap has gotten battered, so she took it off and stored it in a safe place.

D-FRAGMENTS
ディーふらぐめんつ!

Chapter 104: I Said Stop! It's Dangerous!

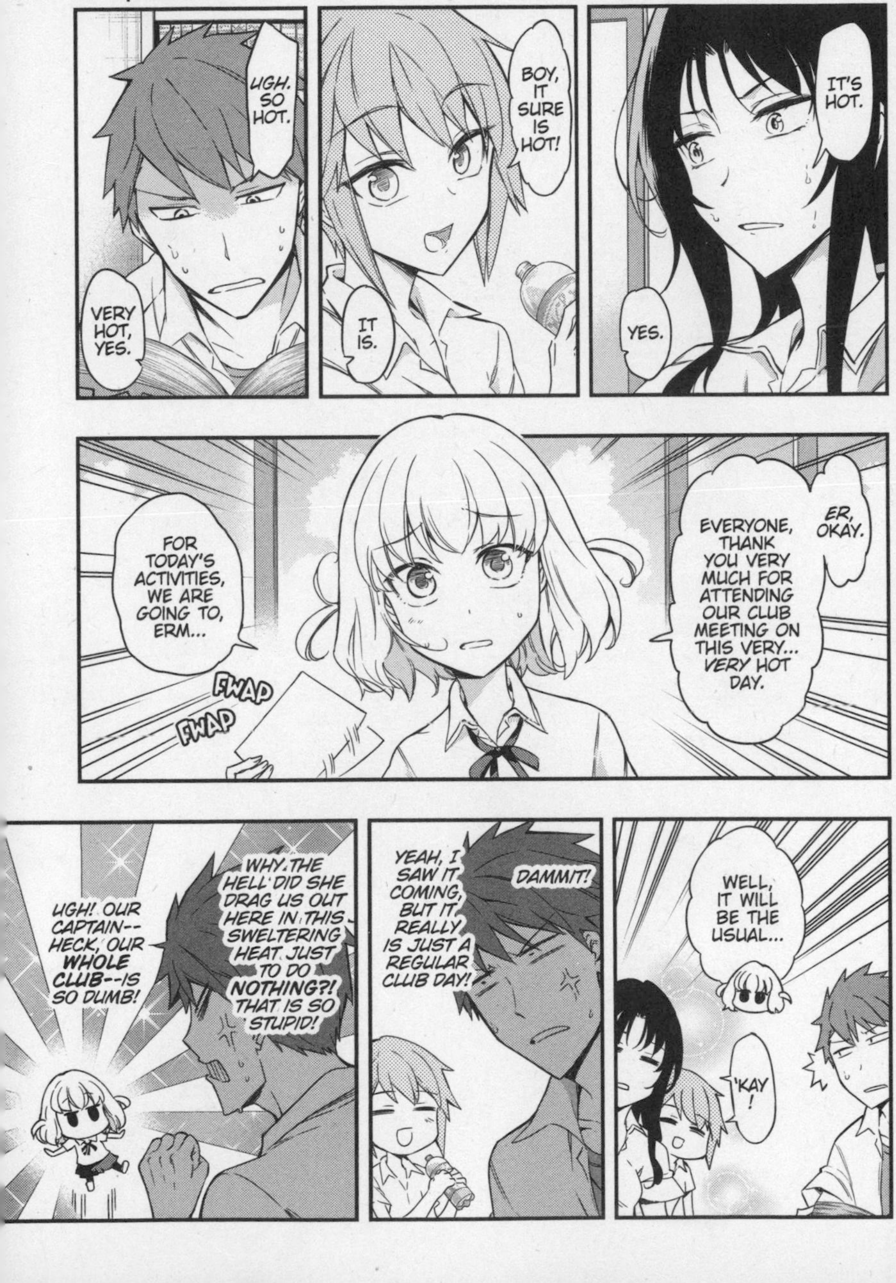
IT'S HOT.
YES.
BOY, IT SURE IS HOT!
IT IS.
UGH. SO HOT.
VERY HOT, YES.
ER, OKAY.
EVERYONE, THANK YOU VERY MUCH FOR ATTENDING OUR CLUB MEETING ON THIS VERY... VERY HOT DAY.
FOR TODAY'S ACTIVITIES, WE ARE GOING TO, ERM...
FWAP
FWAP
WELL, IT WILL BE THE USUAL...
'KAY!
DAMMIT!
YEAH, I SAW IT COMING, BUT IT REALLY IS JUST A REGULAR CLUB DAY!
WHY THE HELL DID SHE DRAG US OUT HERE IN THIS SWELTERING HEAT JUST TO DO NOTHING?! THAT IS SO STUPID!
UGH! OUR CAPTAIN--HECK, OUR WHOLE CLUB--IS SO DUMB!

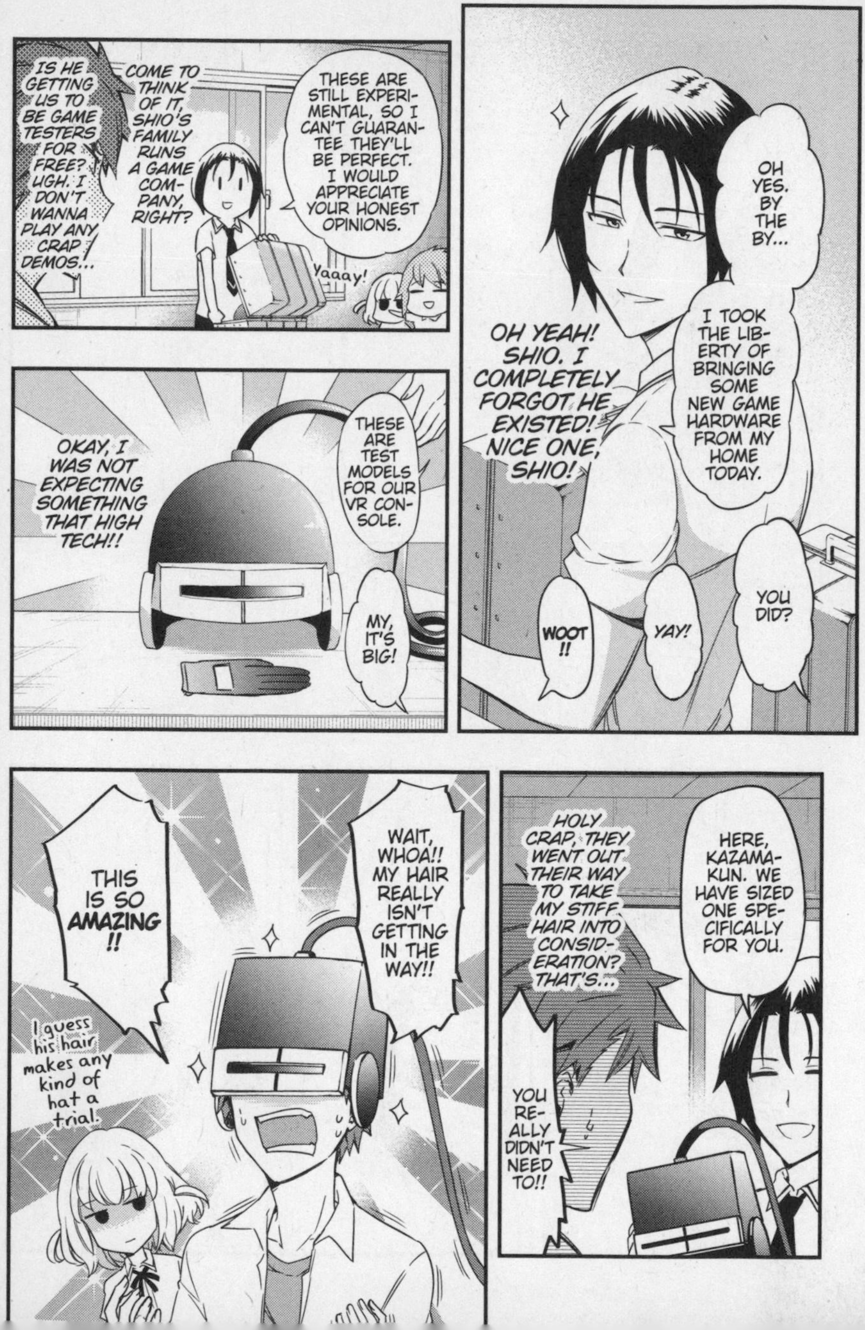
OH YES. BY THE BY...
I TOOK THE LIBERTY OF BRINGING SOME NEW GAME HARDWARE FROM MY HOME TODAY.
YOU DID?
YAY!
WOOT!!
OH YEAH! SHIO. I COMPLETELY FORGOT HE EXISTED! NICE ONE, SHIO!
THESE ARE STILL EXPERIMENTAL, SO I CAN'T GUARANTEE THEY'LL BE PERFECT. I WOULD APPRECIATE YOUR HONEST OPINIONS.
COME TO THINK OF IT, SHIO'S FAMILY RUNS A GAME COMPANY, RIGHT?
IS HE GETTING US TO BE GAME TESTERS FOR FREE? UGH. I DON'T WANNA PLAY ANY CRAP DEMOS...
Yaaay!
THESE ARE TEST MODELS FOR OUR VR CONSOLE.
MY, IT'S BIG!
OKAY, I WAS NOT EXPECTING SOMETHING THAT HIGH TECH!!
HERE, KAZAMA-KUN. WE HAVE SIZED ONE SPECIFICALLY FOR YOU.
HOLY CRAP, THEY WENT OUT THEIR WAY TO TAKE MY STIFF HAIR INTO CONSIDERATION? THAT'S...
YOU REALLY DIDN'T NEED TO!!
WAIT, WHOA!! MY HAIR REALLY ISN'T GETTING IN THE WAY!!
THIS IS SO AMAZING!!
I guess his hair makes any kind of hat a trial.

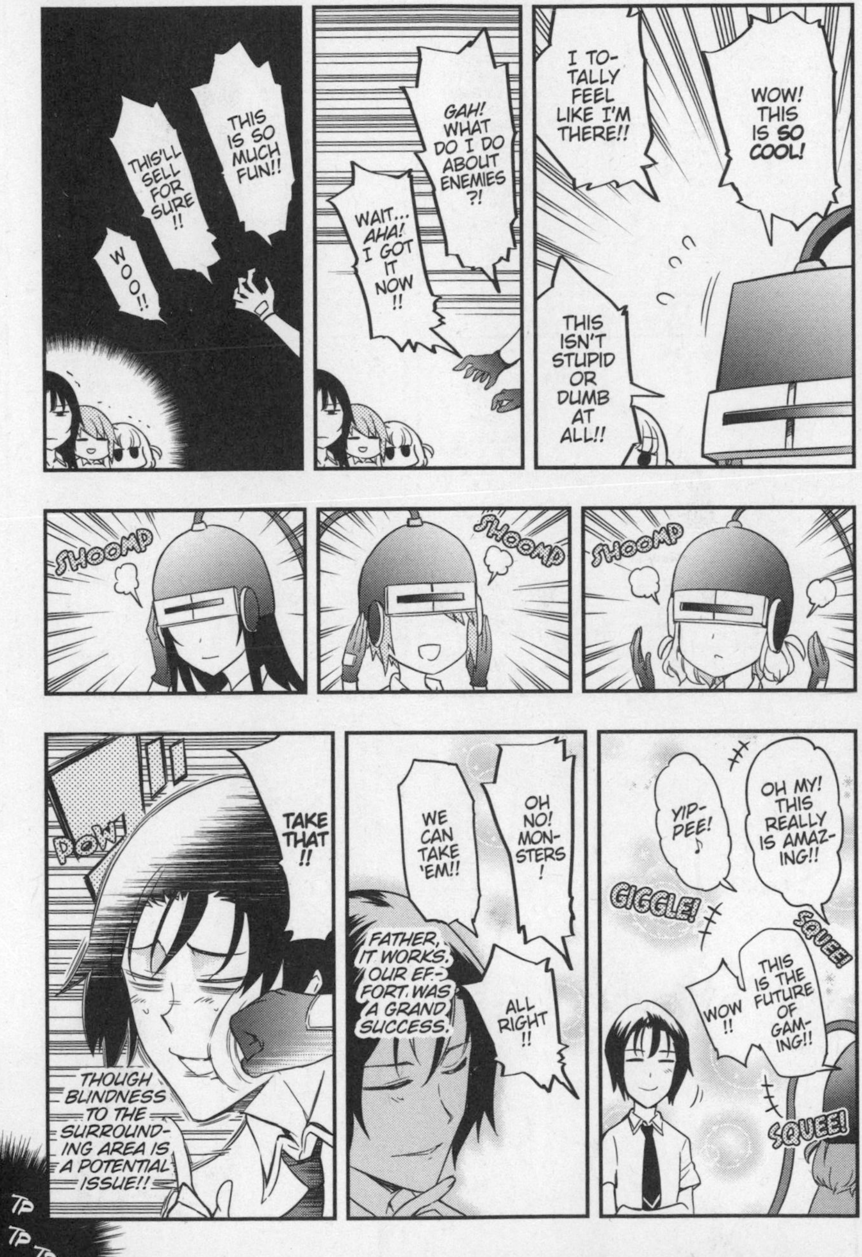
WOW! THIS IS SO COOL!
I TOTALLY FEEL LIKE I'M THERE!!
THIS ISN'T STUPID OR DUMB AT ALL!!
GAH! WHAT DO I DO ABOUT ENEMIES ?!
WAIT... AHA! I GOT IT NOW !!
THIS IS SO MUCH FUN!!
THIS'LL SELL FOR SURE !!
WOO!!
SHOOMP
SHOOMP
SHOOMP
OH MY! THIS REALLY IS AMAZING!!
YIPPEE! ♪
GIGGLE!
SQUEE!
THIS IS THE FUTURE OF GAMING!!
WOW !!
SQUEE!
OH NO! MONSTERS !
WE CAN TAKE 'EM!!
FATHER, IT WORKS. OUR EFFORT WAS A GRAND SUCCESS.
ALL RIGHT !!
TAKE THAT !!
POW
THOUGH BLINDNESS TO THE SURROUNDING AREA IS A POTENTIAL ISSUE!!
TP TP TP

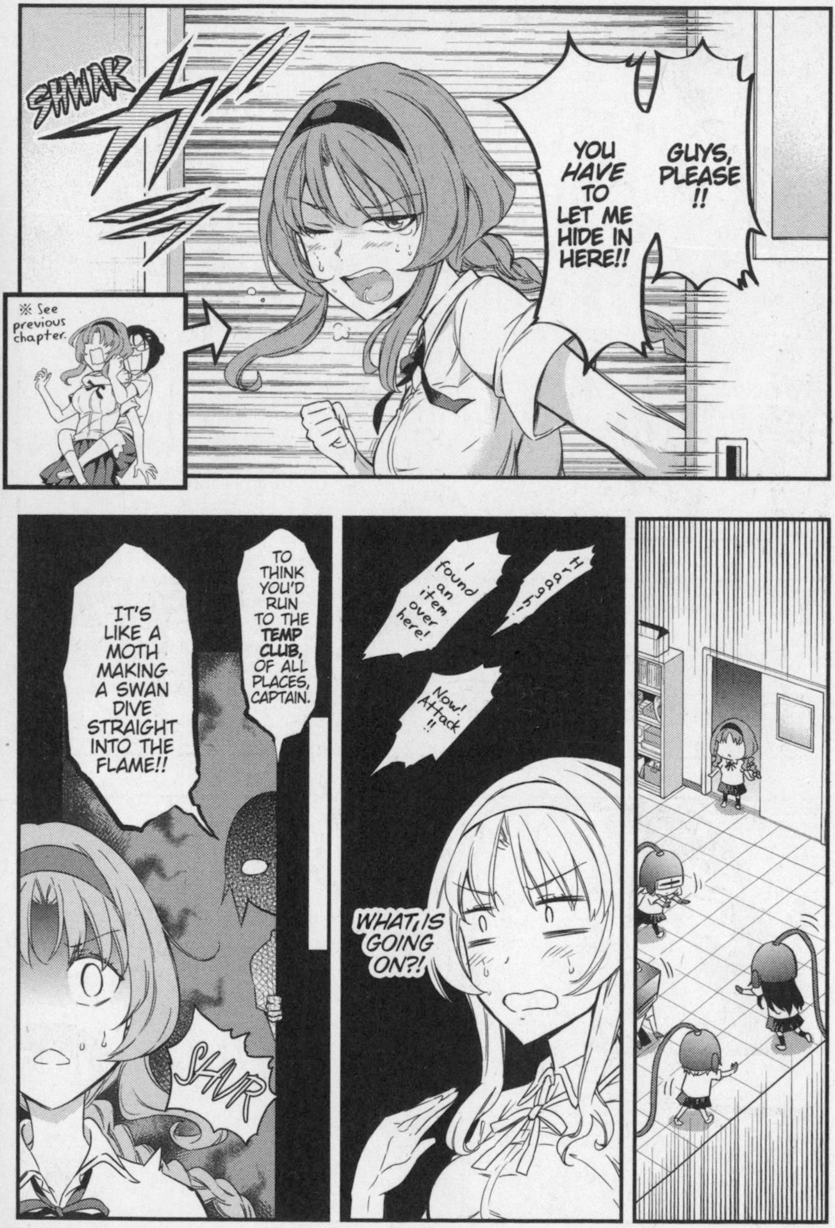
SHWAR
GUYS, PLEASE!!
YOU HAVE TO LET ME HIDE IN HERE!!
※ See previous chapter.
Hrggg...
I found an item over here!
Now! Attack!!
WHAT IS GOING ON?!
TO THINK YOU'D RUN TO THE TEMP CLUB, OF ALL PLACES, CAPTAIN.
IT'S LIKE A MOTH MAKING A SWAN DIVE STRAIGHT INTO THE FLAME!!
SHUR

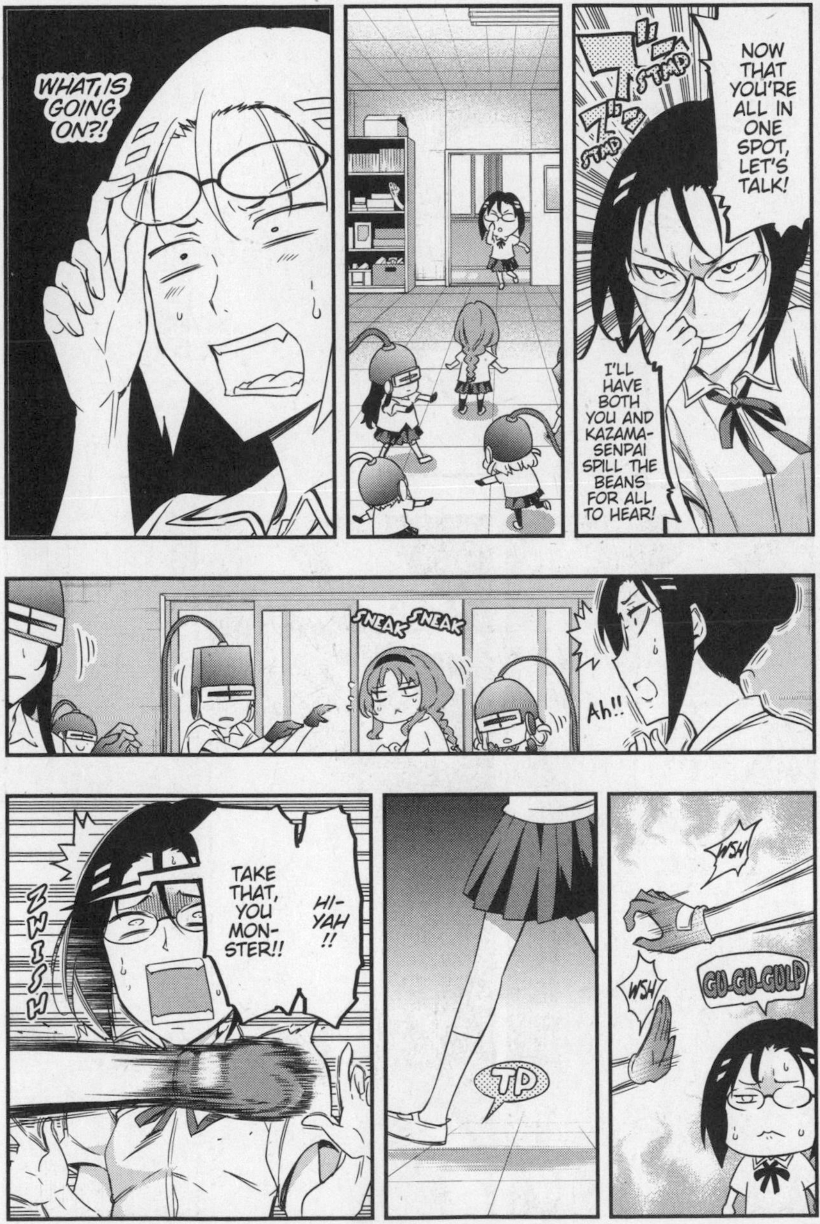
STMP
STMP
NOW THAT YOU'RE ALL IN ONE SPOT, LET'S TALK!
I'LL HAVE BOTH YOU AND KAZAMA-SENPAI SPILL THE BEANS FOR ALL TO HEAR!
WHAT IS GOING ON?!
Ah!!
SNEAK SNEAK
WSH
GU-GU-GULP
WSH
TP
HI-YAH!!
TAKE THAT, YOU MONSTER!!
ZWISH

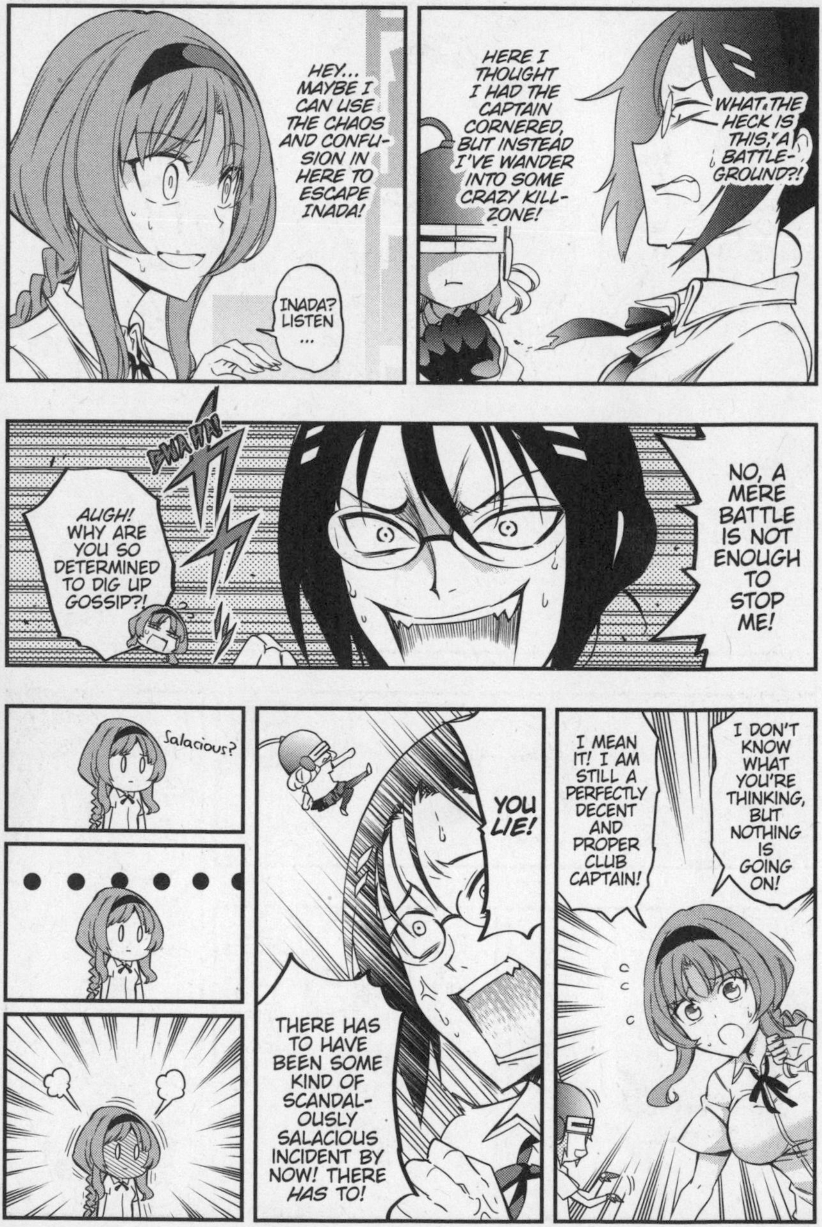
WHAT THE HECK IS THIS, A BATTLE-GROUND?!
HERE I THOUGHT I HAD THE CAPTAIN CORNERED, BUT INSTEAD I'VE WANDER INTO SOME CRAZY KILL-ZONE!
HEY... MAYBE I CAN USE THE CHAOS AND CONFUSION IN HERE TO ESCAPE INADA!
INADA? LISTEN ...
NO, A MERE BATTLE IS NOT ENOUGH TO STOP ME!
DWA HA!
AUGH! WHY ARE YOU SO DETERMINED TO DIG UP GOSSIP?!
I DON'T KNOW WHAT YOU'RE THINKING, BUT NOTHING IS GOING ON!
I MEAN IT! I AM STILL A PERFECTLY DECENT AND PROPER CLUB CAPTAIN!
YOU LIE!
THERE HAS TO HAVE BEEN SOME KIND OF SCANDALOUSLY SALACIOUS INCIDENT BY NOW! THERE HAS TO!
Salacious?

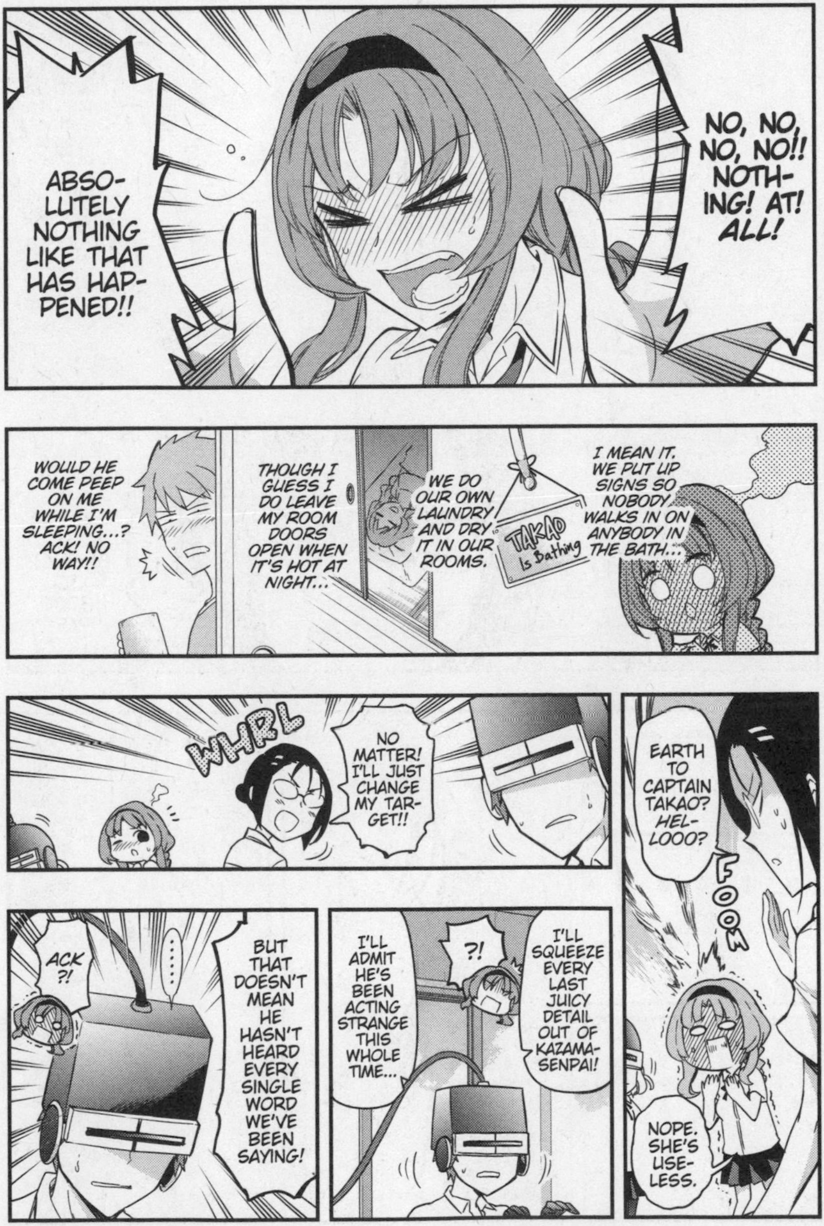
NO, NO, NO, NO!! NOTHING! AT! ALL!
ABSOLUTELY NOTHING LIKE THAT HAS HAPPENED!!
I MEAN IT. WE PUT UP SIGNS SO NOBODY WALKS IN ON ANYBODY IN THE BATH...
TAKAO Is Bathing
WE DO OUR OWN LAUNDRY AND DRY IT IN OUR ROOMS.
THOUGH I GUESS I DO LEAVE MY ROOM DOORS OPEN WHEN IT'S HOT AT NIGHT...
WOULD HE COME PEEP ON ME WHILE I'M SLEEPING...? ACK! NO WAY!!
EARTH TO CAPTAIN TAKAO? HELLOOO?
FOOOM
NOPE. SHE'S USELESS.
NO MATTER! I'LL JUST CHANGE MY TARGET!!
WHRL
I'LL SQUEEZE EVERY LAST JUICY DETAIL OUT OF KAZAMA-SENPAI!
?!
I'LL ADMIT HE'S BEEN ACTING STRANGE THIS WHOLE TIME...
BUT THAT DOESN'T MEAN HE HASN'T HEARD EVERY SINGLE WORD WE'VE BEEN SAYING!
......
ACK?!

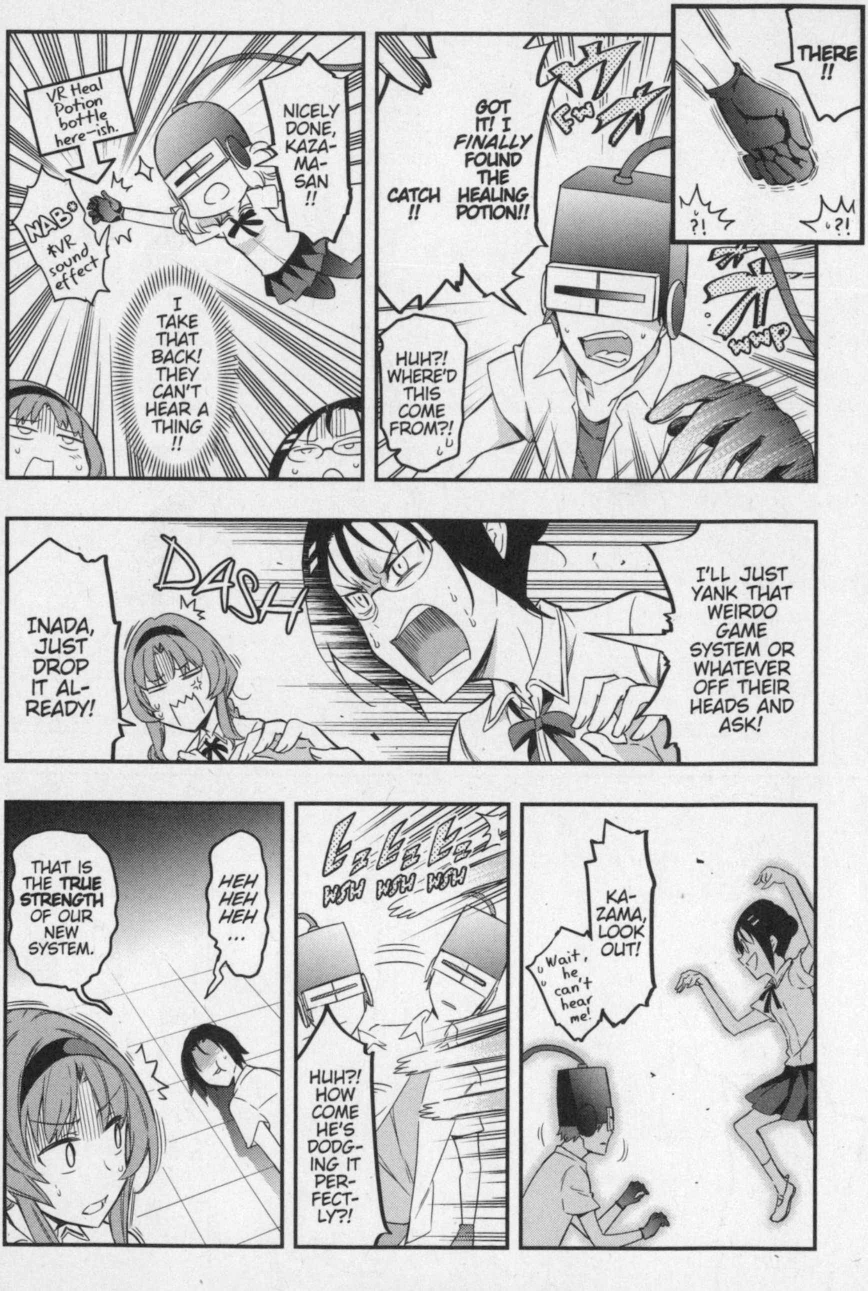
THERE!!
?!
?!
GOT IT! I FINALLY FOUND THE HEALING POTION!!
FW
CATCH!!
WWP
HUH?! WHERE'D THIS COME FROM?!
NICELY DONE, KAZAMA-SAN!!
VR Heal Potion bottle here-ish.
NAB*
*VR sound effect
I TAKE THAT BACK! THEY CAN'T HEAR A THING!!
I'LL JUST YANK THAT WEIRDO GAME SYSTEM OR WHATEVER OFF THEIR HEADS AND ASK!
DASH
INADA, JUST DROP IT ALREADY!
KAZAMA, LOOK OUT!
Wait, he can't hear me!
WSH WSH WSH
HUH?! HOW COME HE'S DODGING IT PERFECTLY?!
HEH HEH HEH...
THAT IS THE TRUE STRENGTH OF OUR NEW SYSTEM.

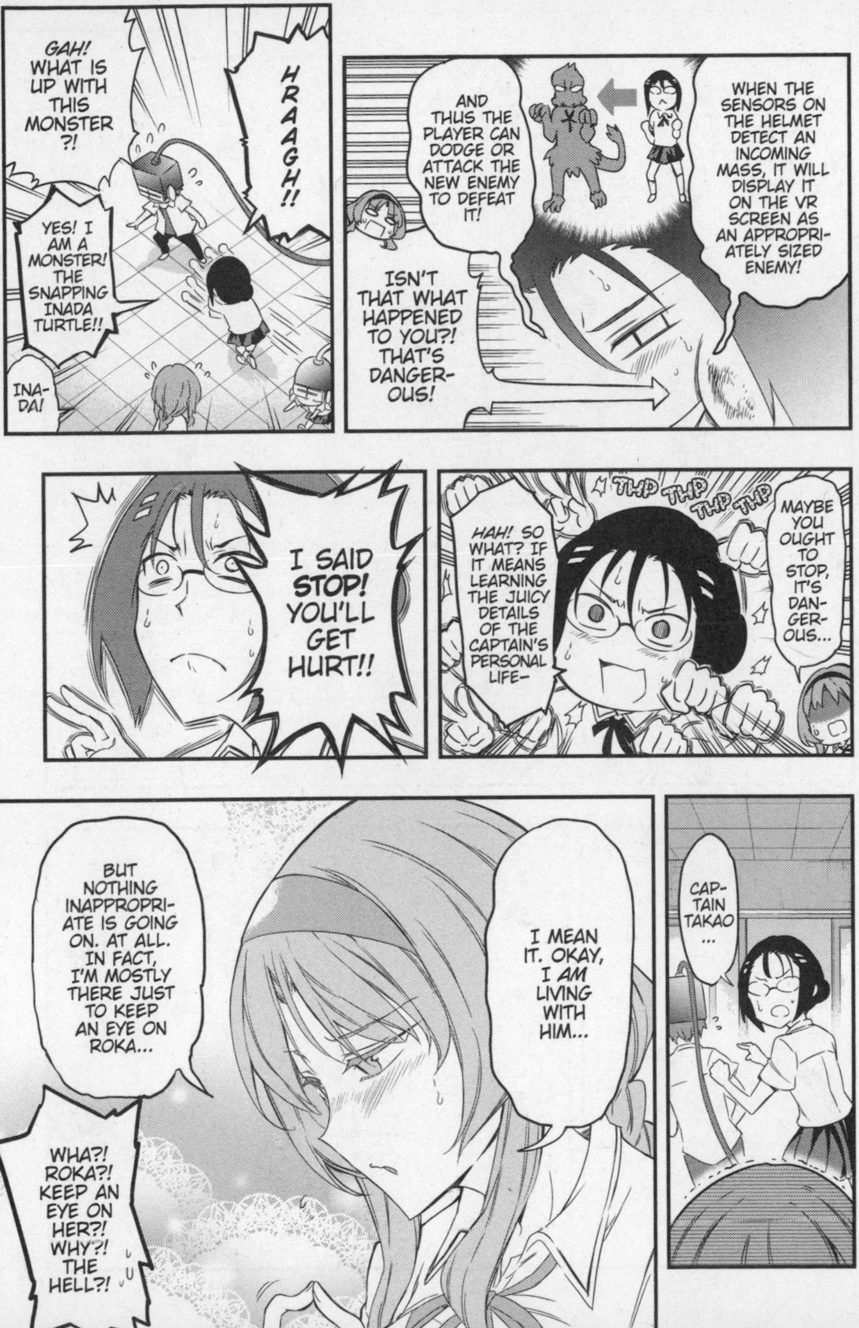
WHEN THE SENSORS ON THE HELMET DETECT AN INCOMING MASS, IT WILL DISPLAY IT ON THE VR SCREEN AS AN APPROPRIATELY SIZED ENEMY!
AND THUS THE PLAYER CAN DODGE OR ATTACK THE NEW ENEMY TO DEFEAT IT!
ISN'T THAT WHAT HAPPENED TO YOU?! THAT'S DANGEROUS!
HRAAAGH!!
GAH! WHAT IS UP WITH THIS MONSTER?!
YES! I AM A MONSTER! THE SNAPPING INADA TURTLE!!
INADA!
THP THP THP THP
MAYBE YOU OUGHT TO STOP, IT'S DANGEROUS...
HAH! SO WHAT? IF IT MEANS LEARNING THE JUICY DETAILS OF THE CAPTAIN'S PERSONAL LIFE-
I SAID STOP! YOU'LL GET HURT!!
CAPTAIN TAKAO...
I MEAN IT. OKAY, I AM LIVING WITH HIM...
BUT NOTHING INAPPROPRIATE IS GOING ON. AT ALL. IN FACT, I'M MOSTLY THERE JUST TO KEEP AN EYE ON ROKA...
WHA?! ROKA?! KEEP AN EYE ON HER?! WHY?! THE HELL?!

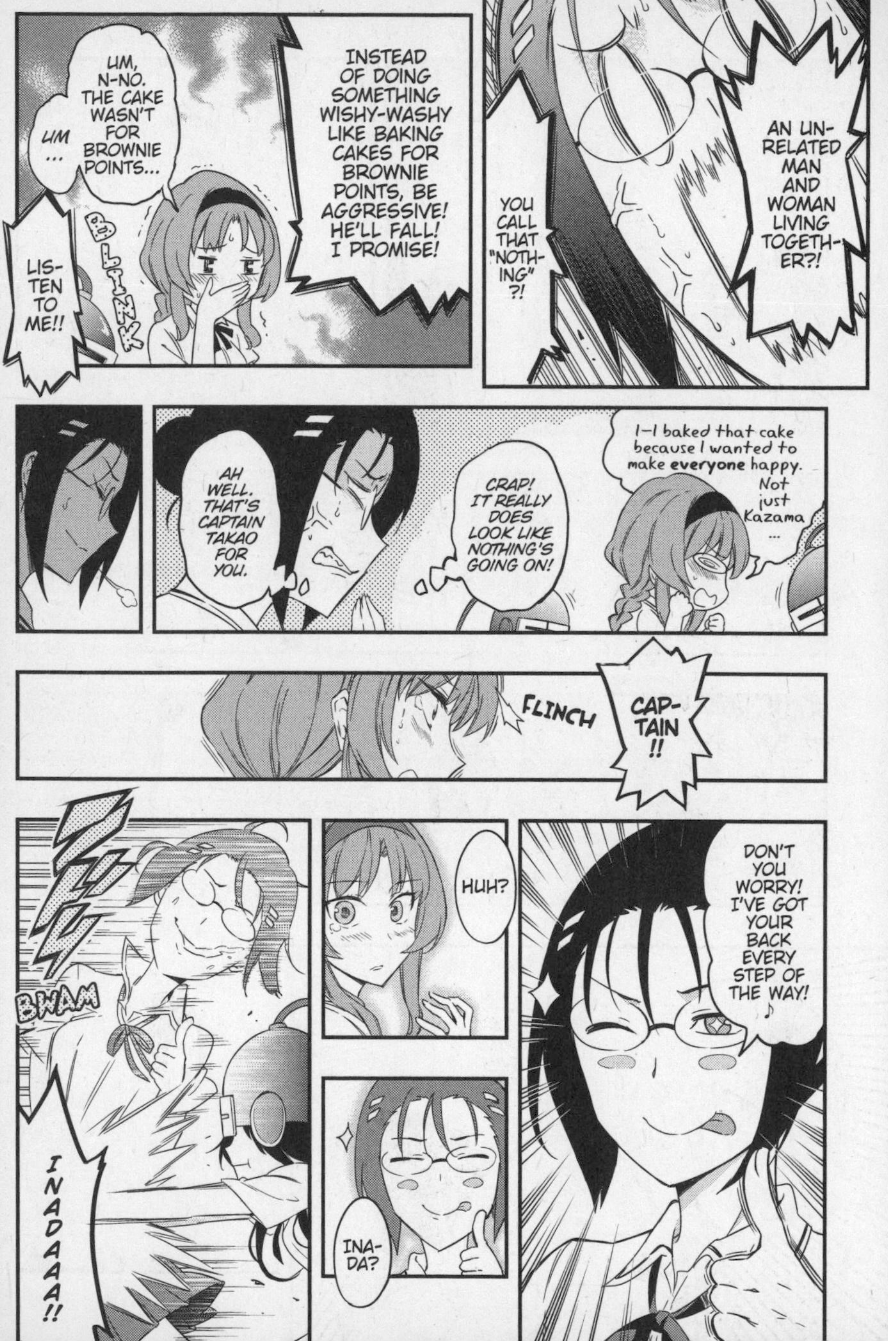
AN UN-RELATED MAN AND WOMAN LIVING TOGETH-ER?!
YOU CALL THAT "NOTH-ING"?!
INSTEAD OF DOING SOMETHING WISHY-WASHY LIKE BAKING CAKES FOR BROWNIE POINTS, BE AGGRESSIVE! HE'LL FALL! I PROMISE!
UM, N-NO. THE CAKE WASN'T FOR BROWNIE POINTS...
UM ...
BLINK
LIS-TEN TO ME!!
I-I baked that cake because I wanted to make **everyone** happy. Not just Kazama ...
CRAP! IT REALLY DOES LOOK LIKE NOTHING'S GOING ON!
AH WELL. THAT'S CAPTAIN TAKAO FOR YOU.
CAP-TAIN !!
FLINCH
DON'T YOU WORRY! I'VE GOT YOUR BACK EVERY STEP OF THE WAY! ♪
HUH?
INA-DA?
BWAM
INADAAAA!!

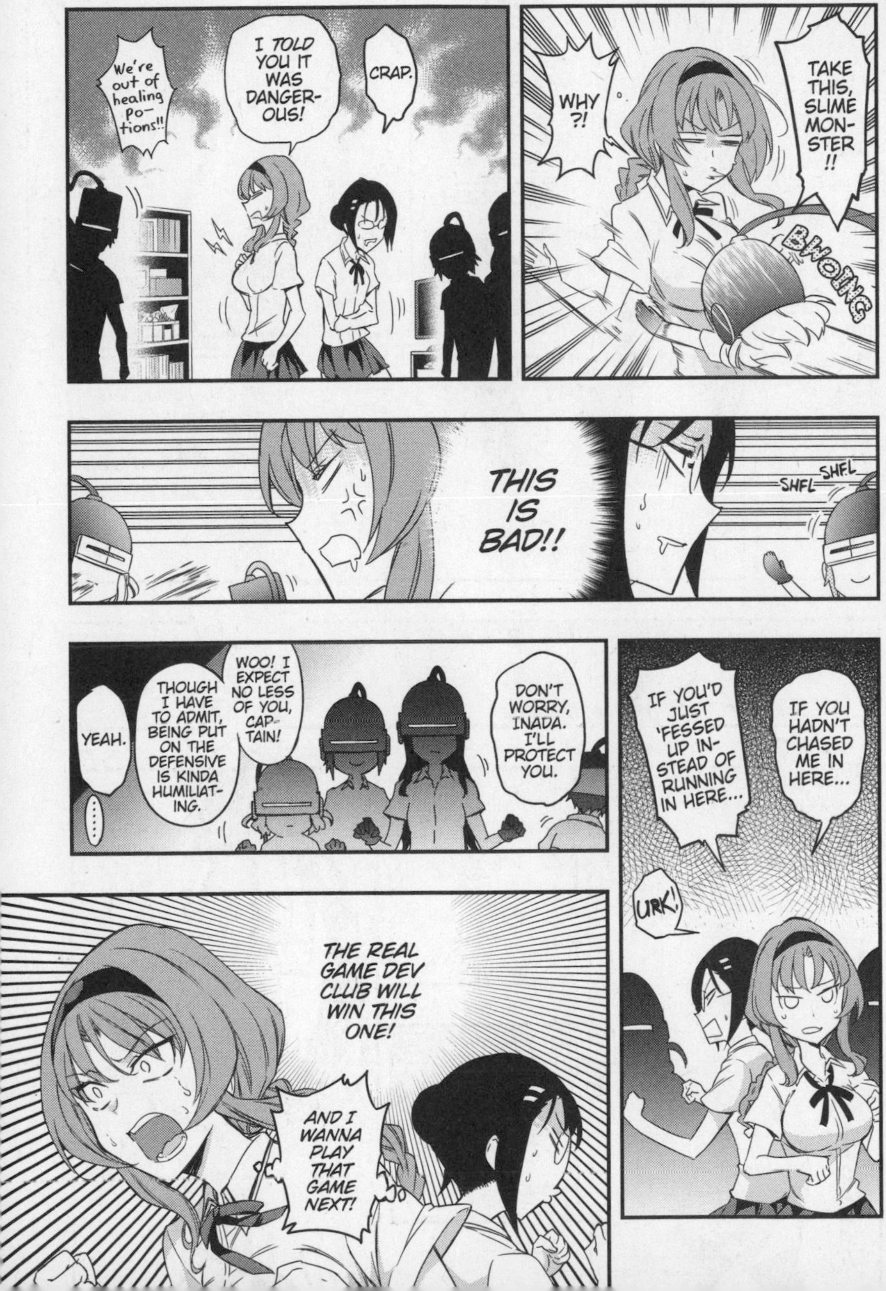
TAKE THIS, SLIME MONSTER!!
WHY?!
BWOING
CRAP.
I TOLD YOU IT WAS DANGEROUS!
We're out of healing potions!!
SHFL
SHFL
THIS IS BAD!!
IF YOU HADN'T CHASED ME IN HERE...
IF YOU'D JUST 'FESSED UP INSTEAD OF RUNNING IN HERE...
URK!
DON'T WORRY, INADA. I'LL PROTECT YOU.
WOO! I EXPECT NO LESS OF YOU, CAPTAIN!
THOUGH I HAVE TO ADMIT, BEING PUT ON THE DEFENSIVE IS KINDA HUMILIATING.
YEAH.
......
THE REAL GAME DEV CLUB WILL WIN THIS ONE!
AND I WANNA PLAY THAT GAME NEXT!

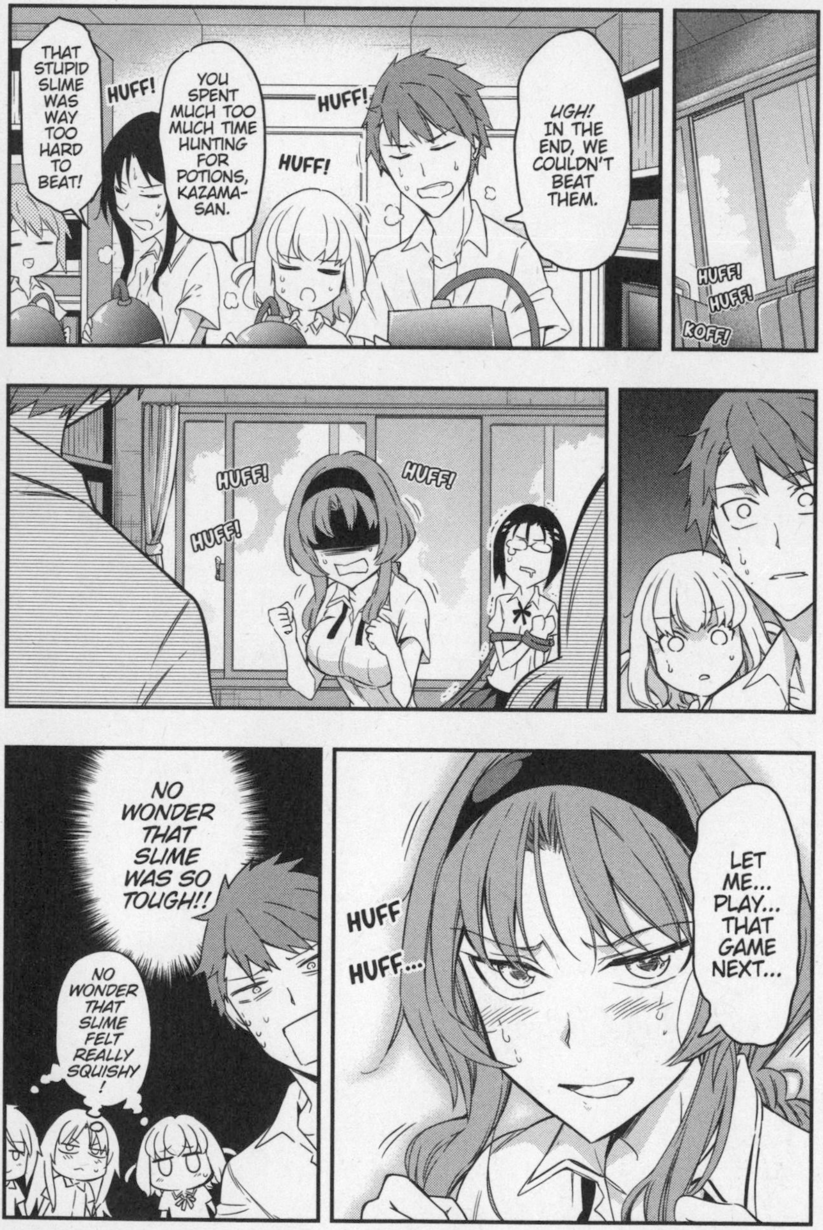
HUFF!
HUFF!
KOFF!
UGH! IN THE END, WE COULDN'T BEAT THEM.
HUFF!
HUFF!
YOU SPENT MUCH TOO MUCH TIME HUNTING FOR POTIONS, KAZAMA-SAN.
HUFF!
THAT STUPID SLIME WAS WAY TOO HARD TO BEAT!
HUFF!
HUFF!
HUFF!
LET ME... PLAY... THAT GAME NEXT...
HUFF
HUFF...
NO WONDER THAT SLIME WAS SO TOUGH!!
NO WONDER THAT SLIME FELT REALLY SQUISHY!

GU-GU-GULP!

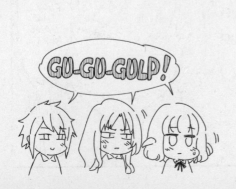

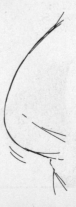

D-FRAGMENTS ディーフラグメンツ!

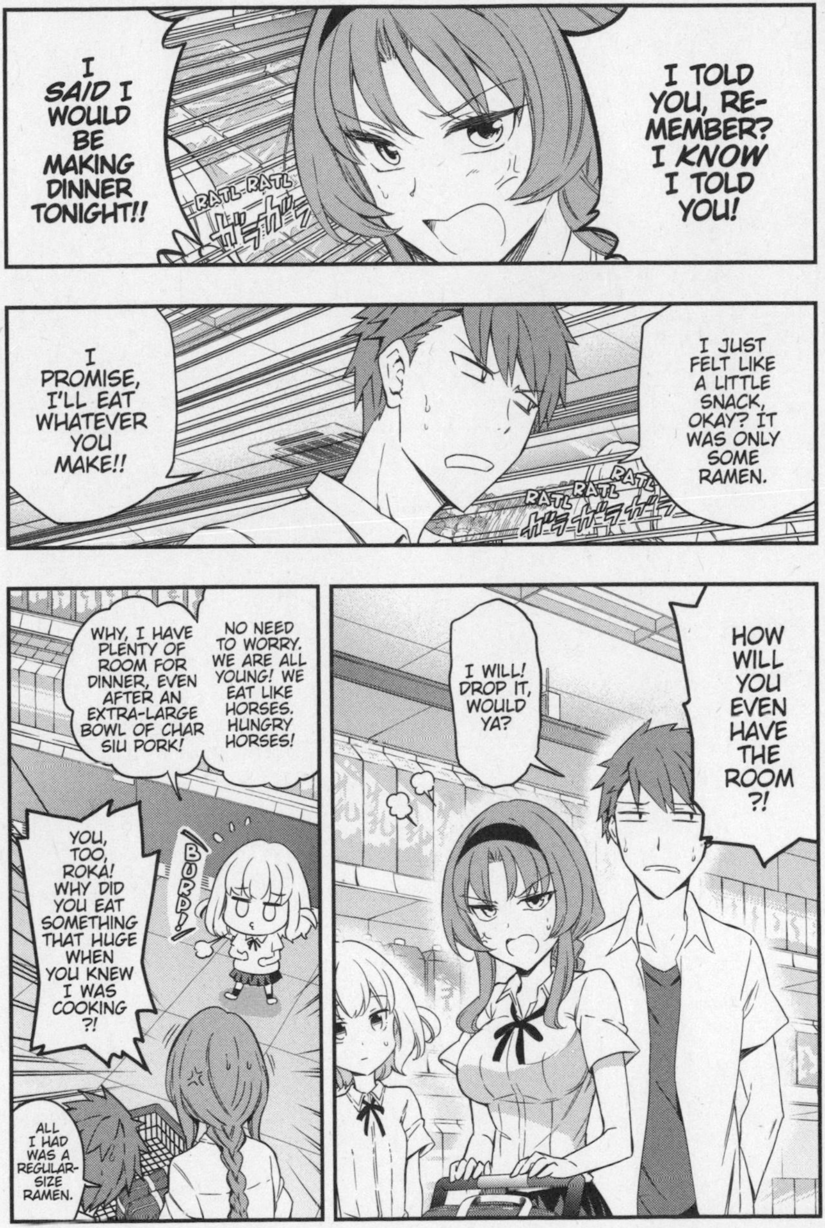
I TOLD YOU, RE-MEMBER? I *KNOW* I TOLD YOU!
I *SAID* I WOULD BE MAKING DINNER TONIGHT!!
RATL RATL
I JUST FELT LIKE A LITTLE SNACK, OKAY? IT WAS ONLY SOME RAMEN.
RATL RATL RATL
I PROMISE, I'LL EAT WHATEVER YOU MAKE!!
HOW WILL YOU EVEN HAVE THE ROOM?!
I WILL! DROP IT, WOULD YA?
NO NEED TO WORRY. WE ARE ALL YOUNG! WE EAT LIKE HORSES. HUNGRY HORSES!
WHY, I HAVE PLENTY OF ROOM FOR DINNER, EVEN AFTER AN EXTRA-LARGE BOWL OF CHAR SIU PORK!
BURP!
YOU, TOO, ROKA! WHY DID YOU EAT SOMETHING THAT HUGE WHEN YOU KNEW I WAS COOKING?!
ALL I HAD WAS A REGULAR-SIZE RAMEN.

Chapter 105: I'd Like Extra Meat

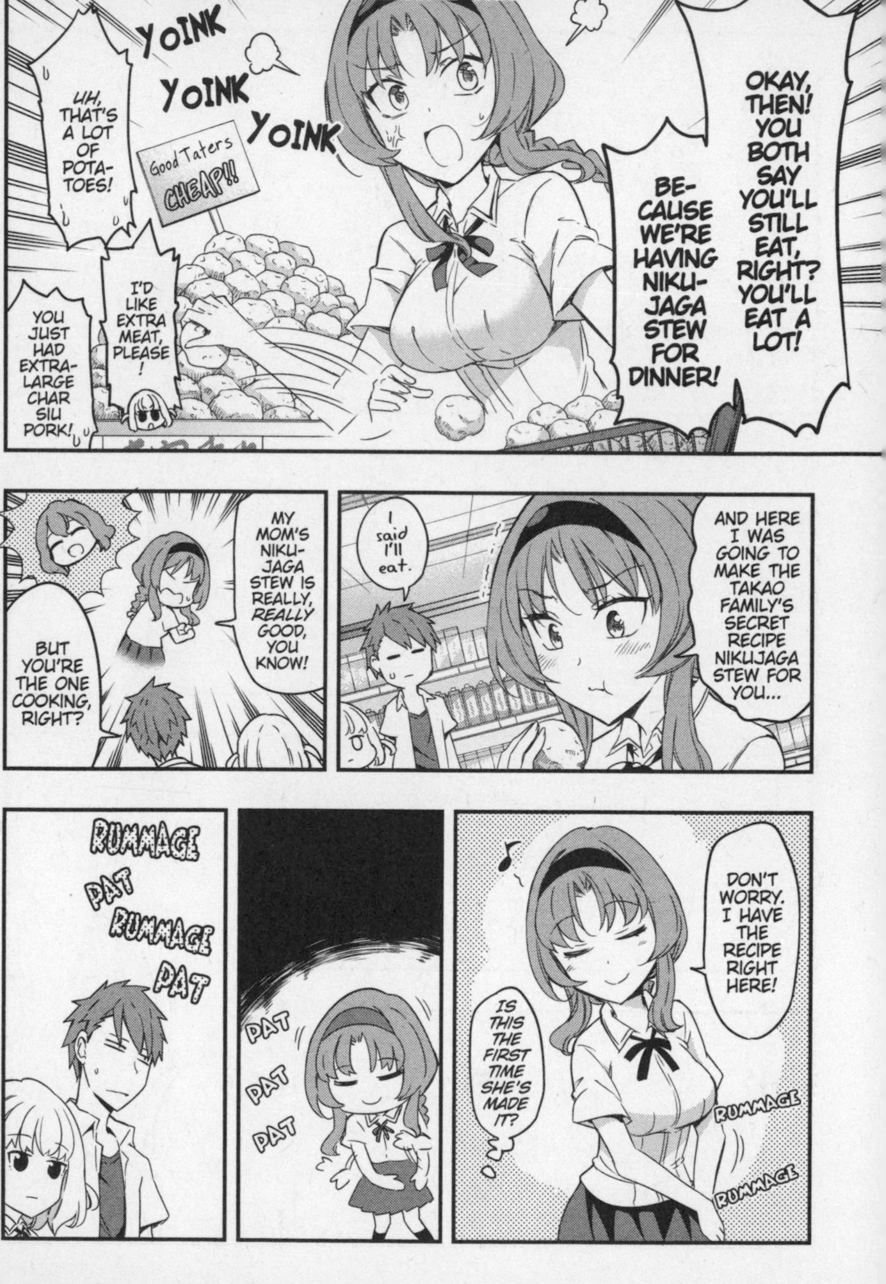
OKAY, THEN! YOU BOTH SAY YOU'LL STILL EAT, RIGHT? YOU'LL EAT A LOT!
BE-CAUSE WE'RE HAVING NIKU-JAGA STEW FOR DINNER!
YOINK
YOINK
YOINK
Good Taters CHEAP!!
UH, THAT'S A LOT OF POTA-TOES!
I'D LIKE EXTRA MEAT, PLEASE!
YOU JUST HAD EXTRA-LARGE CHAR SIU PORK!
AND HERE I WAS GOING TO MAKE THE TAKAO FAMILY'S SECRET RECIPE NIKUJAGA STEW FOR YOU...
I said I'll eat.
MY MOM'S NIKU-JAGA STEW IS REALLY, REALLY GOOD, YOU KNOW!
BUT YOU'RE THE ONE COOKING, RIGHT?
DON'T WORRY. I HAVE THE RECIPE RIGHT HERE!
IS THIS THE FIRST TIME SHE'S MADE IT?
RUMMAGE
RUMMAGE
PAT
PAT
PAT
RUMMAGE
PAT
RUMMAGE
PAT

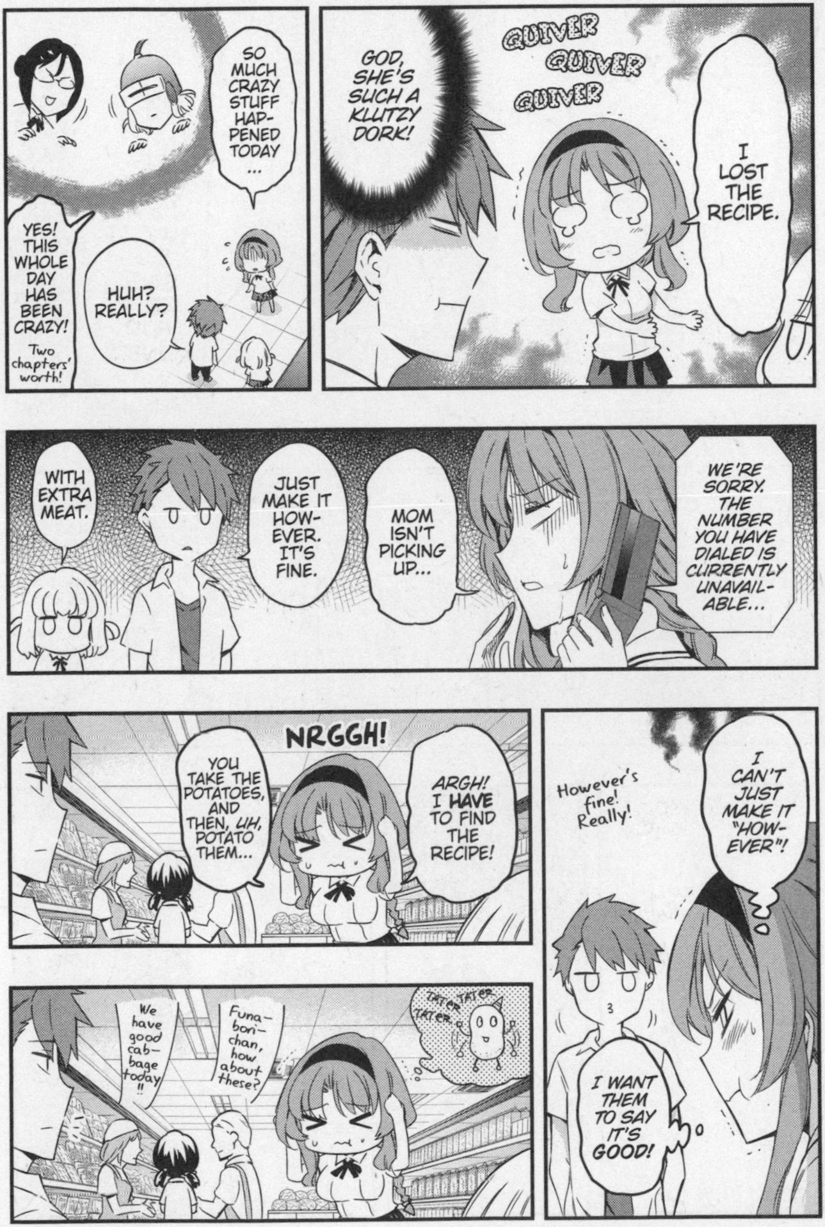
QUIVER QUIVER QUIVER
I LOST THE RECIPE.
GOD, SHE'S SUCH A KLUTZY DORK!
SO MUCH CRAZY STUFF HAP-PENED TODAY...
HUH? REALLY?
YES! THIS WHOLE DAY HAS BEEN CRAZY!
Two chapters' worth!
WE'RE SORRY. THE NUMBER YOU HAVE DIALED IS CURRENTLY UNAVAIL-ABLE...
MOM ISN'T PICKING UP...
JUST MAKE IT HOW-EVER. IT'S FINE.
WITH EXTRA MEAT.
I CAN'T JUST MAKE IT "HOW-EVER"!
However's fine! Really!
I WANT THEM TO SAY IT'S GOOD!
NRGGH!
ARGH! I HAVE TO FIND THE RECIPE!
YOU TAKE THE POTATOES, AND THEN, UH, POTATO THEM...
TATER TATER TATER
Funa-bori-chan, how about these?
We have good cab-bage today!!

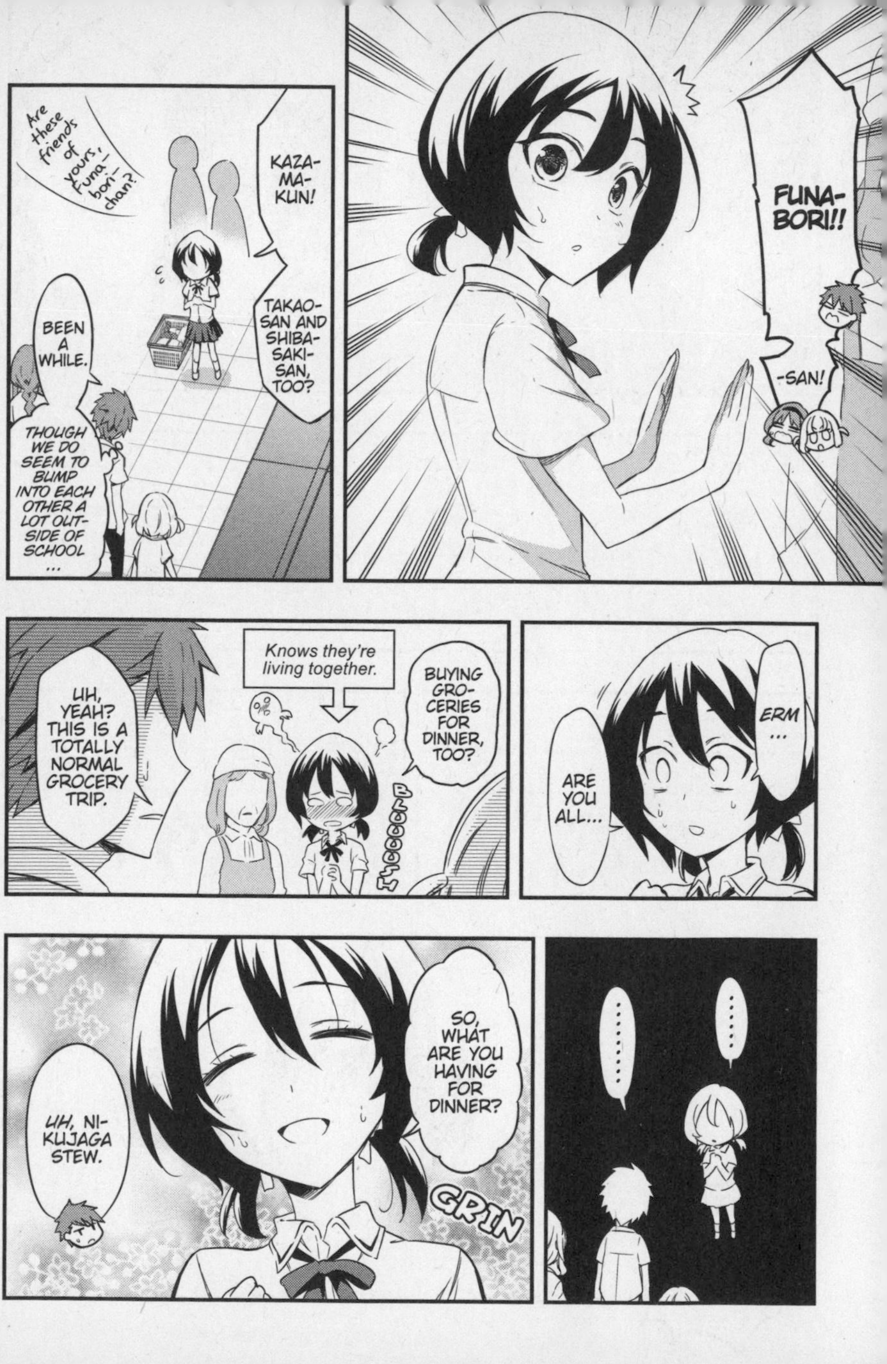
FUNA-BORI!!
-SAN!
KAZAMA-KUN!
TAKAO-SAN AND SHIBA-SAKI-SAN, TOO?
Are these friends of yours, Funa-bori-chan?
BEEN A WHILE.
THOUGH WE DO SEEM TO BUMP INTO EACH OTHER A LOT OUTSIDE OF SCHOOL...
ERM...
ARE YOU ALL...
BUYING GROCERIES FOR DINNER, TOO?
BLOOOOSH
Knows they're living together.
UH, YEAH? THIS IS A TOTALLY NORMAL GROCERY TRIP.
......
......
SO, WHAT ARE YOU HAVING FOR DINNER?
GRIN
UH, NI-KUJAGA STEW.

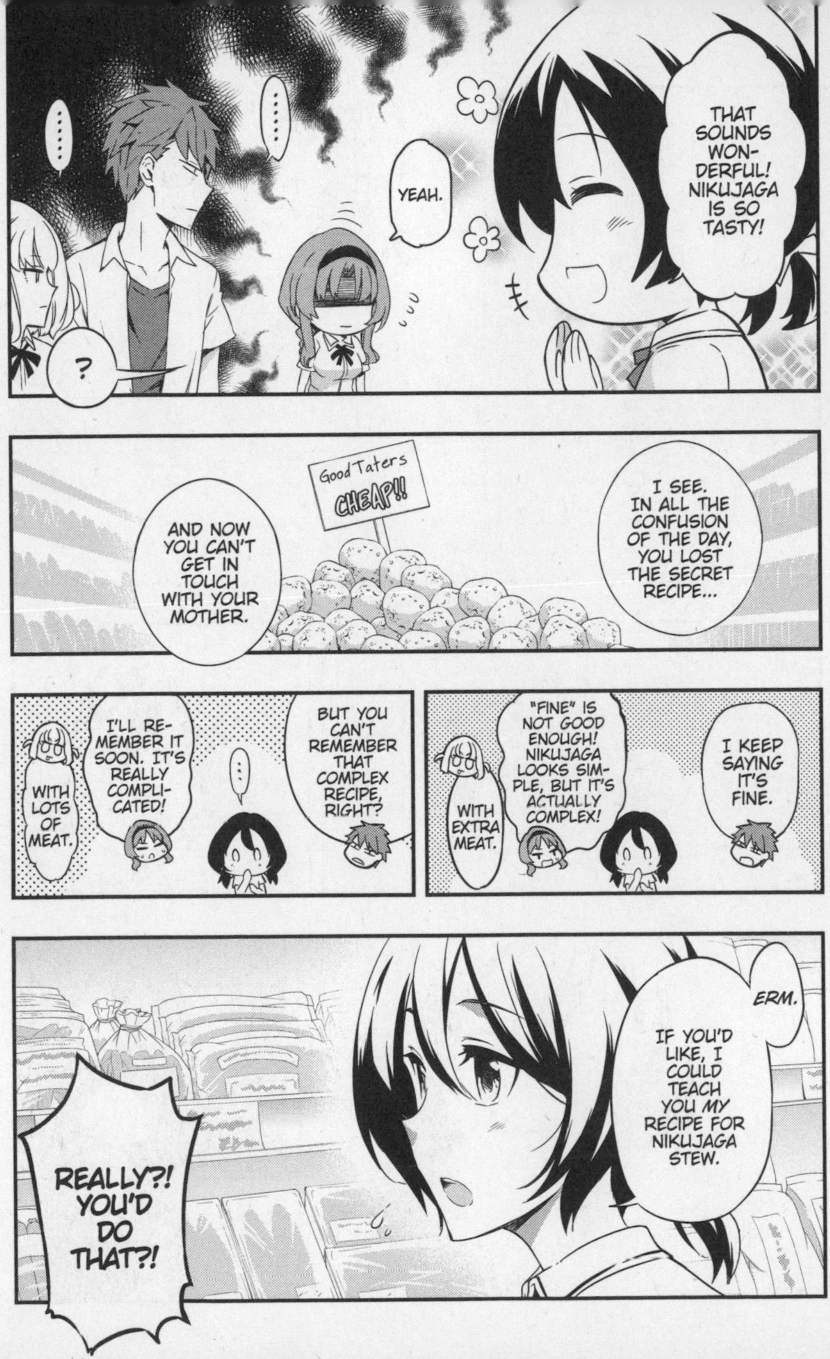
THAT SOUNDS WON-DERFUL! NIKUJAGA IS SO TASTY!
YEAH.
......
......
?
I SEE. IN ALL THE CONFUSION OF THE DAY, YOU LOST THE SECRET RECIPE...
Good Taters
CHEAP!!
AND NOW YOU CAN'T GET IN TOUCH WITH YOUR MOTHER.
I KEEP SAYING IT'S FINE.
"FINE" IS NOT GOOD ENOUGH! NIKUJAGA LOOKS SIM-PLE, BUT IT'S ACTUALLY COMPLEX!
WITH EXTRA MEAT.
BUT YOU CAN'T REMEMBER THAT COMPLEX RECIPE, RIGHT?
...
I'LL RE-MEMBER IT SOON. IT'S REALLY COMPLI-CATED!
WITH LOTS OF MEAT.
ERM.
IF YOU'D LIKE, I COULD TEACH YOU MY RECIPE FOR NIKUJAGA STEW.
REALLY?! YOU'D DO THAT?!

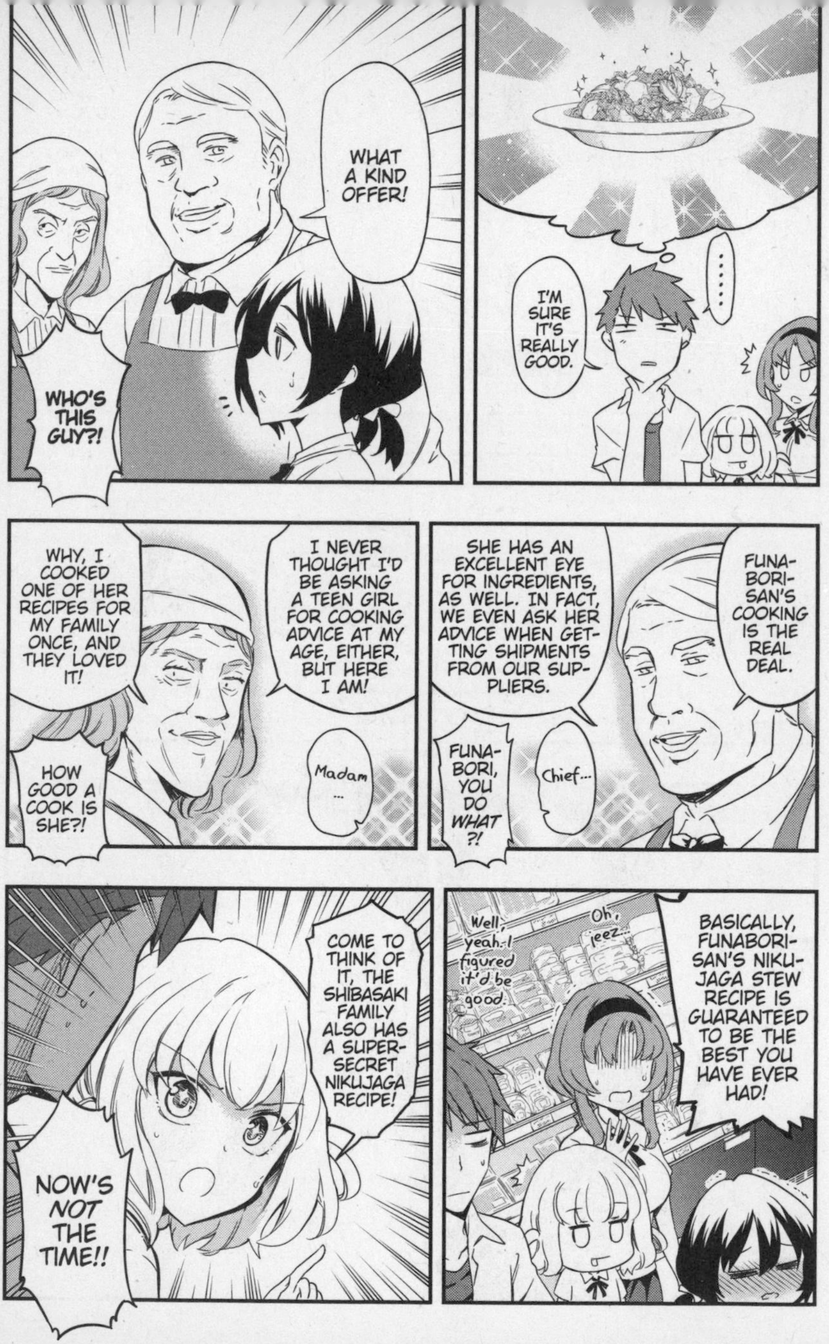
......
I'M SURE IT'S REALLY GOOD.
WHAT A KIND OFFER!
WHO'S THIS GUY?!
FUNA-BORI-SAN'S COOKING IS THE REAL DEAL.
SHE HAS AN EXCELLENT EYE FOR INGREDIENTS, AS WELL. IN FACT, WE EVEN ASK HER ADVICE WHEN GET-TING SHIPMENTS FROM OUR SUP-PLIERS.
Chief...
FUNA-BORI, YOU DO *WHAT* ?!
I NEVER THOUGHT I'D BE ASKING A TEEN GIRL FOR COOKING ADVICE AT MY AGE, EITHER, BUT HERE I AM!
WHY, I COOKED ONE OF HER RECIPES FOR MY FAMILY ONCE, AND THEY LOVED IT!
Madam ...
HOW GOOD A COOK IS SHE?!
BASICALLY, FUNABORI-SAN'S NIKU-JAGA STEW RECIPE IS GUARANTEED TO BE THE BEST YOU HAVE EVER HAD!
Oh, jeez...
Well, yeah. I figured it'd be good.
COME TO THINK OF IT, THE SHIBASAKI FAMILY ALSO HAS A SUPER-SECRET NIKUJAGA RECIPE!
NOW'S *NOT* THE TIME!!

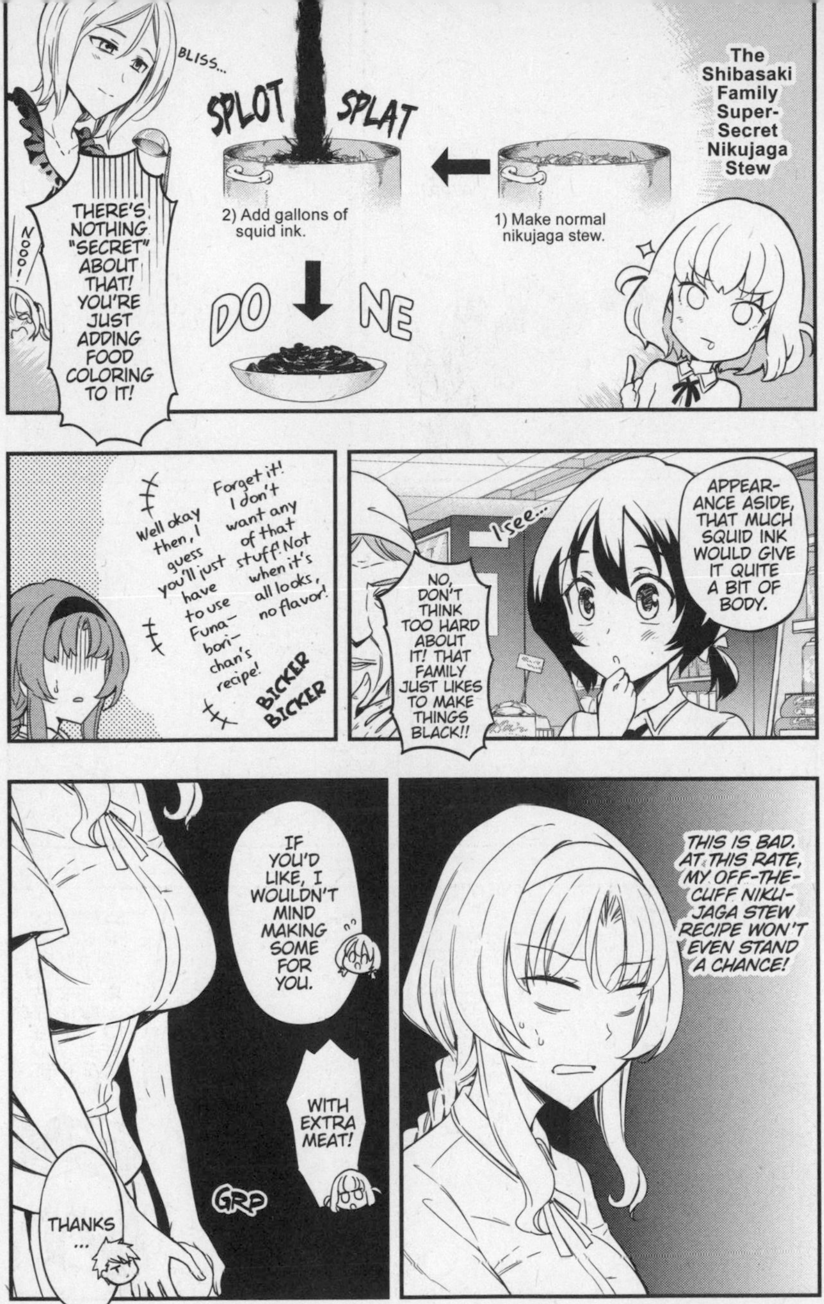
The Shibasaki Family Super-Secret Nikujaga Stew
1) Make normal nikujaga stew.
SPLAT
SPLOT
BLISS...
2) Add gallons of squid ink.
DO NE
THERE'S NOTHING "SECRET" ABOUT THAT! YOU'RE JUST ADDING FOOD COLORING TO IT!
Nooo!
APPEARANCE ASIDE, THAT MUCH SQUID INK WOULD GIVE IT QUITE A BIT OF BODY.
I see...
NO, DON'T THINK TOO HARD ABOUT IT! THAT FAMILY JUST LIKES TO MAKE THINGS BLACK!!
Forget it! I don't want any of that stuff! Not when it's all looks, no flavor!
Well okay then, I guess you'll just have to use Funabori-chan's recipe!
BICKER BICKER
THIS IS BAD. AT THIS RATE, MY OFF-THE-CUFF NIKUJAGA STEW RECIPE WON'T EVEN STAND A CHANCE!
IF YOU'D LIKE, I WOULDN'T MIND MAKING SOME FOR YOU.
WITH EXTRA MEAT!
GRP
THANKS ...

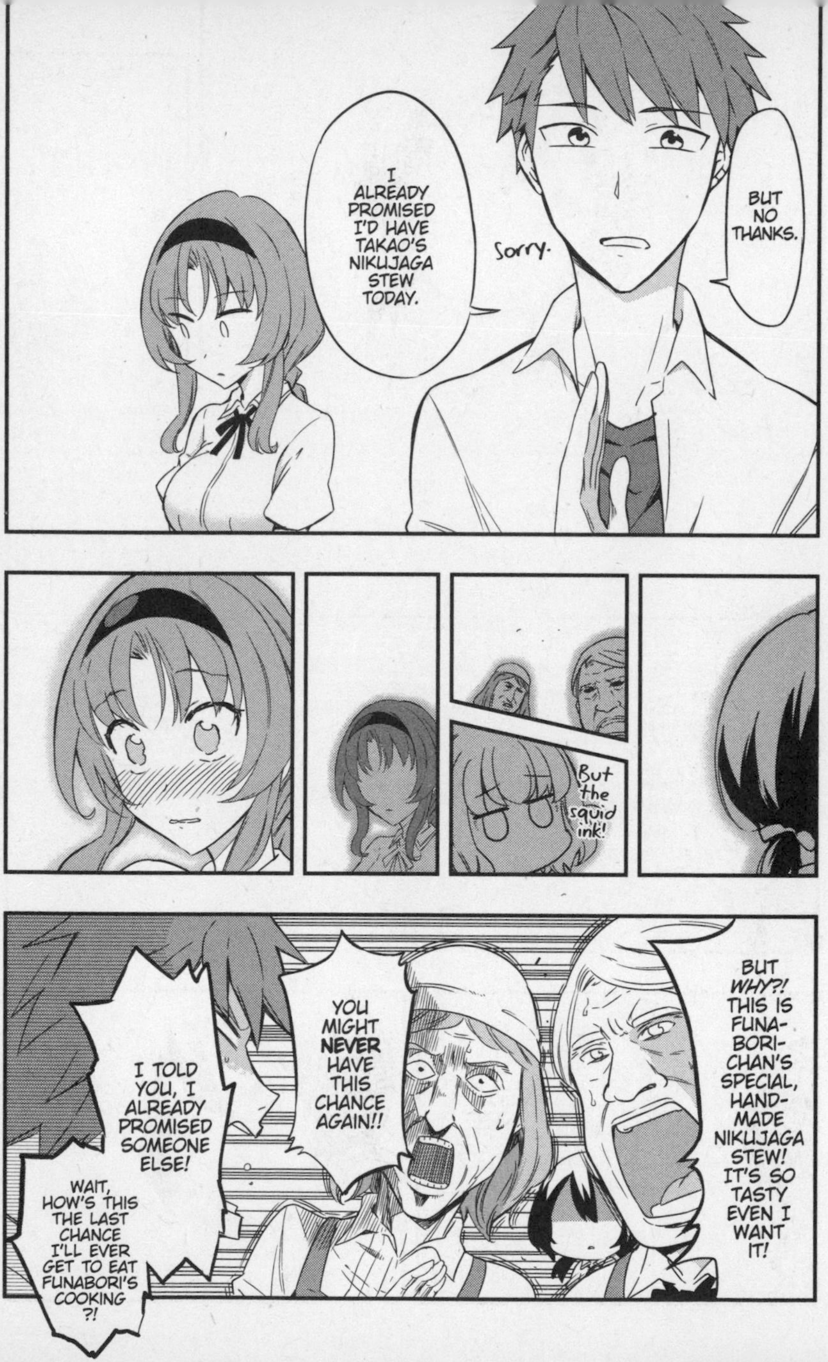
BUT NO THANKS.
Sorry.
I ALREADY PROMISED I'D HAVE TAKAO'S NIKUJAGA STEW TODAY.
But the squid ink!
BUT *WHY?!* THIS IS FUNABORI-CHAN'S SPECIAL, HAND-MADE NIKUJAGA STEW! IT'S SO TASTY EVEN I WANT IT!
YOU MIGHT **NEVER** HAVE THIS CHANCE AGAIN!!
I TOLD YOU, I ALREADY PROMISED SOMEONE ELSE!
WAIT, HOW'S THIS THE LAST CHANCE I'LL EVER GET TO EAT FUNABORI'S COOKING ?!

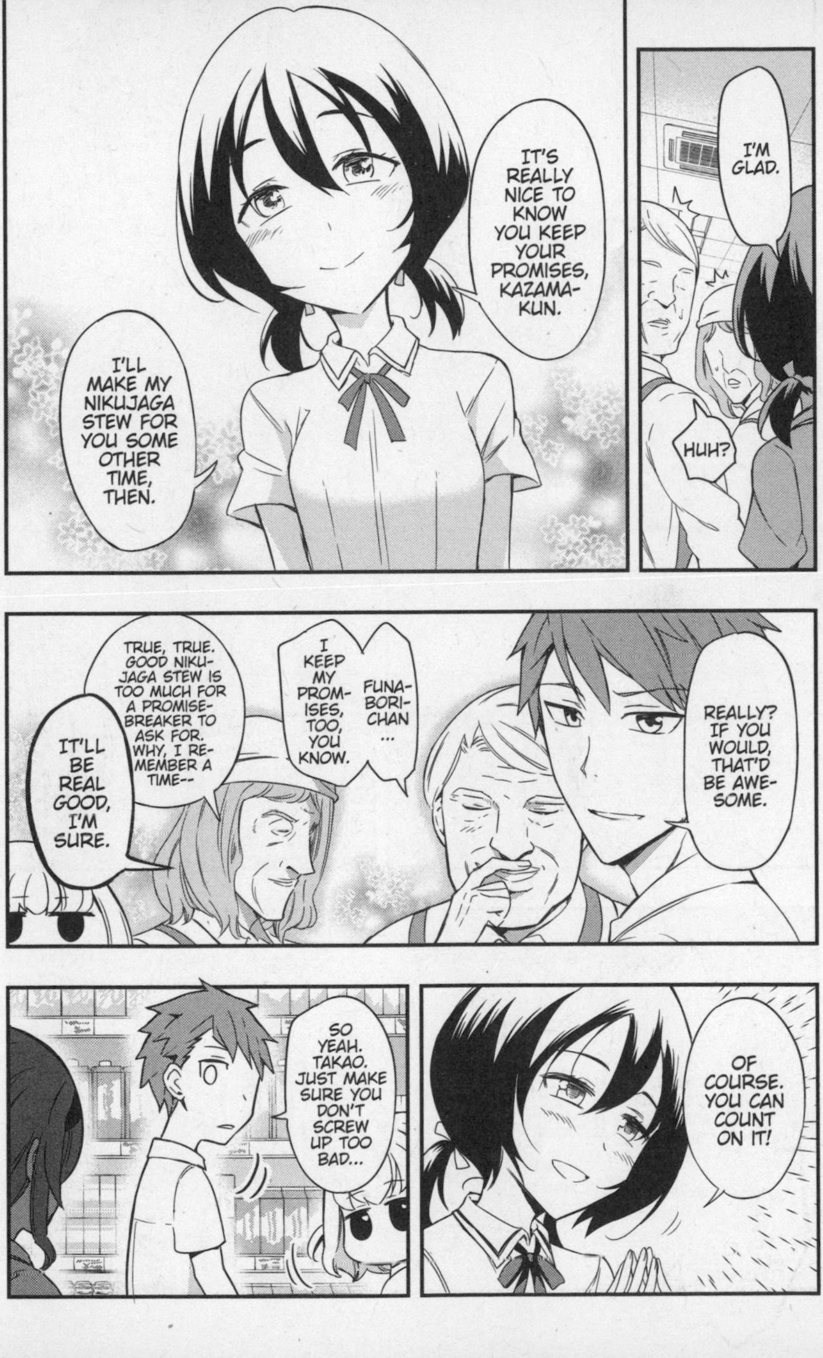
I'M GLAD.
HUH?
IT'S REALLY NICE TO KNOW YOU KEEP YOUR PROMISES, KAZAMA-KUN.
I'LL MAKE MY NIKUJAGA STEW FOR YOU SOME OTHER TIME, THEN.
REALLY? IF YOU WOULD, THAT'D BE AWE-SOME.
FUNA-BORI-CHAN...
I KEEP MY PROM-ISES, TOO, YOU KNOW.
TRUE, TRUE. GOOD NIKU-JAGA STEW IS TOO MUCH FOR A PROMISE-BREAKER TO ASK FOR. WHY, I RE-MEMBER A TIME--
IT'LL BE REAL GOOD, I'M SURE.
OF COURSE. YOU CAN COUNT ON IT!
SO YEAH. TAKAO. JUST MAKE SURE YOU DON'T SCREW UP TOO BAD...

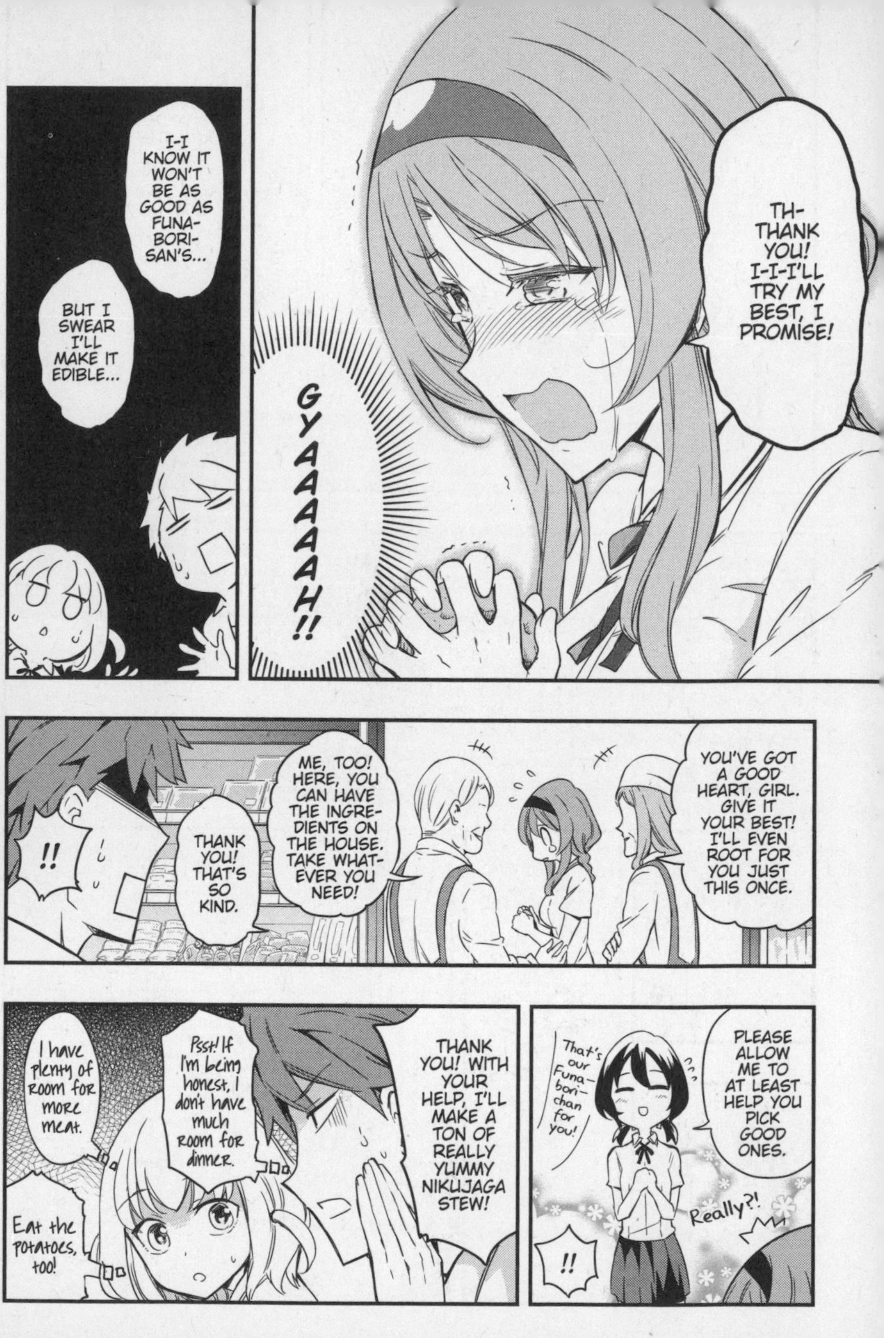
TH-THANK YOU! I-I-I'LL TRY MY BEST, I PROMISE!
GYAAAAAAH!!
I-I KNOW IT WON'T BE AS GOOD AS FUNABORI-SAN'S...
BUT I SWEAR I'LL MAKE IT EDIBLE...
YOU'VE GOT A GOOD HEART, GIRL. GIVE IT YOUR BEST! I'LL EVEN ROOT FOR YOU JUST THIS ONCE.
ME, TOO! HERE, YOU CAN HAVE THE INGREDIENTS ON THE HOUSE. TAKE WHATEVER YOU NEED!
THANK YOU! THAT'S SO KIND.
!!
PLEASE ALLOW ME TO AT LEAST HELP YOU PICK GOOD ONES.
That's our Funabori-chan for you!
Really?!
!!
THANK YOU! WITH YOUR HELP, I'LL MAKE A TON OF REALLY YUMMY NIKUJAGA STEW!
Psst! If I'm being honest, I don't have much room for dinner.
I have plenty of room for more meat.
Eat the potatoes, too!

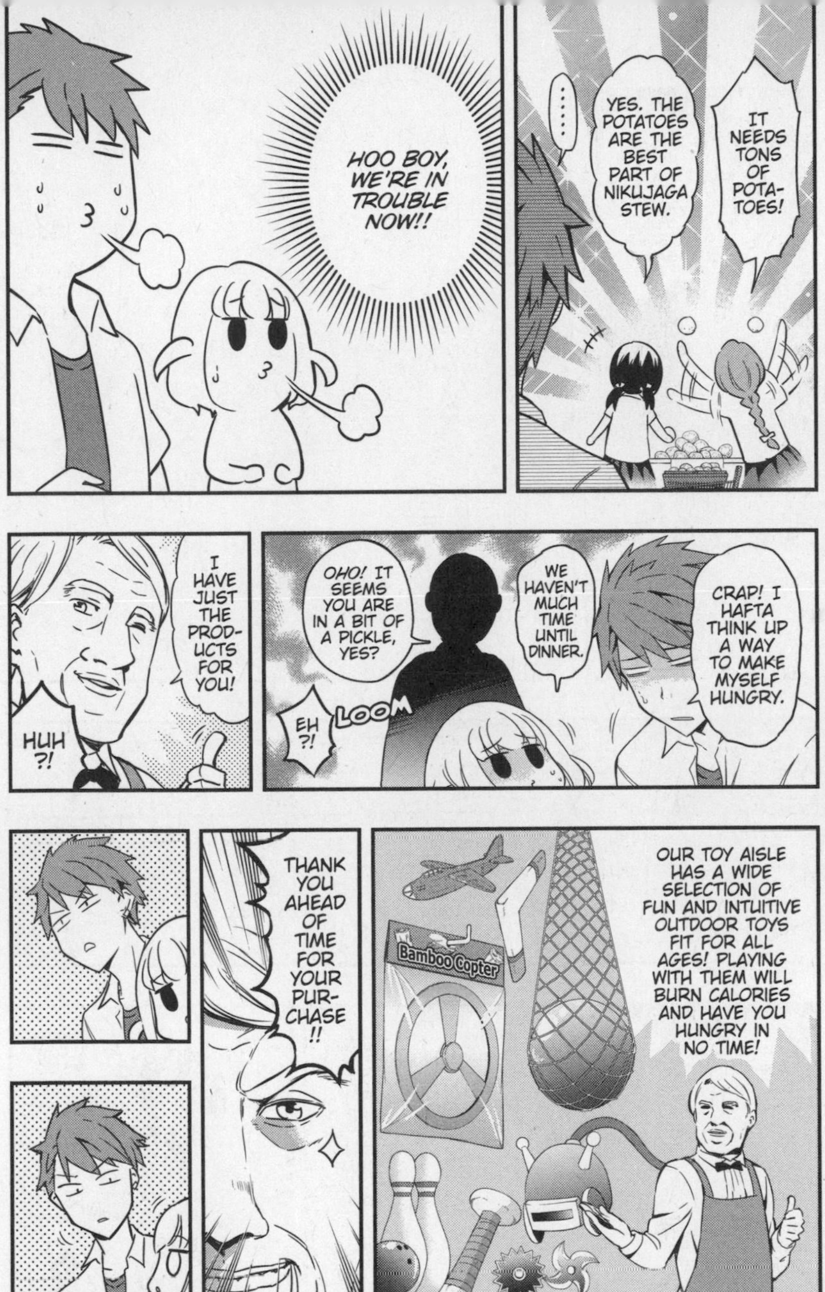
IT NEEDS TONS OF POTATOES!
YES. THE POTATOES ARE THE BEST PART OF NIKUJAGA STEW.
……
HOO BOY, WE'RE IN TROUBLE NOW!!
CRAP! I HAFTA THINK UP A WAY TO MAKE MYSELF HUNGRY.
WE HAVEN'T MUCH TIME UNTIL DINNER.
OHO! IT SEEMS YOU ARE IN A BIT OF A PICKLE, YES?
LOOM
EH?!
I HAVE JUST THE PRODUCTS FOR YOU!
HUH?!
OUR TOY AISLE HAS A WIDE SELECTION OF FUN AND INTUITIVE OUTDOOR TOYS FIT FOR ALL AGES! PLAYING WITH THEM WILL BURN CALORIES AND HAVE YOU HUNGRY IN NO TIME!
Bamboo Copter
THANK YOU AHEAD OF TIME FOR YOUR PURCHASE!!

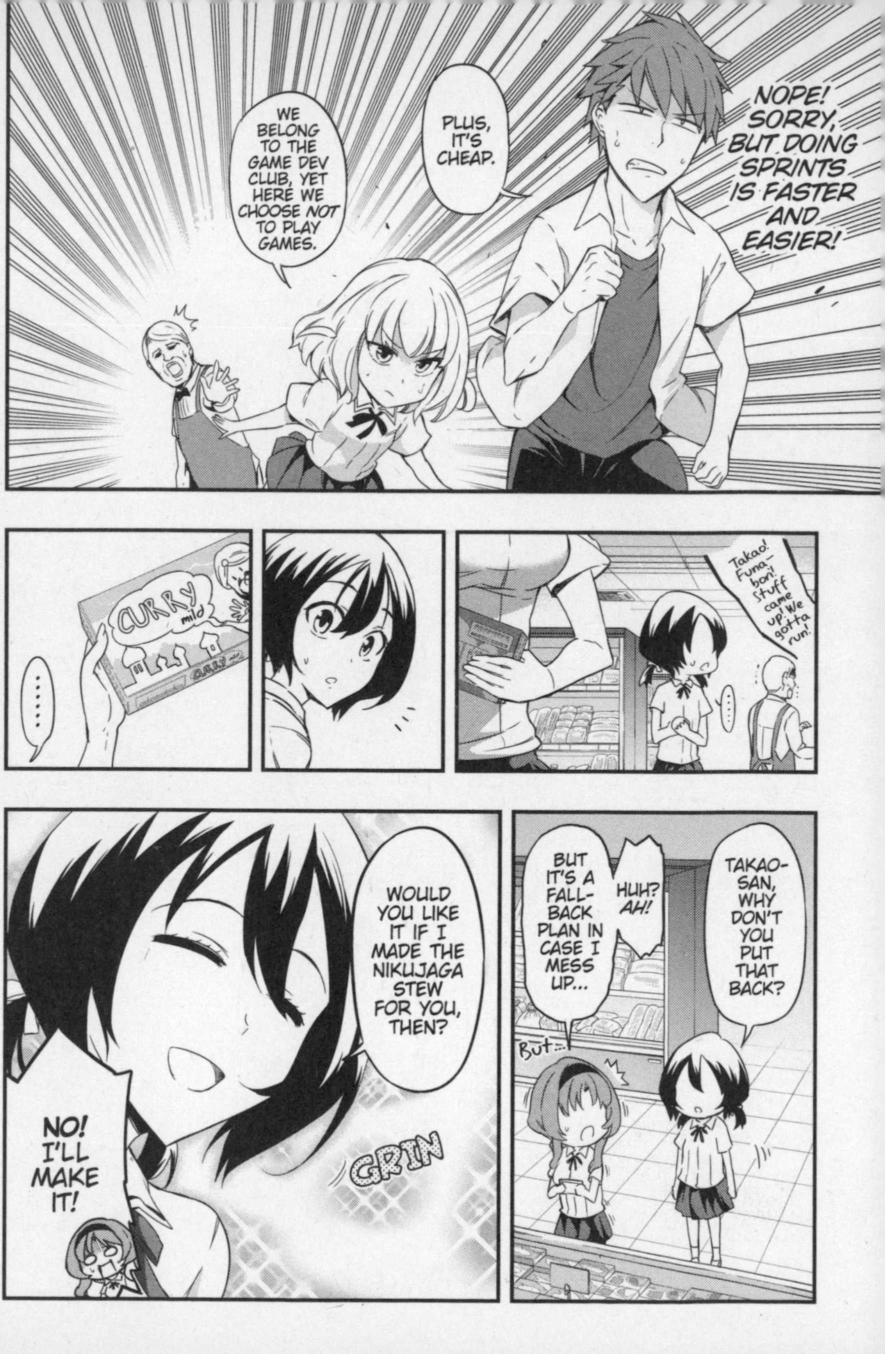
NOPE! SORRY, BUT DOING SPRINTS IS FASTER AND EASIER!
PLUS, IT'S CHEAP.
WE BELONG TO THE GAME DEV CLUB, YET HERE WE CHOOSE NOT TO PLAY GAMES.
Takao! Funa-bori! Stuff came up! We gotta run!
...
CURRY mild
CURRY
......
TAKAO-SAN, WHY DON'T YOU PUT THAT BACK?
HUH? AH!
BUT IT'S A FALL-BACK PLAN IN CASE I MESS UP...
But...
WOULD YOU LIKE IT IF I MADE THE NIKUJAGA STEW FOR YOU, THEN?
GRIN
NO! I'LL MAKE IT!

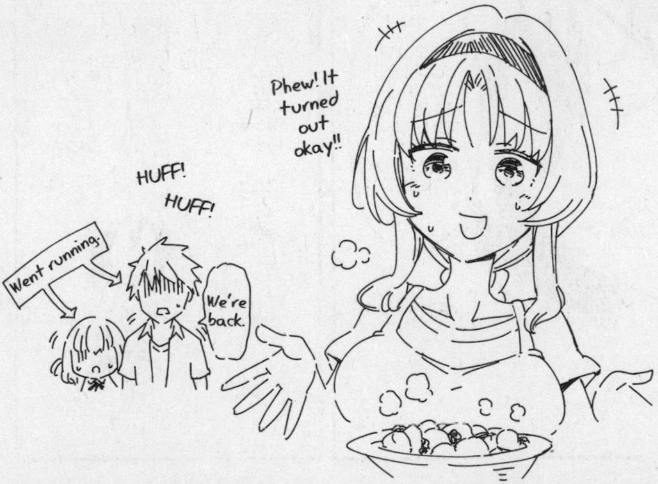
Phew! It turned out okay!!
HUFF!
HUFF!
We're back.
Went running.

D-FRAGMENTS

ディーふらぐ!

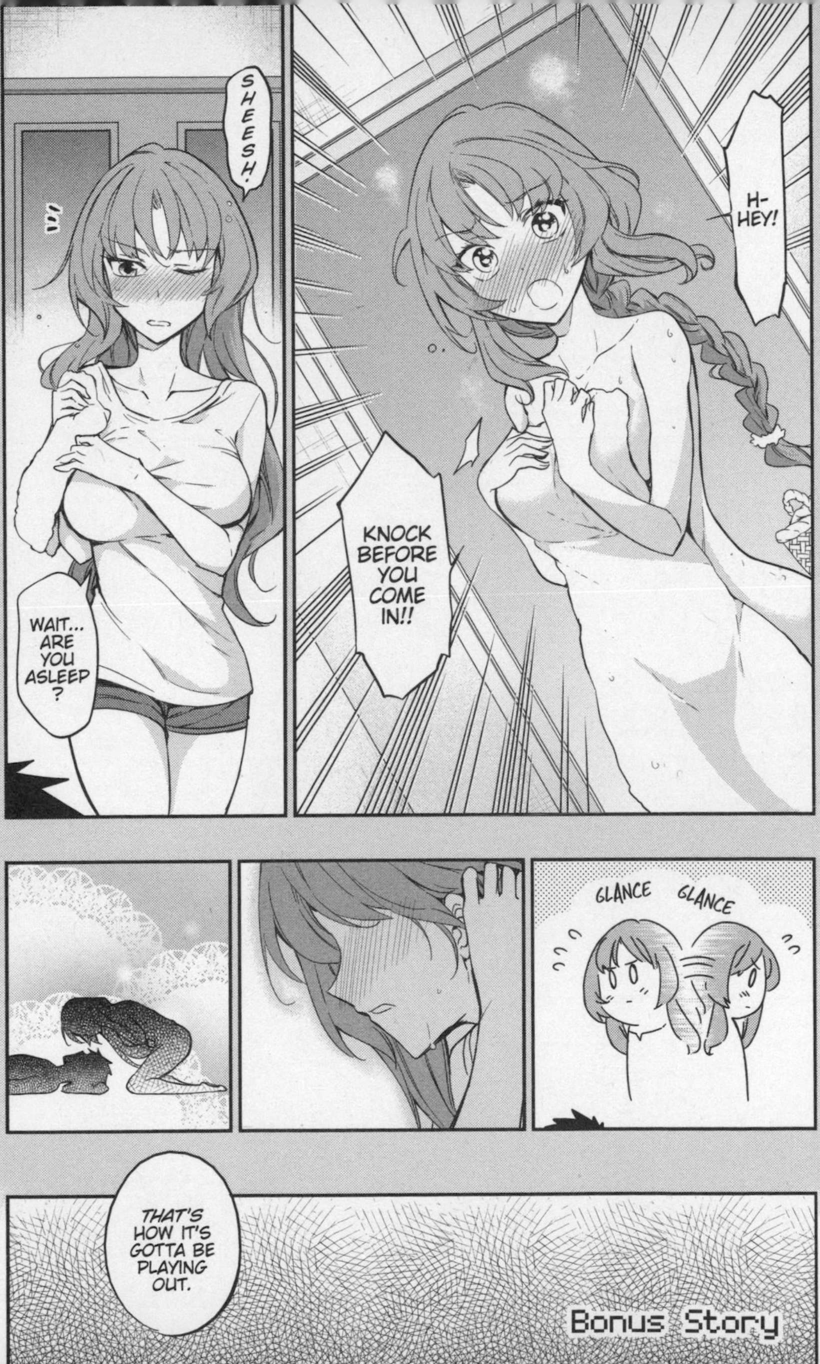
H-HEY!
KNOCK BEFORE YOU COME IN!!
SHEESH!
!!
WAIT... ARE YOU ASLEEP?
GLANCE
GLANCE
THAT'S HOW IT'S GOTTA BE PLAYING OUT.
Bonus Story

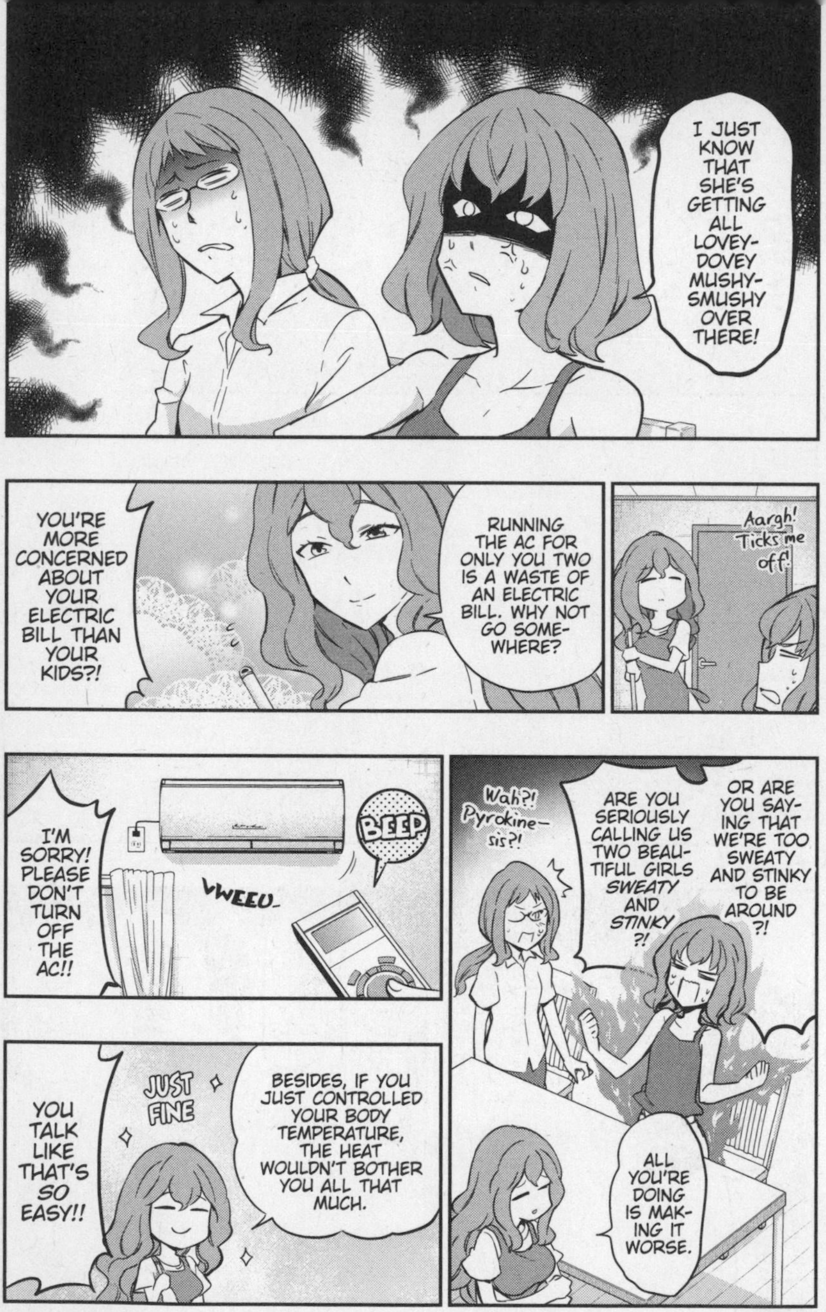
I JUST KNOW THAT SHE'S GETTING ALL LOVEY-DOVEY MUSHY-SMUSHY OVER THERE!
Aargh! Ticks me off!
RUNNING THE AC FOR ONLY YOU TWO IS A WASTE OF AN ELECTRIC BILL. WHY NOT GO SOME-WHERE?
YOU'RE MORE CONCERNED ABOUT YOUR ELECTRIC BILL THAN YOUR KIDS?!
OR ARE YOU SAY-ING THAT WE'RE TOO SWEATY AND STINKY TO BE AROUND ?!
ARE YOU SERIOUSLY CALLING US TWO BEAU-TIFUL GIRLS *SWEATY* AND *STINKY* ?!
Wah?! Pyrokine-sis?!
ALL YOU'RE DOING IS MAK-ING IT WORSE.
BEEP
VWEEU_
I'M SORRY! PLEASE DON'T TURN OFF THE AC!!
BESIDES, IF YOU JUST CONTROLLED YOUR BODY TEMPERATURE, THE HEAT WOULDN'T BOTHER YOU ALL THAT MUCH.
JUST FINE
YOU TALK LIKE THAT'S SO EASY!!

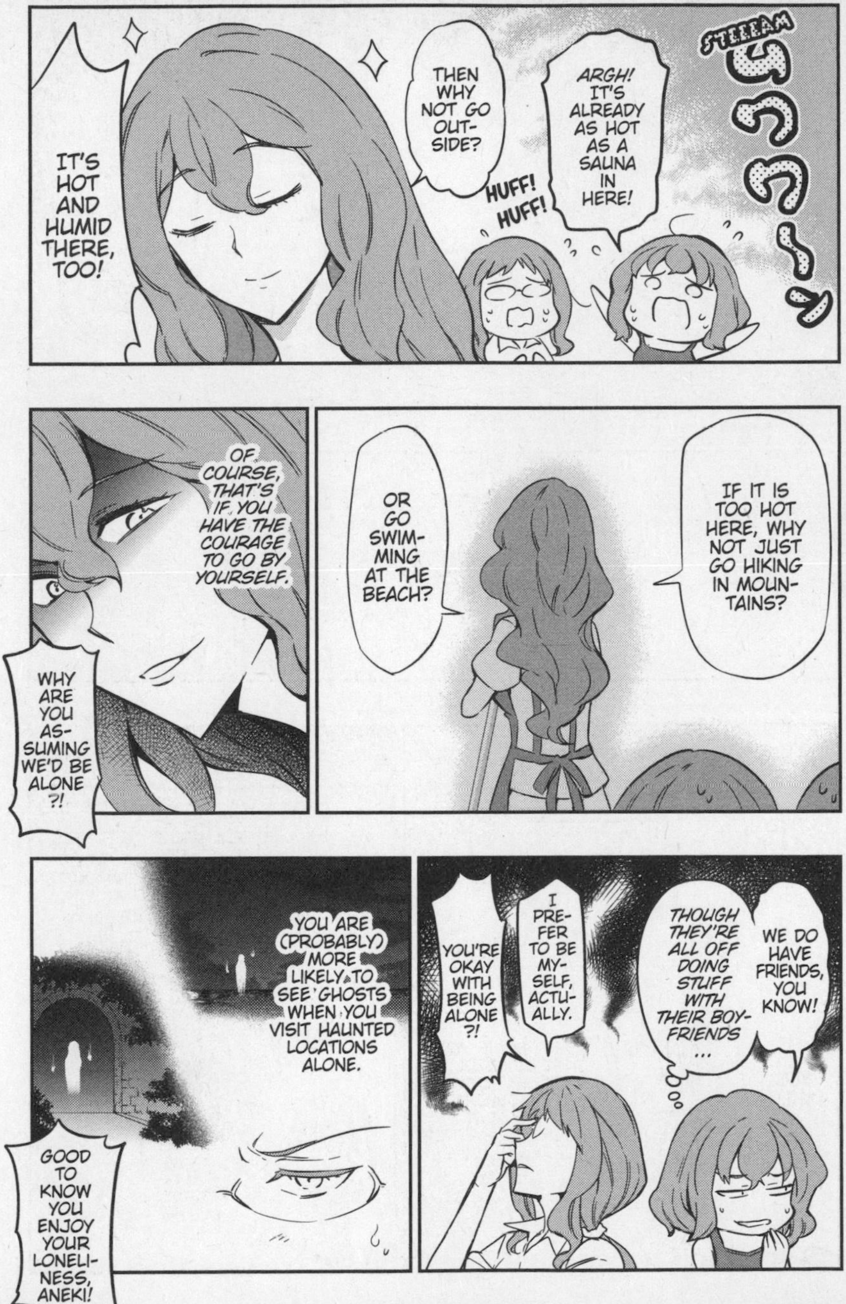
STEEEAM
ARGH! IT'S ALREADY AS HOT AS A SAUNA IN HERE!
HUFF! HUFF!
THEN WHY NOT GO OUTSIDE?
IT'S HOT AND HUMID THERE, TOO!
IF IT IS TOO HOT HERE, WHY NOT JUST GO HIKING IN MOUNTAINS?
OR GO SWIMMING AT THE BEACH?
OF COURSE, THAT'S IF YOU HAVE THE COURAGE TO GO BY YOURSELF.
WHY ARE YOU ASSUMING WE'D BE ALONE?!
WE DO HAVE FRIENDS, YOU KNOW!
THOUGH THEY'RE ALL OFF DOING STUFF WITH THEIR BOYFRIENDS...
I PREFER TO BE MYSELF, ACTUALLY.
YOU'RE OKAY WITH BEING ALONE?!
YOU ARE (PROBABLY) MORE LIKELY TO SEE GHOSTS WHEN YOU VISIT HAUNTED LOCATIONS ALONE.
GOOD TO KNOW YOU ENJOY YOUR LONELINESS, ANEKI!

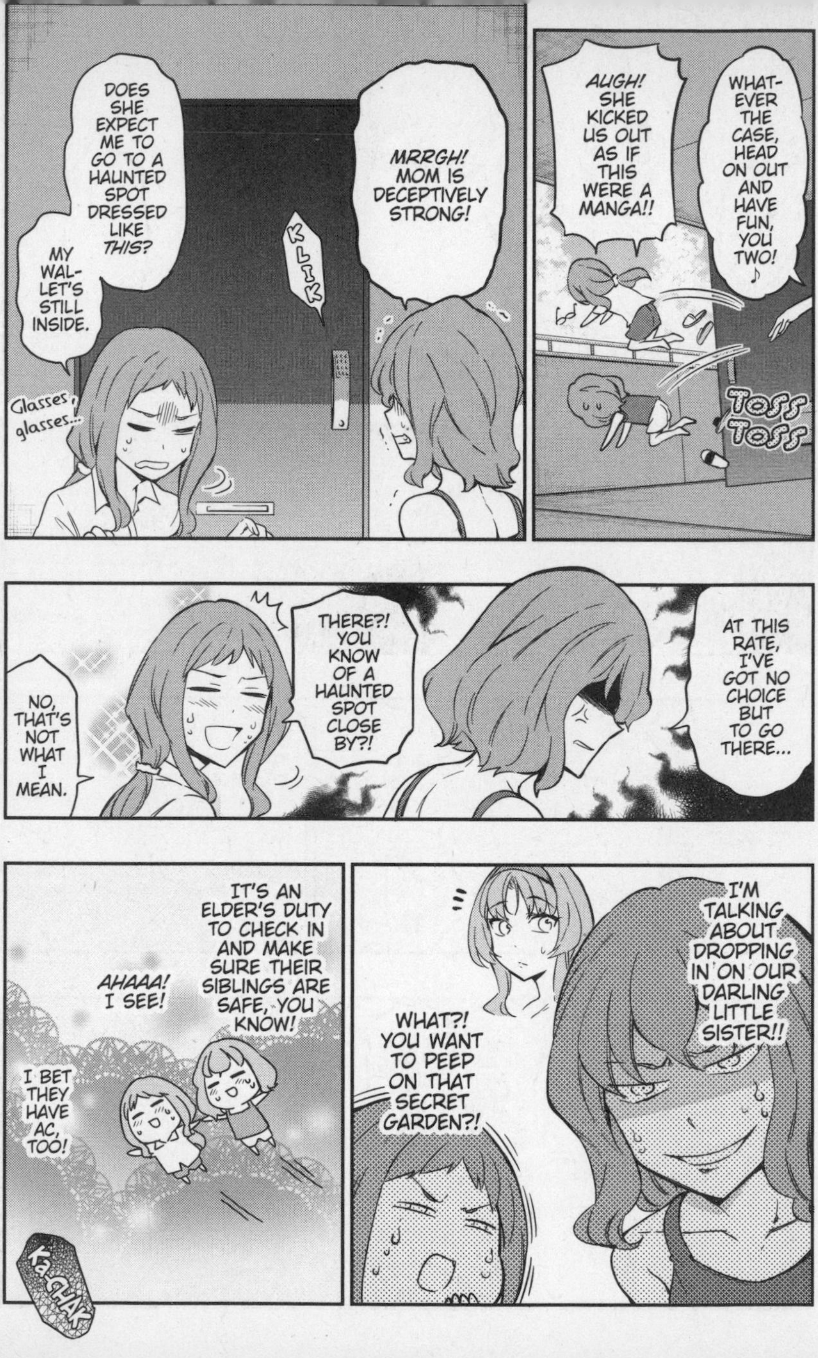
WHAT-EVER THE CASE, HEAD ON OUT AND HAVE FUN, YOU TWO! ♪
AUGH! SHE KICKED US OUT AS IF THIS WERE A MANGA!!
TOSS TOSS
MRRGH! MOM IS DECEPTIVELY STRONG!
KLIK
DOES SHE EXPECT ME TO GO TO A HAUNTED SPOT DRESSED LIKE THIS?
MY WAL-LET'S STILL INSIDE.
Glasses, glasses...
AT THIS RATE, I'VE GOT NO CHOICE BUT TO GO THERE...
THERE?! YOU KNOW OF A HAUNTED SPOT CLOSE BY?!
NO, THAT'S NOT WHAT I MEAN.
I'M TALKING ABOUT DROPPING IN ON OUR DARLING LITTLE SISTER!!
WHAT?! YOU WANT TO PEEP ON THAT SECRET GARDEN?!
IT'S AN ELDER'S DUTY TO CHECK IN AND MAKE SURE THEIR SIBLINGS ARE SAFE, YOU KNOW!
AHAAA! I SEE!
I BET THEY HAVE AC, TOO!
Ka-CHAK

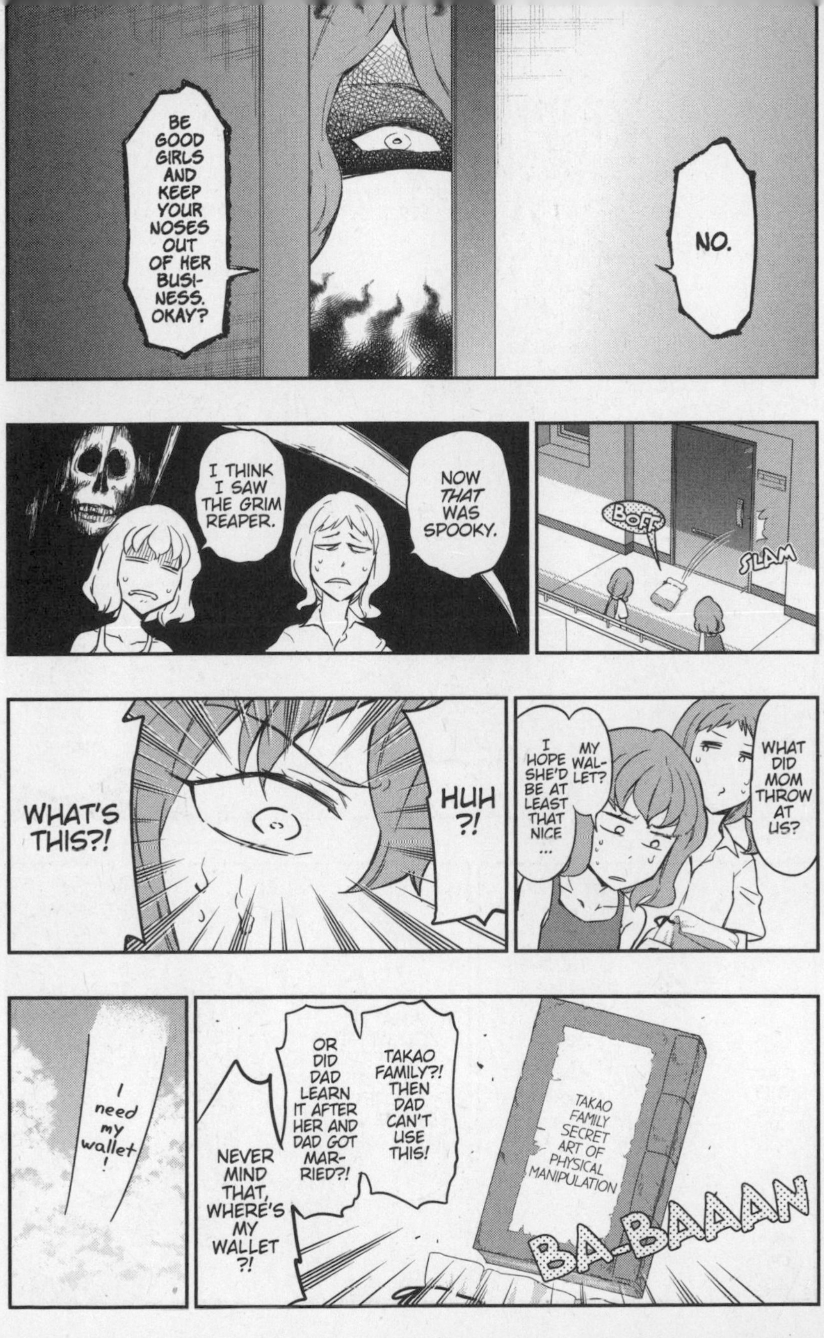
NO.
BE GOOD GIRLS AND KEEP YOUR NOSES OUT OF HER BUSINESS. OKAY?
BOFF
SLAM
NOW THAT WAS SPOOKY.
I THINK I SAW THE GRIM REAPER.
WHAT DID MOM THROW AT US?
MY WALLET?
I HOPE SHE'D BE AT LEAST THAT NICE...
HUH?!
WHAT'S THIS?!
TAKAO FAMILY SECRET ART OF PHYSICAL MANIPULATION
BA-BAAAAN
TAKAO FAMILY?! THEN DAD CAN'T USE THIS!
OR DID DAD LEARN IT AFTER HER AND DAD GOT MARRIED?!
NEVER MIND THAT, WHERE'S MY WALLET?!
I need my wallet!

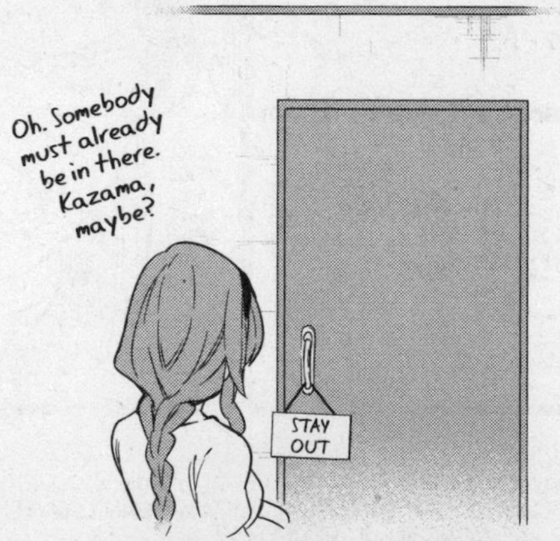
Oh. Somebody must already be in there. Kazama, maybe?
STAY OUT

Backstage Uran is Back

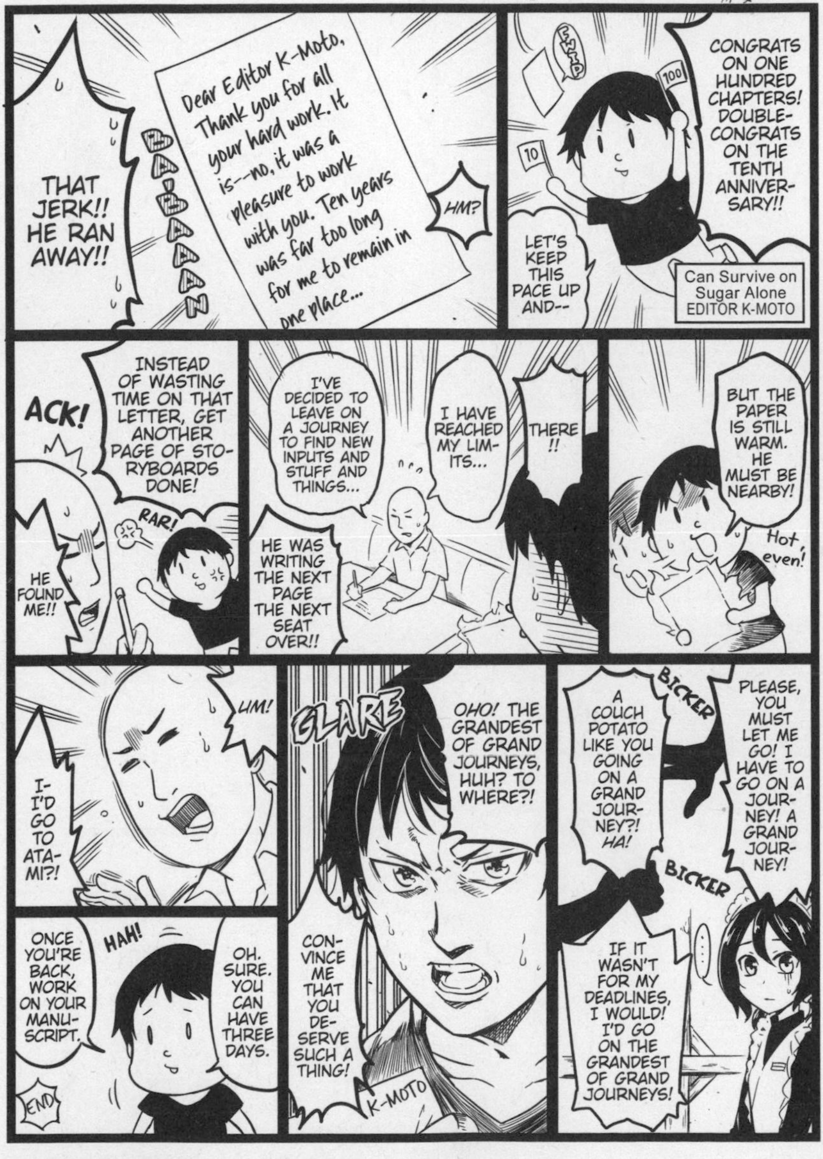
CONGRATS ON ONE HUNDRED CHAPTERS! DOUBLE-CONGRATS ON THE TENTH ANNIVERSARY!!
FWIP
100
10
LET'S KEEP THIS PACE UP AND--
Can Survive on Sugar Alone EDITOR K-MOTO
Dear Editor K-Moto, Thank you for all your hard work. It is--no, it was a pleasure to work with you. Ten years was far too long for me to remain in one place...
HM?
BADAAAN
THAT JERK!! HE RAN AWAY!!
BUT THE PAPER IS STILL WARM. HE MUST BE NEARBY!
Hot, even!
THERE!!
I HAVE REACHED MY LIMITS...
I'VE DECIDED TO LEAVE ON A JOURNEY TO FIND NEW INPUTS AND STUFF AND THINGS...
HE WAS WRITING THE NEXT PAGE THE NEXT SEAT OVER!!
INSTEAD OF WASTING TIME ON THAT LETTER, GET ANOTHER PAGE OF STORYBOARDS DONE!
ACK!
RAR!
HE FOUND ME!!
PLEASE, YOU MUST LET ME GO! I HAVE TO GO ON A JOURNEY! A GRAND JOURNEY!
BICKER
A COUCH POTATO LIKE YOU GOING ON A GRAND JOURNEY?! HA!
BICKER
...
IF IT WASN'T FOR MY DEADLINES, I WOULD! I'D GO ON THE GRANDEST OF GRAND JOURNEYS!
OHO! THE GRANDEST OF GRAND JOURNEYS, HUH? TO WHERE?!
GLARE
CONVINCE ME THAT YOU DESERVE SUCH A THING!
K-MOTO
UM!
I-I'D GO TO ATAMI?!
OH. SURE. YOU CAN HAVE THREE DAYS.
HAH!
ONCE YOU'RE BACK, WORK ON YOUR MANUSCRIPT.
END

SPECIAL THANKS!!
HIGAWA KAKERU-SAN, HOTA-SAN, YUKINOJOU-SAN
KAWAMOTO-SAN (EDITOR) TOMIYAMA-SAN (COVER DESIGN),
AND MY WONDERFUL READERS!!

The Aftermath of Chapter 98

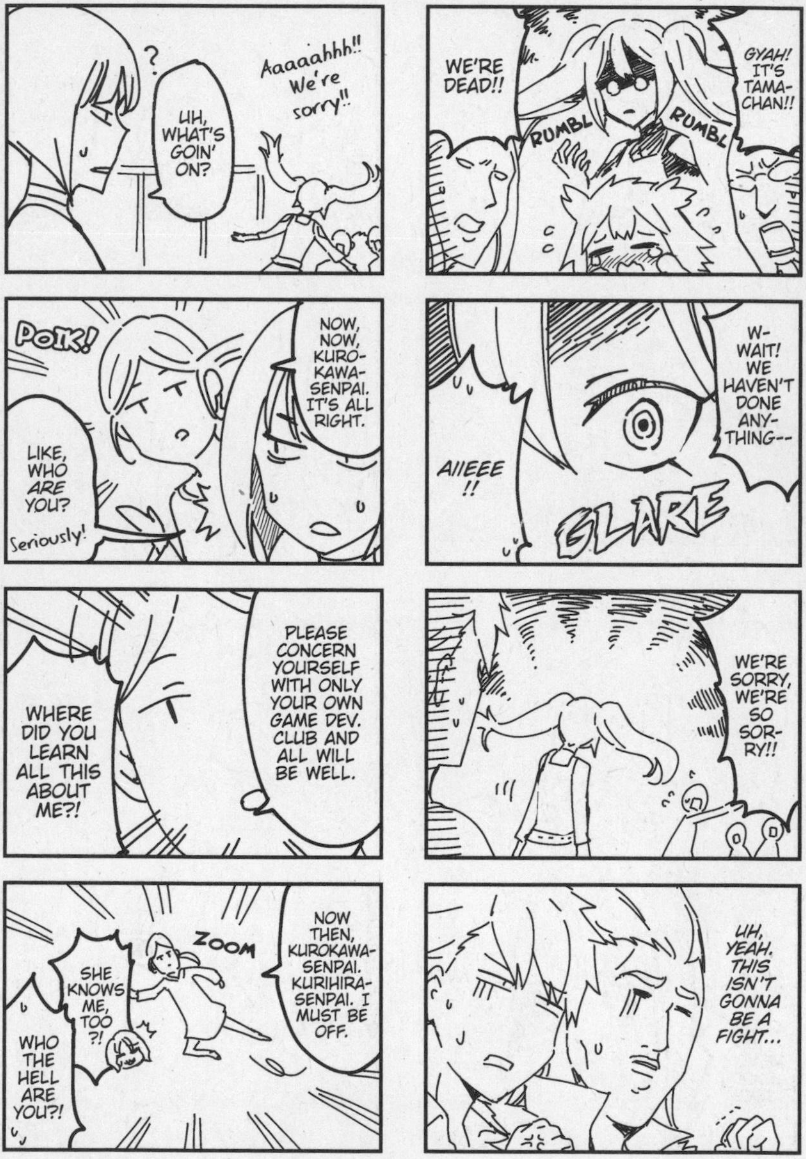
GYAH! IT'S TAMA-CHAN!!
RUMBL
RUMBL
WE'RE DEAD!!
Aaaaahhh!! We're sorry!!
?
UH, WHAT'S GOIN' ON?
W-WAIT! WE HAVEN'T DONE ANYTHING--
AIIEEE!!
GLARE
NOW, NOW, KUROKAWA-SENPAI. IT'S ALL RIGHT.
POIK!
LIKE, WHO ARE YOU?
Seriously!
WE'RE SORRY, WE'RE SO SORRY!!
PLEASE CONCERN YOURSELF WITH ONLY YOUR OWN GAME DEV. CLUB AND ALL WILL BE WELL.
WHERE DID YOU LEARN ALL THIS ABOUT ME?!
UH, YEAH. THIS ISN'T GONNA BE A FIGHT...
NOW THEN, KUROKAWA-SENPAI. KURIHIRA-SENPAI. I MUST BE OFF.
ZOOM
SHE KNOWS ME, TOO?!
WHO THE HELL ARE YOU?!

The Aftermath of Chapter 99

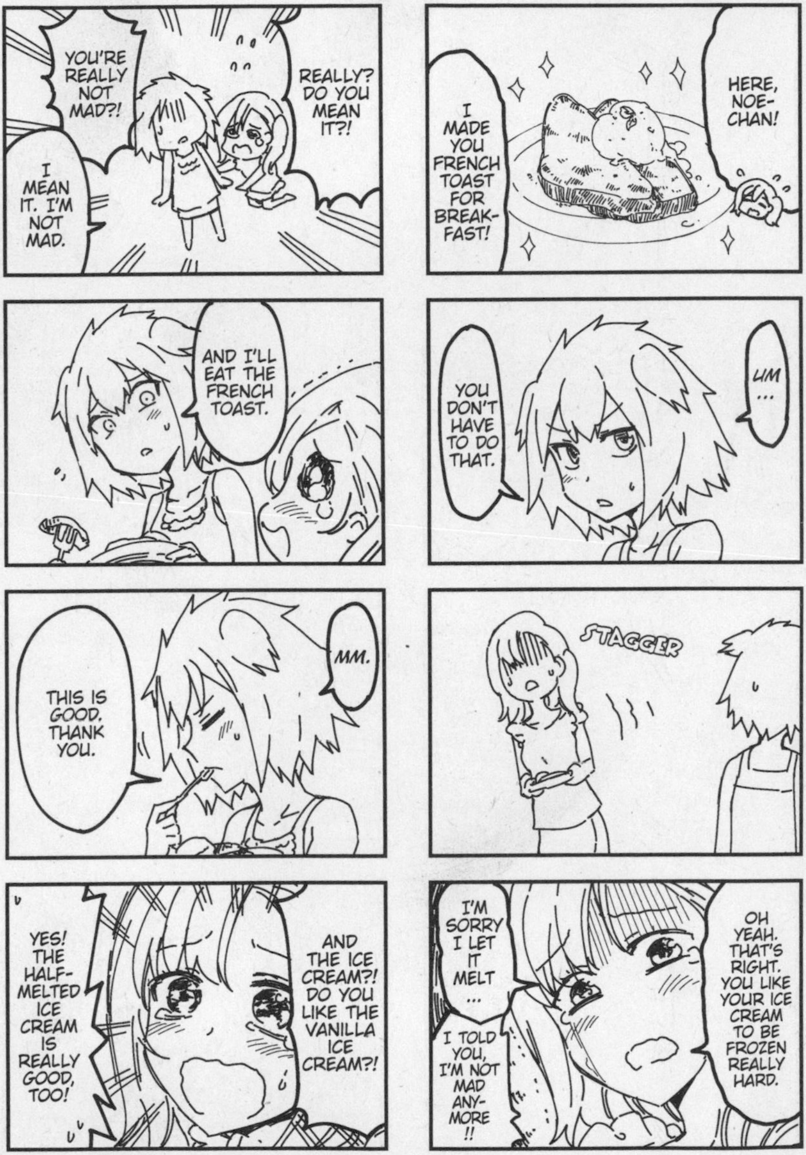
HERE, NOE-CHAN!
I MADE YOU FRENCH TOAST FOR BREAKFAST!
REALLY? DO YOU MEAN IT?!
YOU'RE REALLY NOT MAD?!
I MEAN IT. I'M NOT MAD.
UM...
YOU DON'T HAVE TO DO THAT.
AND I'LL EAT THE FRENCH TOAST.
STAGGER
MM.
THIS IS GOOD. THANK YOU.
OH YEAH. THAT'S RIGHT. YOU LIKE YOUR ICE CREAM TO BE FROZEN REALLY HARD.
I'M SORRY I LET IT MELT...
I TOLD YOU, I'M NOT MAD ANYMORE!!
AND THE ICE CREAM?! DO YOU LIKE THE VANILLA ICE CREAM?!
YES! THE HALF-MELTED ICE CREAM IS REALLY GOOD, TOO!

SEVEN SEAS ENTERTAINMENT PRESENTS

D-FRAG!

story and art by **TOMOYA HARUNO**

VOLUME 13

TRANSLATION
Adrienne Beck

ADAPTATION
Claudie Summers

LETTERING AND RETOUCH
Carolina Hernández Mendoza

LOGO DESIGN
Courtney Williams

COVER DESIGN
KC Fabellon

PROOFREADING
B. Lana Guggenheim
Cae Hawksmoor

EDITOR
Shannon Fay

PRODUCTION MANAGER
Lissa Pattillo

EDITOR-IN-CHIEF
Adam Arnold

PUBLISHER
Jason DeAngelis

D-FRAG! VOL. 13
© Tomoya Haruno 2018
First published in Japan in 2018 by KADOKAWA CORPORATION, Tokyo.
English translation rights reserved by Seven Seas Entertainment
under the license from KADOKAWA CORPORATION, Tokyo.

Seven Seas press and purchase enquiries can be sent to Marketing Manager
Lianne Sentar at press@gomanga.com. Information regarding the distribution
and purchase of digital editions is available from Digital Manager CK Russell
at digital@gomanga.com.

ISBN: 978-1-64275-104-8

Printed in Canada

First Printing: July 2019

10 9 8 7 6 5 4 3 2 1

FOLLOW US ONLINE: *www.sevenseasentertainment.com*

READING DIRECTIONS

This book reads from ***right to left***, Japanese style.
If this is your first time reading manga, you start
reading from the top right panel on each page and
take it from there. If you get lost, just follow the
numbered diagram here. It may seem backwards at
first, but you'll get the hang of it! Have fun!!

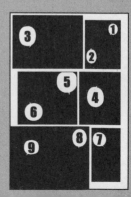